'Letters to

> *Brian King is among the most un-pastorly pastors I've known. Without pretense or pomp, he writes as a "regular guy" who, when it comes to pain, has been there, done that, felt that. From the get-go, he lets the reader knows it's OK not to feel OK, even to be angry about it. But he complements his empathetic approach with a scholar's zeal for data, his biblical foundation fortified with nuerological studies. And infuses it all with no small sense of courage and honesty. To read* To My Friends in Pain *is to take a journey with someone who cares deeply about the people he's writing to; indeed, we the readers become the "friends" he's addressing the book to. The result: deep salve to the wounded soul.*
>
> —BOB WELCH, author of *Lessons on the Way to Heaven*

> *Brian King has provided us with wise counsel and good company with the friend nobody wants—pain. He knows the presence of pain in his life and the impact it has on every part of each day. Brian is no stranger to this strange friend. Each of us will have close encounters with pain. Now we have a guide and faithful companion for our journey. I recommend this book to you. You will find wise counsel and deep comfort here.*
>
> —JOE CHAMBERS, pastor and author of *Walking Ancient Paths: A Daily Liturgy for the Sacred Journey*

> *When I hear the name Brian King, it always brings a smile to my face. I remember the day Brian made public his profession of faith in Jesus. I also remember the day Brian let it be known that God was calling him to preach. I was Brian's pastor. He was one of those young people who was serious about his walk with the Lord from the first day he met Jesus. Brian has been used as a successful pastor. And now his ministry has spread to the written word.*
>
> *You are about to read a book that will encourage you. Brian is writing about how we as believers—or even non-believers—can handle pain. But Brian is writing through his personal experience. He is not only expressing biblical truth, he is expressing personal truth through which he and his family have lived. Read this work carefully and slowly. Let the Lord use it in your life. You are going to be glad you read this book. And you are going to enjoy getting to know Brian King.*

This is a book you will want to read and recommend to others. You are about to begin ministry you can use in your life and in the life of others.
—DR. TED KERSH, pastor, Edmond, Oklahoma

In the past, I've tried to run from pain, but that's not a sustainable mission. Likewise, running toward pain is a fruitless exercise, too. In these pages, Brian King helps the reader to flip a switch that reveals the distorted illusions that typically accompany physical pain, regardless of the harshness and severity of that pain. While medications can numb or deaden sensitivities to pain, these pages provide tangible insights in the way of mindset shifters—never-ending journeys that move us from just accepting and coping with pain to realizing how these inflictions can bring us closer to our creator.
—MARK GANDY, business consultant and podcast host

Letters to My Friends in Pain

Brian King

SoulCare Press

Copyright © 2024 by Brian King

All rights reserved. No part of this book may be reproduced in any form without written permission from the author, except by reviewers or authors who may quote brief passages in support of their works.

All Scripture quotations are from the New International Version (NIV) of the Bible, unless otherwise noted.

Front cover photograph by Brian King

Front and back cover design by Bob Welch

SoulCare Press
  Eugene, Oregon

ISBN: 9798871752647

Printing 012124.0724p

Also available as an e-book and soon as an audio book, read by the author, on amazon.com

To contact the author:

brian@myfriendsinpain.com

To My Savior

There are not enough words to express my gratitude for Your presence in my life. But when it comes to pain, I'm so thankful You get the final word.

To My Wife

Through all your pain and mine, and the sheer fact that I am sometimes a pain, I've never walked alone since you came into my life. Thank you is not enough.

To My Daughters

You are a blessing beyond measure. Nothing will ever change that.

When we honestly ask ourselves which person in our lives means the most to us, we often find that it is those who, instead of giving advice, solutions, or cures, have chosen rather to share our pain and touch our wounds with a warm and tender hand.
— Henri Nouwen

Table of Contents

Prologue 15

Part I: The Big Picture 19

1. Why Pain Sucks 21
2. The Way Forward Through Pain 29

Part II: The Mindsets and the Letters 39

MINDSET 1: Rediscovering Your Identity 40

3. Loved:
   To My Friend Who Doesn't Feel Loved 49

4. Joy:
   To My Friend Who Doesn't Realize That Her Circumstances Will Never Make Her Happy 55

5. Humility:
   To My Friend Who's Wrestling with Insecurity and Pride 61

6. Breathe:
   To My Doctor Friend Who's Struggling with Burnout 67

7. Redemption:
   To My Friend Who Feels Like a Failure 73

MINDSET 2: Embrace Your Life Despite Your Pain 78

8. Peace:
   To My Friend with Neuropathy 89

9. Hope:
To My Friend Who Just Lost Her Husband   97

10. Providence:
To My Friend Who is Angry at God   105

11. Lament:
*To My Pastor Friend Who is Suppressing
the Hurt and Trauma That Comes from Leading a Church*   113

12. Gratitude:
*To My Friend Who's Trapped in the Vortex
of Complaining and Negativity*   123

MINDSET 3: *Finding a New Power Source*   128

13: Weakness:
To My Friend with No Energy Left in the Tank   137

14. Self-Honesty:
To My Friend Who Hit the Wall   145

15. Resurrection:
To My Friends Who Lost Their Child   153

16. Waiting:
*To My Friend Who's Struggling
with Disappointment and Discouragement*   161

17. Confidence:
To My Friend Who Feels Like Life is a Perpetual Crisis   169

MINDSET 4: Choosing a New Support Network   176

18. Vulnerability:
*To My Friend Who's Freaking Out
but Doesn't Want Anyone to Know*   183

19: Reaching Out:
To My Friend Who's Thinking about Suicide   189

20. Forgiveness:
To My Friend Who's Bitter and Doesn't Feel Like Forgiving   197

21. Community:
To My Friend Who's Ready to Give up on Church   205

22. Love:
To My Bi-racial Friends Who've Experienced Racism in the Church   211

MINDSET 5: *Experiencing Growth*   218

23. Transformation:
To My Friend Who's Passing on the Pain to His Family   225

24. Acceptance:
To My Friend Whose Teen is Leaving for College   231

25. Momentum and Growth:
To My Friend Who Feels Like a Deer in the Headlights   237

26. Grace:
To My Friend Who's Living in Enemy Mode   241

27. Glory:
To My Friend Who's Watching His Wife Wilt Before His Eyes   249

Part III: Digging Deeper — 257

28. The Pity Vortex — 259

29. The Perseverance Revolution — 267

30. Addiction and The Perseverance Revolution — 283

31. Where to Begin When You Don't Know Where to Start — 291

32. Overcoming:
    To My Friend Who Still Has Pain — 297

Endnotes — 303

Acknowledgments — 309

Prologue

the questions of God

the alarm sounds
questions abound
will today be the day
the ache goes away?

when—when will the pain end?
what—what is the point?
who—who cares enough to really help out?
where—where were you Jesus when the tempest blew loud?

why—why the weight of this grief?
why the burden of stress?
why the struggle to live
wishing they'd be less?

in this season of wounds
i ache for escape
temptations swirl 'bout to drown out the misery
the enemy pounces with illusions of trickery

now this is your life
pain defines who you are
there is no hope; your life is a mess
you have no hope; why deal with this stress?

i wrestle with God
blame is the game
i question why me
i fight through my pain

Jesus breaks through
no word from God will ever fail
pain sucks: agony is real
but the broken sting of sin's thorns will not prevail

strength is not found in running away
strength is not found in the games that we play
i plead and i plead—please take my pain away
He said my grace is sufficient; my perfect power is in play

now answer my questions God responds with a look
do you remember the end of The Book?
pain will not last—no more death or mourning or crying or pain
for the pain of this world will itself pass away

have you ever considered the gift in your pain?
thought deeply about the blessing you would miss if you skipped the
    strain?
the pleasures, the joys, the sorrows, the troubles
all flow through the same nerves; they're part of the struggle

have you reckoned with the cross—the necessity of it all?
have you wept at the feet of the suffering of God?
have you considered that Jesus is not immune to the agony?
have you wept at the loss, the death of God on a cross?

have you forgotten the moments you've grown through the pain?
do you know what you'd lose if the pain never came?
have you considered the times others carried your sting?
would you give up the bonds that pain jumping would bring?

you wonder why God is moving so slow
you don't understand how this makes you grow
God's time is eternal, your rush to numb is a blunder
would you look at creation and trust Him in wonder?

yes, the pain of this world is indeed impossible
would you dream that a God who suffers is probable?
yes, the troubles and nightmares make us scream at God's throne
would you dream of a King willing to suffer in His bones?

now can you bow in surrender, the empty tomb to concede?
He is not here. He has risen, defeating sin, pain, and death, indeed
will you let go of control, find strength in His thorns,
cling to hope through the struggle to be healed by His wounds?

strength is not found in running away
strength is not found in the games that we play
i plead and i plead—please take my pain away
He said my grace is sufficient; my perfect power is in play

and so, may you know the gifts of grief and of comfort
of darkness, of light, of despair, and of hope
of the pain of this world and the work of God with His might
in the wrestling of questions in your soul's dark night

PART I

The Big Picture

1.

Why Pain Sucks

He said, "Look! I see four men walking around in the fire, unbound and unharmed, and the fourth looks like a son of the gods."
—Daniel 3:25

Two things I want you to know. First, pain sucks. Second, you are not alone. Now, here's one thing you might want to know: "Brian, if you're writing a book about pain, what do you really know about it? About trouble? About hardship? About grief?"

Fair question. Fair concern. Here's my story:

Today, I woke up with a headache. That's not unusual. Everyone gets headaches now and then. And many people struggle with migraines.

What is unusual about this particular headache is that I woke up with it on October 16, 2021. And I still have this same headache today, more than two years later. Every morning, I wake up, stretch, and lay with my head on the pillow wondering, "Will today be the day the ache goes away?"

Not that I haven't tried. I've seen doctor after doctor. I've taken test after test. I've tried treatment after treatment. I bet you have, too, for all your pains. After a while, my life begins to feel like I'm a monkey swinging on a vine from one appointment or test to another.

My headache is an interesting animal. Some days, it is tolerable, and others, it's more overpowering, like a migraine. I can barely remember the last day it didn't ache or throb. The headache is mostly on one side of my head. On days when the pain is more tolerable, it aches. On days that are more overwhelming, it throbs from back to front, pulsating with tremendous pressure behind my left eye. My life feels a lot like *Groundhog Day*, the movie. Different day, same painful reality.

Most days, the headache includes dizziness and light-headedness. Any quick movement or bending down might cause the room to spin. After multiple MRIs, several specialists, lots of tests, and plenty of failed treatments, I'm still living daily in 2024 with a headache that varies in intensity but never goes away.

Every night, when I lay down in bed, I wonder if tomorrow might be different. But this headache is not the only pain in my life.

My first concussion happened in elementary school. At a baseball practice, I took a line drive to my right temple that knocked me unconscious. I spent several days in the hospital. Recently, I found out I suffered permanent brain damage from that concussion, but the original doctors didn't catch it. I'm lucky to be alive. Who knew? (If my family and friends are reading this, this revelation of brain damage explains a lot!)

These days, in addition to my headache, I also battle neuropathy in my legs and feet. It started in the early 2010s when I noticed a pricking pain in the bottom of my feet when I walked long distances. I did not know that this pain was nerve pain. I did not know what nerve pain was or what it felt like. Nor did I know that it wasn't a foot problem. Nor that the source of this pain was generated "up river," so to speak. All I knew was that my feet hurt when I walked, and I had some lower back and hip pain as well.

By 2015, this unexplained pain became a daily occurrence. Every step felt like walking on nails. Late that year, my chiropractor helped me discover the source of my nerve pain—spondylosis and a grade 3 spondylolisthesis in my spine at L5, S1. Big words, esoteric letter-number combos, but in a nutshell, my vertebrae weren't working the way they were supposed to. The nerves that control the lower half of my body were slowly getting cut off by that vertebrae because of slippage forward of L5 over S1. During that year, my walking aged by 40 years. One day, I was walking like a relatively normal 42-year-old, and six months later, I walked like an 80-year-old.

That winter, my wife and I went to the mall to walk, a necessity in the rainy Pacific Northwest, where I live. One day, a couple in their 70s lapped us. Not only did I feel great physical pain, I felt greatly discouraged, even depressed. As my ability to walk deteriorated, so did my self-confidence. As I awaited surgery that my insurance initially declined as unnecessary, my fears grew stronger every day, reaching the point where I thought I might never walk again. For some of you, that fear inside of me is your reality. You have my utmost respect.

I worried not only about nerve damage, but about my family, my career, and truthfully, my ego.

I probed my neurosurgeon. *What was the cause? Why did this happen?* I probed God too. *Why me? Why now?*

Anyone with this kind of pain would tell you that this sort of neuropathic pain is exhausting. On top of the pain, fatigue and depression are common companions; one day to another, you never know whether you'll have the energy to get done what you need to do.

Long story short, in March 2016, my neurosurgeon fused my spine at L5/S1. I was hopeful this would end my neuropathy, my pain, and my struggle with walking. It did and didn't.

I woke up from surgery as sick as I've ever felt in my life. Did you know that while spinal fusion is major surgery, it is now considered day surgery? Between the excruciating pain, the nausea from the anesthesia, and the need to wake up quickly to leave the surgery center, I was spent. I was given a little something to help with the nausea via an IV and wheeled out to the car. My IV pain meds wore off quickly, but I was so nauseous from the anesthesia that I couldn't hold down any food or medicine. So I spent the first 24 hours recovering from surgery with no meds in my system. If I ever wanted to know what it feels like to be stabbed, cut open, have some parts cut out, then rods and screws drilled into my spine, this was it. Who wouldn't sign up for that?

Do you know the word "excruciating" comes from the Latin "*excruciatus,*" meaning to torment or torture? To inflict severe pain. Look in the middle of the word. "Excruciating" and "crucify" come from the same Latin word. I'm not comparing what I went through to what Jesus went through, but if you've ever felt excruciating pain, you can know beyond a shadow of doubt that Jesus has felt the same and more.

How did the surgery turn out? Technically, it was a great success. I can walk. *This fact is not lost on me. Not everyone can walk. It's a privilege that most of us don't even think twice about.*

I can walk far better than I could in 2015, but I still wrestle with neuropathy from my knees down. Back pain persisted for years. Physical therapy, spinal injections, and massage therapy have been tremendously helpful. I've tried medicine after medicine. But nothing has been able to change the burning sensation I feel in my lower legs. Some days, it's like someone is using sandpaper on my legs. Most days, it feels like my calves and feet are on fire. And when I go for a long walk, I sometimes still feel like I'm walking on nails. Furthermore, wearing socks and shoes is extremely uncomfortable. You know that guy you see at Walmart in winter wearing shorts and sandals even when it's 36 and raining? That's me. (Say hello next time!)

Here's the nitty gritty truth: Every single day, I must choose whether I will focus on the headache and the lingering neuropathy or the fact that I can walk. I must choose between the pain that is so distracting and the purpose Jesus has for my day. It's my choice. Some days, I choose wisely. Many days, I do not. Today, what am I focusing on? I can still walk. Something I wasn't sure would happen before the surgery.

Think my pain list is done? Nope. Headaches and difficulty walking aren't the only "fires" I've been through. You'll learn more as you read through the book. Like you, I've been through plenty. What I discovered walking through the fire is that I am not walking alone. Like Shadrach, Meshach, and Abednego in the fiery furnace in Daniel 3, I'm walking through my fire with "one who looks like a son of the gods." We know Him as Jesus. Interestingly, this same fire walker walks on water in Mark 6 in the New Testament. In both of those stories, I am not alone, and He is walking through and on what I am worried about.

It might be helpful to make a list of the fires you've walked through in your life. The key word here isn't "fires." It is "through." I've been "through" a lot of them, thanks to the goodness of God in my life. And I will get through my current ones as well. Have you ever paused to consider that God has brought you through 100% of the fires in your life up to this point? Seriously, if you are still here, God has brought you through it.

That's the good news: I'm still here today and Jesus is still good. How do I know that? I walked through the fire. In every single one of these fires, whether I was aware of it or not, I was not alone. Jesus was with me. (I realize that some of you readers may not believe in Jesus. You're welcome here whether you see God the way I do or not. Either way, I'm honored.)

These are not the only pains I've ever felt. These are just some of the physical ones. There's physical pain, and then there's also ongoing physical struggles. Did I mention that I'm also asthmatic, suffer from chronic neck pain, and struggle with severe allergies in one of the most allergy-prone locations on the planet? Beyond that, I know the mental pain of depression and discouragement. Like you, I've struggled with rejection and failure. I've experienced the pain of guilt and regret. Grief has overwhelmed my life at times. I've battled the desire to escape the pain and escape it all.

Of course, my pains are not the only pains I have experienced. As a pastor, I often walk with people through their own pain. I have:

- Sat in the ICU praying with family for healing after a stroke.
- Rushed to the ER after a friend had a heart attack.
- Wept with family after the suicide of a husband and father.
- Stood at the grave side as family members express their goodbyes to a loved one.
- Shared coffee with fellow pastors who were so despondent they weren't sure they could or wanted to do their jobs anymore.
- Worked with drug addicts.
- Listened to friends as they've lamented being the targets of racism and judgment in a previous church.

This is just the tip of the iceberg. I'm sure you've experienced and walked with others through pain as well. I'm not going to pretend that I have pain or overcoming pain all figured out. I'm not a physician nor am I a snake oil salesperson. But I do know pain.

And here's what I've learned, and I hope you will learn: Pain might define my feelings in any given moment, but pain doesn't have to define my life because, as difficult as pain is, Jesus is stronger than my suffering.

Pain is powerful. That goes without saying. The battle is not only physical, but emotional, mental, and spiritual. Physically, pain focuses the body intensely on the specific point inside of you that feels like it is suffering the most. The muscles around the painful spot begin to guard the place that is hurting, sometimes creating more problems and eventually, more pain. Emotionally, pain intensifies our feelings, struggles, and reactions. What physical pain does to focus our muscles, emotional pain does to our emotions to guard and protect that place inside our soul that is hurting. Mentally, pain leaves us wondering what to do, how to fix it, and who to blame. The questions never end. And spiritually, pain leads to temptation—a lot of it.

In fact, pain possesses within itself a very distinct temptation for us: to focus on the feeling of the moment and believe that whatever pain I am feeling most is the only thing that matters. Severe pain, whether physical or emotional, tempts me to believe deep in my soul that what hurts inside of me is the most important thing in my life and the most important thing about my life. And that this most important thing defines what is most important about me and God.

Pain tempts me to feel something specific about God. In short, pain tempts me to feel something other than God's goodness and to miss the thousands of other times that God has been good to me. In an instant, pain in one place makes me forget the good and normal feelings in other places.

Anyone who has stubbed a toe knows that. Pain makes us forget the good and forget God. Pain tempts me to focus on what God hasn't done and what God isn't doing. Pain even tempts me to blame Jesus, believing that He isn't good, because if He was, I wouldn't be feeling this much pain. Many people have abandoned their faith in God for this exact reason.

Pain tempts me to abandon the goodness of God, and God himself, because pain doesn't feel good. It tempts me to think that it is more powerful than my savior, Jesus Christ. Every single day, I need a reality check.

Two things can be true at once. *Pain can suck, and God can still be good.* Today, I'm doing what I can to face my pain. But I'm also facing Jesus, who is so good.

Today, I woke up with a headache. That's not good.

Today, I still have neuropathy in my legs and feet. That's not good either.

But, today, I ... woke ... up.

And for that, I am grateful.

2.

The Way Forward Through Pain

I have told you these things, so that in me you may have peace. In this world you will have trouble. But take heart! I have overcome the world.
—John 16:33

Then he said to Thomas, "Put your finger here; see my hands. Reach out your hand and put it into my side. Stop doubting and believe."
—John 20:27

The choice we want: Pain or no pain. The choice we have: Pity or perseverance. OK, so perhaps we can agree on this: Pain sucks. There's no way around it. You might not like my language. You might think I understated the truth about pain and should have used more colorful words. Growing up, you might have heard people say, "No pain, no gain." But let's be honest, you don't like pain, and neither do I.

We do like when the story ends the way we want. The pain ends. The girl gets the guy. The hero survives. The cancer is healed. The marriage is put back together. We celebrate these moments. And in real life, we give credit to God for the miracles. But what about when the story doesn't end the way we want? When the cancer doesn't disappear? When the stroke leaves life-altering consequences? When the persistent depression won't fade no matter what you try? What about the moments when it feels like chronic pain defines your life? Where is God then? Is Jesus still a miracle-working God deserving of our praise even when the immediate outlook remains dim?

The answer is *"Yes, He is!"*

Examine your Bible for the story where God always heals the pain and suffering of those He loves. Couldn't find one? That's because that story isn't there. At least not on this side of eternity. On the other hand, search the Scriptures deeply for the storms where God's people endured and overcame. As you read your Bible, pay close attention to the part where Jesus suffered and died.

I know, we like how it turns out, but before you fast forward to the part of the Easter story you love, read slowly about Jesus praying in the Garden of Gethsemane and the agony of the cross that Jesus wondered out loud if He could skip. Read bit by bit through the moments where He is treated unfairly in kangaroo courts. Make your way deliberately through the physical suffering and agony as He is beaten, whipped, and pushed beyond suffering that you know you could not endure. Read again where He is nailed to a cross in moments that will literally take His breath away. Listen as He cries out about being forsaken, as the consequence of your sins and mine is poured out on Him. He suffered excruciating pain. Read slowly about the moment when He died. Think about what that means: God died an agonizing death. Read about His scars after the resurrection, and believe.

Jesus didn't skip any of the unfair moments of life, including pain. Read one more time about how He was buried in a borrowed grave. Again, we all know the story. He is risen. But don't skip the moment between Good Friday and Easter Sunday. We call that day Holy Saturday.

Most of our lives are more like Holy Saturday than Good Friday or Easter Sunday. We live between what God has already done and what Jesus will still do. We live in the period of life that we least like, the period where God often says *wait*. You and I know that Jesus is resurrected. And when you are a believer in Jesus Christ, you will be too. But until that day, we must learn to wait with Jesus in our pain, with our grief, with our suffering, trusting that his grace is still sufficient for you and me. We live between the brokenness of this world and the remaking of the next where all will be as it was created to be. We must learn to embrace this life even amid our pain. It's part of how we grow to overcome it.

Here's where we're headed in this book: Everybody experiences pain. There's no way to avoid it. Some of this is about what is going on in your body, but much more if it is about what is going on in your mind and in your soul. Many discoveries in neuroscience point to the fact that much of our experience of pain is in our brain, not just the rest of our body. In the end, our thinking about suffering influences our experience of pain, and the health of our souls influences our capacity to cope with what life throws our way. Understanding our nervous system is helpful because, as believing neuroscientists and believing doctors know, understanding more about our nervous system is discovering more about what God has created.

Understanding pain is the first step toward demasking the monster of pain. Let's start with the obvious. I am not a neurologist, and I am not a doctor. I am a pastor trying to understand what neuroscience and God teach us about pain. I don't pretend to have neuroscience all figured out, but then again, I don't pretend to have Jesus all figured out either.

I'm going to introduce you to some authors who specialize in neuroscience, the brain, and pain.

- Dr. Richard Ambron, a pain specialist, and author of *The Brain and Pain.*
- Dr. Bessell Van der Kolk, a trauma specialist, and author of *The Body Keeps the Score.*
- Dr. Stephen L. Macknik and Dr. Susana Martinez-Conde, neuroscientists, magicians, and authors of *Sleights of Mind: What the Neuroscience of Magic Reveals About our Everyday Deceptions*

Since God made the body, we are learning about God and His ways as we study the brain, the nervous system, and the body. New discoveries in neuroscience provide a fresh understanding of pain, our experience of pain, and our recovery from pain.

I know this may sound like mumbo jumbo, but neuroscience teaches us that there's a significant difference between our *actual* pain and our *experience* of that actual pain. Many new discoveries in neuroscience help us understand the role our brain plays in processing pain. Our experience of pain includes perceptions, awareness, attention, expectations, and several other factors. If we could learn to change those factors, our experience of pain can be modified from the actual sensation of pain. Ambron writes:

> The complexity of pain actually arises when the brain receives this information because the degree to which pain is experienced is highly subjective and is influenced by past experience, present circumstances, beliefs, and a variety of other factors. Until recently, we had no inkling as to how these factors could modulate pain. This all changed when advances in real-time imaging enabled clinicians and neuroscientists to visualize the activity within the brain of patients in pain.[1]

In addition to neuroscience, we're going to explore two different paths in life:
- The path of pity
- The path of perseverance.

On one path, we decide that, like it or not, pain defines our life, and we will often unintentionally make decisions that trap us in our pain and pity. Later in the book, I'll call this path *"The Pity Vortex"* because we get sucked deeper and deeper into the belief that life will always suck because pain sucks.

The superior path is the path of perseverance, defined by the choices we make that allow Jesus to make us an overcomer. I'll call this path *"The Perseverance Revolution."* The overcomer is not the person who attempts to escape their pain. Overcomers move forward to embrace life *despite* their pain. The difference between these two paths lies in—and is mirrored by—the choices we make.

Specifically, I'll unpack five mindsets that can change our experience of our pain and suffering:

- **Mindset 1: Resdiscovering Your Identity.**
- **Mindset 2: Embracing What's Most Important.**
- **Mindset 3: Finding a New Power Source.**
- **Mindset 4: Choosing a New Support System.**
- **Mindset 5: Experiencing Growth.**

Each mindset, or choice, is a decision between pity and perseverance.

Note: These are not one-time decisions. We make these choices every day of our lives. In the rest of this book, I'll outline these five choices, and share some letters to real people I know, letters I've written about how our choices change us as we learn to walk with Jesus through the pain of this world. In the last part of the book, I'll dig deeper into how our choices work *for us* to make us stronger or *against us* to make us weaker.

Identity
The Choice Between Illusion and Truth

Your source of identity provides meaning, value, guardrails, and direction for your life. Pain can be the defining force in our lives. Escaping pain can become our god as we begin to tell ourselves a lot of lies to justify the escape. Will I build my identity in these illusions, or will I accept my identity in what God says about me in the Bible?

What's Most Important
The Choice Between Escaping Pain and Embracing Life

Pain screams and echoes in the soul. Will I allow this reverberating echo to define what is most important in my life and most important in the moment? Will escaping the pain become my Prime Directive, albeit through numbness, poor coping mechanisms, and the corresponding damage to my life? Will I prioritize my escape of pain or will I prioritize my broken but beautiful life with Jesus?

My Source of Strength
The Choice Between Living Self-Sufficient and Jesus-Dependent

When life is comfortable, we become self-sufficient. When faced with knee-dropping pain, am I limited to the strength I can find within myself or does God provide a source of strength that is well beyond what I can manifest on my own? What will be my source of strength when I run out? Are the resources that I have within me enough to go on, or can I admit that I am not enough and turn to God for a strength infinitely beyond what I bring to the equation?

Relationships
The Choice Between Isolation and Community

Pain roars into our soul with this message: no one else understands our pain, leaving us isolated in a world where every other soul we know is experiencing pain that we likely know nothing about. Were we meant for this kind of isolation and self-reliance? God and his people offer care, support, and accountability. When the pain is more than I can bear, will I retreat into isolation or reach out to the community Jesus provides for my life? Am I willing for my life to become a testimony to others about what God can do?

Change
The Choice Between Stagnation and Next Steps

Pain is a paralytic. When overwhelmed by our pain, we often become the proverbial deer in the headlights, unsure about whether to run right or left. Pain often leaves us feeling not only alone, but trapped in this state we're in. Will we surrender to stagnation, or will we choose to embrace the next step before us and trust Jesus for what's next? Will we succumb to inaction, or will we embrace the opportunity to take action toward health and change?

A lot of Bible verses talk about suffering, pain, disease, comfort, healing, and salvation; we'll explore a lot of those. But for now, as a preview of where we are headed, think about these:

> Therefore, since we are surrounded by such a great cloud of witnesses, let us throw off everything that hinders and the sin that so easily entangles. And let us run with perseverance the race marked out for us, fixing our eyes on Jesus, the pioneer and perfecter of faith. For the joy set before him he endured the cross, scorning its shame, and sat down at the right hand of the throne of God. Consider him who endured such opposition from sinners, so that you will not grow weary and lose heart.
> —*Hebrews 12:1-3*

> Consider it pure joy, my brothers and sisters, whenever you face trials of many kinds, because you know that the testing of your faith produces perseverance. Let perseverance finish its work so that you may be mature and complete, not lacking anything.

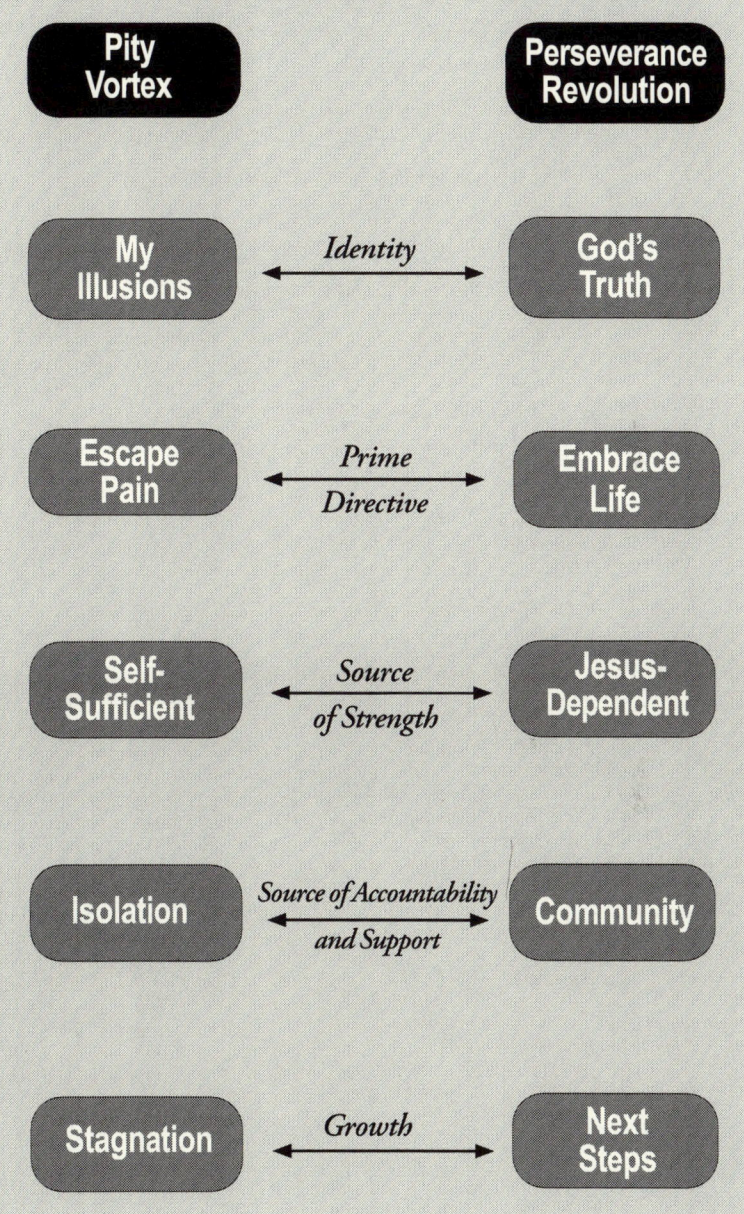

—*James 1:2-4*

If we believe that Jesus came to give us a comfortable life without pain, we are mistaken. Likewise, Jesus didn't die just to end our pain. He died to put a finish to our sins. When we acknowledge that sinful living brings with it plenty of pain, the Bible points us toward something quite remarkable—not simply how to escape our pain, but how to do something far more valuable. Something that will leave us stronger and closer to Jesus.

> How to *thrive even in the midst* of our pain.
> Not just to survive our pain but to
> *thrive despite the problems and pain of this world.*
> The Bible helps me to *embrace life in all its joy and pain,*
> *knowing that Jesus, and only Jesus, is enough.*

Pain sucks for everyone. What I am going to share with you is not a way *out*. It is a way *forward*. No one signs up for suffering. That's what makes what Jesus did so remarkable. He makes all the difference. Pain sucks, but with Jesus living inside of me and with real hope for eternity beyond, my life doesn't have to.

PART II

The Mindset Changes
& The Letters

MINDSET 1
Rediscovering Your Identity

Even if I should choose to boast, I would not be a fool, because I would be speaking the truth. But I refrain, so no one will think more of me than is warranted by what I do or say.
—2 Corinthians 12:6

I must totally disown my self-rejecting voice and claim the truth that God does indeed want to embrace me.[2]
—Henri Nouwen

The spooky truth is that your brain constructs reality, visual and otherwise. What you see, hear, feel, and think is based on what you expect to see, hear, feel, and think. In turn, your expectations are based on all your prior experiences and memories. What you see in the here and now is what proved useful to you in the past ... the brain mechanisms that elicit perceived illusions, automatic reactions, and even consciousness itself essentially define who you are.[3]
—Stephen L. Macknik and Susana Martinez-Conde

Think about some of the illusions we sell ourselves in this life:
- A pain-free life would be a complete life.
- All pain is bad and should be avoided.
- It's OK to ignore my pain.
- My pain defines my life.
- My inabilities, limitations, and failures caused by my pain define my life.
- If there was a God, He would understand my need to escape my pain.
- My sin is OK because of my circumstances. God gives an

exception in my case.
- No one is really hurt by me numbing my pain.
- If God really cared, I wouldn't be in pain.

I love illusions, but not these lies we sell ourselves. I've watched in wonder at the magic of Penn and Teller, David Copperfield, Danny Goldsmith, and Juan Tamariz. I've always been fascinated by coin tricks, card tricks, misdirection, magical moments, and believing the unbelievable.

That said, I'm also fascinated by human nature as well, but not in a good way. We love our illusions. Not in the magician sense, but in the sense of fooling ourselves. Penn and Teller would be proud. Whether our lives are full of comfort or pain, we have an enormous capacity to live in our illusions.

Neuroscientists Stephen Macknik and Susana Martinez-Conde, along with Sandra Blakeslee, wrote *Sleights of Mind: What the Neuroscience of Magic Reveals about Our Everyday Deceptions* to show the rest of us what magicians have known for hundreds of years. Every single day, our minds fool us. They say:

> Perception means resolving ambiguity ... alas, you simply cannot trust your eyes. You also make up a lot of what you see.[4]

True or False: the easiest person to fool in this life is yourself? What does neuroscience say about that? Lots, it turns out. Because your brain can only process so much information at one time, and because your brain has one significant sphere of focus at a time, it's natural for it to fill in the gaps with information based on your past experiences.

This means that you fool yourself regularly into seeing things in perception that you are not actually seeing in reality. Visually, it happens with optical illusions or an oasis in the desert. Internally, it might be as simple as thinking that binging one more episode on Netflix won't make us tired in the morning. We must learn to let God define our reality and adjust our perceptions to God's truths rather than our illusions.

Macknik and Martinez-Conde write:

> You believe you are aware of your surroundings, but at any given moment you're blocking out 95 percent of all that is happening. Magicians use these various perceptual pitfalls and brain processes against you in a form of mental jujitsu. The samurai invented jujitsu as a way to continue fighting if their swords broke in battle. Striking an armored opponent would be futile, so jujitsu is based on the principle of using an attacker's own energy against him rather than opposing it. Magicians have a similar MO. Their arts are founded on the principle of using your mind's own intrinsic properties against you. They reveal your brain for the liar that it is.[5]

Think about how many of our common illusions revolve around our identity: *I am what I do. I am what I have. I am who others think I am.* Or, *I am how I feel.* For those of us in pain, we can easily fall into the trap of believing we are the sum total of our pain. It dominates and dictates not only what we do each day, but how we feel. We get so used to accommodating this and working on our pain that we conclude, "My pain is the most important thing about me." That's where people in pain tend to find their identity.

Generally speaking, as humans, we find our identity in one of several places:

- I am my past.
- I am my wealth.
- I am my career.
- I am my successes or failures—sports, business, kids, and more.
- I am my tribe—political, religious, social standing.
- I am my victimhood.
- I am my followers on social media.
- I am my sexual attractions.

When life is comfortable, it's easy to live in our illusions. Thus, it often takes the removal of comfortability and an experience with pain or suffering for us to pry our fingers off our illusions and drive us to this most basic truth: *I am not who I think I am. I am not who others think I am. I am who God thinks I am.* I am His child. Being His child, there are several implications. I am not God, but I am His. I am not in control, but I am in a relationship with the One who is. I am not perfect, and God still loves me. I am not immune to pain, but I can find hope and help in my relationship with Jesus.

When we embrace our illusions long enough, they become delusions. Illusions and delusions exist in part because we make things, accomplishments, feelings, and experiences into idols, into minigods and demigods. We even fool ourselves into believing we are god. We fool ourselves into believing what no one else believes about us and we delude ourselves into behaving in ways that are not true to who God created us to be. We delude our thinking to rationalize our poor decisions.

But there's nothing helpful nor energizing about a two-faced life. The life of pretending is a life of delusion, exhaustion, and shame. Letting go of my illusions provides real energy because I no longer must spend energy hiding what's really going on inside of me. Authenticity provides the breeding ground for strength, trust, and improved relationships. When God breaks down our illusions and delusions, He's doing what's best for our souls.

In this sense, we need to be dis-illusioned—we need God to dis-illusion some of our biggest illusions about pain. Maybe you recognize some of these in your life and realize that you need God to dis-illusion some of the following in you:

- The illusion of pretending to have it all together.
- The illusion of perfection.
- The illusion that God wastes my pain.
- The illusion that everyone else is to blame.
- The illusion that God is responsible for all my pain.
- The illusion that I am not responsible for any of my pain.
- The illusion that I am better than most other people.
- The list goes on and on.

One of God's biggest tools to dis-illusion you in life is difficulty, hardship, and pain. To bring you to the end of your illusion and the end of you. I'm not saying that God causes our pain for this purpose. I am saying that we should allow God to use our pain to drive us back to Him.

Our capacity to deceive ourselves never ceases to amaze me.

> The heart is deceitful above all things and beyond cure. Who can understand it?
> —*Jeremiah 17:9*

Jeremiah knew it. I know it. And, if you are honest, you know it too. In this sense, I need to be dis-illusioned. By God. Everyone who loves an addict knows exactly what I am talking about.

Our illusions comfort us and distract us. My illusions justify all the poor decisions I make and selfish attitudes I embrace. In the end, my illusions distort my perspective such that I cannot admit what is true or real in my life. Even worse, my illusions prevent me from seeing God's perspective of me and others. When we feel the need to escape our pain, excuse our sin, or explain our problems away, we deceive ourselves in an attempt to deceive others about what is really going on.

Illusions, in this sense, are like cancer. They can be ignored, but they tend to metastasize anyway. And the results can be catastrophic, not only for our lives, but for those closest to us.

How often do the things we struggle with end up distorting how we actually live our lives and end up destroying our lives, our relationships, and our futures? The emotions we battle, the feelings we have during conflict, the thoughts and feelings we have about ourselves, the assumptions we make about other people, the wrong things we believe about God—how often do such assumptions, perspectives, and lies cause chaos in our lives?

Too often.

There are many things we have believed about ourselves that have become "truths" to us—but they are actually lies. Think about all the ways our thoughts become toxic based on illusions rooted in a confused or mistaken identity. "I hate myself and I'm worthless." Or "There's no hope for me."

In fact, our thoughts are often trapped in toxic illusions. We say toxic things to ourselves all the time. We live in those thoughts, refuse to deal with them, and defend them when others point them out. And we use those toxic thoughts and illusions to justify bad behavior. I need Jesus to bring freedom to my mind when I'm trapped by toxic illusions. I need Jesus to bring truth to my life and my core identity.

I need Jesus. Period.

Pain does not—or should not—define our lives. Neither does pretending. Despite what we tell ourselves, our world is not all good. I am not all good either. But the One who is good is at work in your life and mine. And when you can focus on that, there is hope. In Him, you find truth. And in Him, you find our true identity.

Let me be clear: My hope isn't in the healing. It's in the healer. If my hope is in the healing, I must get the outcome I want, or I really don't have hope but rather wishful thinking for the outcome I want. But, if my hope is in the healer, I've got genuine hope no matter what, because my relationship with Him is secure.

When we think about our experience with pain, the last thing we want to think about is some theoretical naval gazing. We want something that will stop our pain or, at least, ease our pain. If you think that way, I don't blame you. I'm in pain and that's what I want, too. But, as we will see, how we think about our pain makes a significant difference not only in our brains, but in our experience of the pain itself. Furthermore, how we think about ourselves (our identity) makes a world of difference as we try to sell ourselves on the reason we deserve to escape pain. Even more, how we think about our identity influences every decision we make, every attitude we embrace, and every next step we take.

It matters that we back up a little bit to explore how we define our identity. My identity will be formed by one of three constructs:

- Option one: I will let other people define who I think I am, giving them a tremendous amount of power over my life.

- Option two: I will define who I think I am based on my thoughts and feelings. Given how easy it is to deceive myself, this gives a tremendous amount of power to my temptations and sins. Often, we define ourselves in terms of our pain. It's easy to think that I'm defined by something that I think I don't deserve.
- Option three: I will trust how Jesus defines who I am. Rather than rely on myself or others to construct my personal identity, I can seek out, work to understand, and trust the truth as revealed in the Bible about how Jesus defines my life.

Since my personal identity is such a big part of whether I choose my myths, illusions, and lies, or whether I choose God's truths, I need Jesus' perspective and Jesus' grace before I am ever in pain. As a Christian, the question is a little stronger than just "Who am I?" The question is, "Who am I in Christ?" That's the starting point for every believer.

Have you noticed that the more we live in our toxic illusions, the more we run from one thing to the next seeking after something that will stroke our false identity? It's easy to fill our lives, even overfill our lives, chasing the wind. We hurry after our illusions.

I love what Pastor John Mark Comer says about this:

> All too often our hurry is a sign of something else. Something deeper. Usually that we're running away from something—father wounds, childhood trauma, last names, deep insecurity or deficits of self-worth, fear of failure, pathological inability to accept the limitations of our humanity, or simply boredom with the mundanity of middle life. Or we're running to something—promotions or purchases or experiences or stamps on our passports or the next high—searching in vain for something no earthly experience has to offer: a sense of self-worth and love and acceptance. In the meritocracy of the West, it's easy to feel like we're only as good as our next sales commissions or quarterly reports or music singles or sermons or Instagram posts or new toys. So we're constantly out of breath, chasing the ever-elusive wind. Sometimes our hurry is less dramatic: we're just overbusy, more victims of the rights and responsibilities of the modern world than perpetrators of escapism. But either way, the effect is the same.[6]

All of this leads to two gigantic questions I must answer daily:

- What am I believing is true about me that Jesus would say is not true?
- What do I think I need to pursue that I do not need to pursue because I have Christ?

When I stop chasing after the wind long enough to work deeply through these questions, my thinking is changed, my feelings are pointed toward Jesus, and my soul is reminded of the grip of grace on my life. *My thinking about life and pain will change when I refocus my thoughts not just on who I am, but who I am in Christ.* My life is not about me and my pain nor my past. My life is about me and Jesus.

> *Dear Jesus, I acknowledge that I'm often trapped with toxic illusions in my thoughts. That there's a lack of grace rolling through my mind. Jesus, I pray that your grace would wash through my mind like the waves that wash up on the beach. I ask that you work your grace in my identity so that I can refocus my thoughts on who I am in You. Help me to retrain my brain to constantly replace toxic thoughts with graceful ones: compassion, kindness, humility, gentleness, patience, forbearance, forgiveness, and love. In Jesus' name, Amen.*

3.

Loved

Every time you feel hurt, offended, or rejected, you have to say to yourself: These feelings, as strong as they may be, are not telling me the truth about myself.[7]
—Henry Nouwen

(Jesus) said to her, "Daughter, your faith has healed you. Go in peace and be freed from your suffering."
—Mark 5:34

To my friend who doesn't feel loved,

It hurts so much to feel unloved. Not just by someone you care about, but by friends and your church family. You recently experienced what none of us want when we say "I do": A broken marriage, leaving you feeling hurt, grief, and rejection.

Most people don't know the details of what happened, and they do not need to. But you've already started to experience the cold stares and the uncomfortable conversations. In your mind, you wonder: "Do these people at church still love me, and what does that say about Jesus' love for me?" Let me be clear: You are loved by Jesus. There is no scarlet letter around your neck that changes how God sees you. So it doesn't change how I see you either.

Rejection is one of life's deeper pains, and when people treat us like we're invisible, it hurts. Back in middle school, I think we all went through something like this. Sadly, many adults still treat people today like they don't matter. Some people have never moved beyond the "you're not one of the cool kids" mentality from seventh grade or the "you don't belong here anymore" thinking that goes on in country clubs. You've experienced some of that in your life from family or friends. I can see why you feel so much pain.

It's easy to feel like no one cares. Life is difficult for many of us. Add to that the ways in which we misinterpret and overinterpret other people and their actions, and it almost guarantees that we feel unloved at some point in our journeys. Others of us "know" we are loved, but we just don't *feel loved*.

When I think about feeling invisible and unloved, I think about a woman in the New Testament, in Mark 5. We don't know her name, but we know her reputation. We call her "the woman with the discharge of blood." Think about it. That's probably how most people thought of her in her day. They didn't know her name either. But they knew this about her: She was ceremonially unclean. She couldn't participate in religious or social functions. In fact, anyone who touched her was ceremonially unclean. She lived an isolated life. She had spent everything she owned to overcome this disorder or disease, yet it kept getting worse. Certainly, she knew something about pain and feeling unloved. Not just the physical pain, but the emotional pain that came with it.

Think about all the ways she could have defined her life. "I am unclean." "I am a failure." "I am unimportant and unloved."

Not only did she have this reputation, but she was also interrupting Jesus as He made his way to heal an important official's daughter. Even the official probably thought of her as an interruption. Certainly, the disciples considered her an insignificant person who was interrupting something important.

We sometimes feel this way. *I don't matter. I am a nobody. I am just my reputation. I'm not important. I'm just an interruption.*

But she had faith that Jesus could heal her. She comes to Jesus, thinking to herself, "If I can just touch him, maybe I will be healed."

She wasn't allowed to touch anyone, but she touched Jesus.

She was even willing for it all to happen anonymously. She was willing, and maybe even wishing, for it all to happen in secret. She didn't want more attention. She just wanted so desperately to be whole. Can you blame her? Don't you long to be whole?

Jesus asked, "Who touched me?" With this question, Jesus makes several things clear. The power is not in some magical touch or even the cloak itself. Jesus has the power. Jesus is not clueless. He knows and He cares when someone puts personal faith in Him. She needed more than His touch. And she needed this to be more than a secret. She eventually came forward in gratitude and fear.

His response: "Daughter, your faith has healed you."

Before you move on and miss it, realize a subtle something He said that's uber significant. He called her "daughter." Daughters are valued. Daughters are important. Daughters are loved. This is important because this is the only recorded time that Jesus called anyone daughter. He saved it just for this woman. I have two daughters. Daughters are *always* loved.

She was content to be anonymous, to be a nobody. Jesus was not. She was content with the illusion. Jesus knew she needed truth, and so did everyone else. Everyone needed to know she was a daughter. Everyone needed to know she was healed. Everyone needed to know that she was no longer suffering. Everyone needed to know that she was loved by Jesus and that Jesus loves women just like her. If you don't believe, and you're thinking that Jesus wouldn't love you if He knew everything you've done, guess what? He does know, and He does love you.

I think that's why Jesus stopped everyone that day. This can't be emphasized strongly enough. She needed to know she was loved. Everyone around her needed to see her as someone Jesus loves.

He said, "Daughter, your faith has healed you. Go in peace and be freed from your suffering."

He commended her faith. He acknowledged she was healed. Actually, the word is "saved." He tells her to go in peace. You can call her life a lot of things. Peace was not her past, but Jesus says it is her present. She has been freed from her suffering. Not just her physical suffering. But the suffering of what everyone else thinks about her. Now everyone knows she has been freed. Now, she is no longer suffering from personal insecurity, nor feelings of being unloved, nor social isolation, nor religious judgment, nor the inner struggle of thinking that God had doomed her. She. Is. Loved.

So next time you look in the mirror, you find yourself in a crowd thinking, "God can't possibly love me," look into the Word of God and hear the words of Jesus for you that call you His child. Read the Gospels again and listen to the voice of Jesus who is the voice of truth.

You are loved,
Pastor Brian

> *Jesus, I admit, I often don't feel loved. But, today, I am going to put my faith in what you say. I'm going to believe your truth that I am loved. Help me to reject all the illusions I build around my identity. Help me to never stop believing this truth—that I am a child of God. In Jesus' name, Amen.*

4.

Joy

Be joyful in hope, patient in affliction, faithful in prayer.
—Romans 12:12

Rejoice always.
—1 Thessalonians 5:16

To my friend who doesn't realize that your circumstances will never make you truly happy,

I know you are struggling internally. You've chased money, success, and one relationship after another, believing that this time you will be happy. Yet you've found that while you feel good momentarily, you're often left feeling emptier.

Some days, your circumstances and the anxiety that comes with them convince you that you will never be happy. Not that you haven't tried. But it's just one thing after another in the wrong direction. Like you, I've also tried to create happiness by constantly changing my circumstances.

Happiness is illusive. We're always chasing it, and rarely if ever, finding it. Every time we think we are there, the goal posts move once again. The reality is that we're always looking for it in the wrong places. The word "illusive" and the word "illusion" share the same root. Both involve deception or trickery.

When it comes to happiness, we're chasing something *internal* but attempting to fill it with something *external*. And what we really need is something *eternal*.

Here's a lesson that most of us never learn: I can't control what happens *to* me. But I must learn to choose what happens *in* me. What happens to me is *external*. What happens in me is *internal*. What Jesus has done for me is *eternal*. Choosing joy is simply the choice to focus my inner soul on the eternal work of Jesus inside my soul, a work that will never end.

It's a paradox really. We often do the exact opposite. We do everything we can to control circumstances, things, and people that we cannot control. We expend enormous amounts of mental anguish trying to control something that we cannot control. On the other hand, we often neglect to take control of feelings that happen within us. We believe those feelings are uncontrollable. Funny how we try to control the feelings of other people while telling ourselves we cannot control our own.

Control is an illusion.

I need to learn to manage my feelings the way Jesus would. After all, joy is generally the mood of Jesus. Happiness comes from the word "happenstance," from which we get the word "circumstance." It depends on happenings. Happiness is external. Joy, on the other hand, is internal. You have a happy time at Disneyland, you leave, and you lose your happiness, often in the parking lot—if not before, say, when two of your kids are crying over a dropped Churro or the Small World ride breaks down and the song keeps playing. And playing. And playing. Joy, on the other hand, can be constant.

Can you have happiness despite what is going on in your life? It sounds good, but life doesn't work that way. On the other hand, you can have joy regardless of your circumstances.

"Hap" is the Old Norse and Old English root of happiness, and it just means luck or chance, as did the Old French "heur," giving us "bonheur," good fortune or happiness. German gives us the word "gluck," which to this day means both happiness and chance.

Here's a real-life question for you to answer:

Life is ____% what happens to me and _____% how I react to it.

The truth is ... Joy is not *chance*, it's a *choice*!

You might think, "Loving life depends on what happens to me in life, right?" You might say, "You don't know my life—if you did, you wouldn't love it." You might say, "If you knew my pain, you wouldn't like your life either." You might say, "My life hasn't been very lucky. Karma has not been good to me."

If you think about it, joy is an accurate word to describe the mood of Jesus when you read the Gospels. Did Jesus get angry? Yes. Was Jesus overwhelmed with grief? Yes. Did Jesus suffer deeply? Yes. But generally, what kind of mood was Jesus in much of the time? Joyful. I think He chose joy—and so can we when we walk with Jesus.

How can we learn to choose joy the way that Jesus did—no matter what?

> I have told you this so that my joy may be in you and that your joy may be complete.
> —*John 15:11*

> Rejoice in the Lord always. I will say it again: Rejoice!
> —*Philippians 4:4*

Rejoice means to make the daily choice to choose joy.

First, since joy is not dependent on my circumstances, I must see my circumstances for what they are. They are a laboratory. They are a learning lab. They are an opportunity to practice joy. Certainly, difficult times clarify some things. Tough times are particularly good at removing the illusion of self-security, the illusion of circumstantial happiness, and the illusion of control.

Second, I must remember that my purpose in life is not to glorify me, it is to glorify my Father in Heaven. It's to glorify Jesus and the Spirit. When I live to glorify myself, my circumstances become all about me. When I live to glorify Jesus, my learning lab is a constant opportunity to point my life to Jesus Christ.

Third, I must learn to look for the work of Jesus in my life, not for the quick fix to my circumstances. I can embrace joy because I am a child of the King. I can choose joy because He is always present and working in my life, even in my most difficult circumstances.

One more thought. Learn to be personable, but don't take things personally. I heard the phrase from a doctor several years ago. It's good advice for doctors. It's even better advice for people looking for more joy in their life.

You are a child of the King,
Pastor Brian

> *Jesus, please help me to release my circumstances to you. Help me to pry my heart and hands off of what I cannot control. Jesus, I ask you to fill me with your joy. I release the illusion of self-security, happiness, and control. I put my trust in you. I confess that I tend to think of myself first, but I ask you to help me consider what you are doing in me and find my joy in your work in this season. In Jesus' name, Amen.*

5.

Humility

The Christian Gospel is that I am so flawed that Jesus had to die for me, yet I am so loved and valued that Jesus was glad to die for me. This leads to deep humility and deep confidence at the same time. It undermines both swaggering and sniveling. I cannot feel superior to anyone, and yet I have nothing to prove to anyone. I do not think more of myself nor less of myself. Instead, I think of myself less. [8]
—Timothy Keller

To my friend who is wrestling with insecurity and pride,

It's one thing to wrestle with an insecurity. It's another to know what to do about it.

You said to me, "I'm struggling with not being good enough. I fear rejection. I don't know who I can really trust, and I'm regularly disappointed in myself. I'm so tired of beating myself up. What is wrong with me and what am I supposed to do?"

I struggle with pride and insecurity too. The reality is we all do, whether we are tuned into it or not.

A long, long time ago in a land far, far away … my wife and I were visiting a beach in Galveston, Texas. As we walked up to the beach, she noted numerous jellyfish scattered on the sand. We had not been to the beach together much, and I suggested we go swimming. She declined, pointing out the jellyfish. I told her that jellyfish were common in the ocean, but that didn't mean we would be stung.

We swam. I got stung. Pride always insists it won't happen to me. Pride always says I know better. I learned a powerful lesson that day. My wife's instincts are usually spot on, and I let my own pride get in the way.

If you think you don't wrestle with pride, you're already living in an illusion. If you are human, you wrestle with pride. Not just the pride of being puffed up, but also the pride of insecurity and obsession with self. We all wrestle with these. Truthfully, insecurity and pride are two sides of the same coin because they both involve an obsession with self.

What we often don't realize is that wrestling with pride is wrestling with God. Let me explain.

> But he gives us more grace. That is why Scripture says: "God opposes the proud but shows favor to the humble."
> —James 4:6

Think about all the ways pride and insecurity are destructive in our lives. My pride:

- Craves to be the center of attention.
- Convinces me that I am always right.
- Feels the need to always air my opinion.
- Makes me feel like I should be able to control other people.
- Believes that I have the right to be angry and stay angry when I've been hurt.
- Refuses correction and continues to make the same mistakes while expecting different results.
- Blames others and refuses to accept responsibility.
- Plays the victim and wallows in pity.

- Obsesses with me and ignores you.
- Convinces me I deserve a life without any pain and suffering.
- Expects change to happen in my life without having to do any of the work.

In the end, it's pride that traps me in The Pity Vortex. The more we are full of ourselves, the less aware we are of our need for Jesus.

Here's the thing we all need to be able to embrace:

Pride and insecurity open the door for everything wrong in my life. Pride creates the illusions of my life. It tells me that I don't need God. That no one will notice my destructive behaviors. That I deserve everything I want.

On the other hand, *humility opens the door for more of Jesus in my life.* Think about the value that humility brings to our lives and relationships. And contrast humility with what pride does.

> He mocks proud mockers but shows favor to the humble and oppressed.
> —*Proverbs 3:34*

Think about what else pride does:

> Haughty eyes and a proud heart—the unplowed field of the wicked—produce sin.
> —*Proverbs 21:4*

Pride opens the door for sin in my life. At the core of my sin is a selfishness rooted in pride. It's the sin behind many of my sins. Humility opens the door for salvation. There's no Jesus in my life if I never find enough humility to confess that I need Him.

> Whoever loves discipline loves knowledge, but whoever hates correction is stupid.
> —*Proverbs 12:1*

Pride opens the door for excuses. Do you ever get defensive? I do. It's easy to make excuses. It's easy to blame everyone else. It's natural to look for something or someone else to blame. You know why? Pride. Humility opens the door for repentance and change in my behavior.

> Where there is strife, there is pride, but wisdom is found in those who take advice.
> —*Proverbs 13:10*

Pride opens the door for conflict and tension in our relationships. Think about how many arguments you've had over the years about some issue or another that no longer really matters. In fact, I bet right now when you look back to the worst arguments you've ever had, you probably forgot what even triggered it. But you can be certain about what fueled it: pride. Humility opens the door for grace in our relationships.

> When pride comes, then comes disgrace, but with humility comes wisdom.
> —*Proverbs 11:2*

> Humility is the fear of the Lord; its wages are riches and honor and life.
> — *Proverbs 22:4*

Pride opens the door for disgrace and destruction in my life. Humility opens the door for honor from the God of the universe—honor from Jesus when I absolutely do not deserve honor from Jesus.

Think about it: Humility was His way of operating. Humility was the culture He worked hard to mold into the disciples. Humility was what He had that everyone else needed. And it's humility that establishes the healthy culture of His church.

Look at this another way. Most everyone acknowledges that the secret to life is love. What most of us don't know is that the secret to love is humility because an obsession with self is the exact opposite of love.

You are secure in the grip of Jesus,
Pastor Brian

Dear Jesus, I humble myself before you. I confess that I wrestle with pride. Please make it evident in my life when I am wrestling with you. Show me how my pride enhances the pain in my life and others. Break through my illusions. And bring more of Jesus to my life, and more humility to my soul. In Jesus' name, Amen.

6.

Breathe

Jesus said to them, "Surely you will quote this proverb to me: 'Physician, heal yourself!' And you will tell me, 'Do here in your hometown what we have heard that you did in Capernaum.'" "Truly I tell you," she continued, "no prophet is accepted in his hometown."
—Luke 4:23-24

To my doctor friend who is struggling with burnout,

When we got together for coffee, you shared that you're struggling to stay focused and find the energy to do what you need to do with patients. You drag yourself to work, find that you are irritable when you shouldn't be, and feel an internal ache that you can't explain. As a doctor, you realize that these are classic symptoms of burnout, right?

It's hard to be the patient when you're used to being the doctor, the one with all the answers. And it's hard to be the one needing healing when you are used to being the healer.

Can we be honest about something? Burnout is so common and oh-so-painful, especially after we've invested so much of our lives in our careers. I'm a pastor. You're a doctor. We're not supposed to struggle with these things, but we do struggle—often underneath the surface. In fact, our professions encourage us to push forward on the outside while we are quietly struggling on the inside. I feel for you because I, too, know the struggle.

I want to say thank you for all you endured during the COVID-19 pandemic. While most people pontificate about origins and whether the threat was real, many of your profession were knee-deep in sickness and death, trying to find a way to prevent people from dying. It's only natural that, somewhere along the way, the pain of all that sickness and death would catch up to you.

In 2022, nearly two-thirds of all U.S. doctors reported burnout because of the pandemic.[9] Between 1 in 10 and 1 in 6 doctors will develop a problem with substance abuse during their career.[10] The suicide rate among male physicians is 1.41 times higher than the general male population, and among female physicians, the relative risk is even more pronounced—2.27 times greater than the general female population.[11]

All healers are wounded healers. All of us need healing in our souls, not to mention our bodies. If you think you are exempt, you're not only living in an illusion, but you're also creating your own delusion.

It's hard to not be able to accomplish precisely what you set out to do. Doctors, by profession, are odds breakers. You are the top of your class. You set goals—academic, professional, financial—and you achieve them. You do what most of us come up short attempting to do.

But at some point, you bump into something you cannot change, and you're not used to that. So, it hurts and aches, often below the surface.

You spend your days consumed with the human body, with flesh and blood, so much so that I'm guessing it would be easy to neglect the soul aspect of your own body. You may or may not believe we have a soul. But surely, you've helped enough people who struggle internally to know there is something beyond flesh and blood.

So, if you are used to being the healer, and yet something is nagging you that you can't place your finger on deep down in your soul, what are you to do?

Slow down long enough to pay attention to what is going on below the surface.

Let's face a harsh reality: Being part of the healing profession does not make you immune to pain, sickness, depression, addiction, or suicidal thoughts. If anything, it puts you at greater risk in all such areas. You bear a burden that often feels like more than a burden. You notch a few wins, but far more defeats.

I want you to look into the mirror and answer this question: *How is my soul really doing underneath the surface?*

What do I mean by soul? The inner and outer part of you. The totality of who you are.

I wonder some days: Who heals the soul of the healers? Who takes care of the people who take care of everyone else? If you ever feel the need to talk, there are plenty of us who provide soul care who would care to listen.

With all the "unhealth" you deal with daily, it's a wonder any in your profession are able to stay healthy. So, as I said, slow down. Breathe.

I know, slowing down seems counterproductive. Slowing down seems so unrealistic in your world. But consider for a moment the ultimate healer. Consider Jesus.

> But Jesus often withdrew to lonely places and prayed.
> —Luke 5:16

Jesus, God in the flesh, is The Healer. He spent time, made time, and gave time to healing others. When the broken and lame were brought to Him, he gave much energy to heal both their bodies and their souls. But consider this: The Healer, with the power of God to heal running through His veins, took time to tend to His soul. The Healer, who is unlimited in power, chose to lay down His power to make time to find renewal. He modeled the need we have as human beings to create space, to withdraw from those who need healing, and to tend to our own souls.

I'm not suggesting that He needed healing in His soul, but that He chose a path that would create health or keep health in His soul.

If you've been ignoring that nagging pain deep inside, and you've found ways—healthy or unhealthy—to mask that pain, what would it take for you to admit this truth to yourself? *I am not sufficient to heal myself. I need to slow down and focus on the deeper parts of my life.*

I have a story that you might relate to: My neighbor's tree almost fell on me in my backyard. Almost. I barely escaped harm. While working in my backyard, I heard the crack and immediately knew what was happening. For years, my daughters joked that the neighbor's tree was going to come down on our house. This was the day. I heard the crack and ran. A large limb fell on our garage, then to the ground.

Later, I asked the arborist why the branch fell that day of all days. It wasn't particularly windy. It wasn't raining or snowing. He said, "It has been diseased a long time. It's just that nobody knew. Why today? Who knows. It seems like it came down all of a sudden, but that's not what happened. It had been diseased for a long time, but no one could see it on the outside."

As a doctor, I'm sure you can relate. Maybe because your branch already fell, or maybe because you know there's a weak one ready to fall, but you keep whistling in the dark, pretending it won't.

What happens below the surface has an exponential and compounding impact on what happens above the surface. What's happening inside the soul exponentially impacts what's happening on the outside.

Based on the life of Jesus, I would encourage you to come to a place of admission. At best, I am a wounded healer. In fact, I am a greater healer when I am a wounded healer. I can embrace greater empathy as a wounded healer. I can embrace improved care as a wounded healer. And I can sustain a longer life of health care when I tend to my own woundedness.

Slowing down and creating time to deal with your own health will make you a better doctor. Your patients will appreciate your care more when you heal better, faster, and stronger from this place. You and I can succeed at helping others with their health when we are healthy, not only in our bodies, but in our minds, spirits, and souls.

Many spiritual writers associate the concept of the wounded healer with Henri Nouwen. He borrowed the idea from Carl Jung, who borrowed it from Greek mythology.

> Jung drew on this metaphor for his understanding of psychotherapy: "The doctor is effective only when he himself is affected. Only the wounded physician heals … . The pains and burdens one bears and eventually overcomes is the source of great wisdom and healing power for others."[12]

You're used to being the helper. The healer. The doctor. The physician. Is it time to slow down and reach out to another for help since as a physician and healer, you cannot heal yourself?

On the TV show M*A*S*H, in a letter written to Sigmund Freud addressing how doctors in war can be strong and find resourceful ways to face the hidden problems below the surface, psychiatrist Sydney Friedman writes, "They look everyday into the face of death. On the surface, they may seem like other doctors and nurses, but underneath, ah Sigmund, underneath."[13]

>You're better when in tune with your woundedness,
>Pastor Brian

> *Jesus, I admit that I am not all mighty. And I admit that my soul needs care and healing. I live in the world of flesh and blood, and frankly, I'm uncomfortable in the world of soul care. Where I am unhealthy, please help me to know what to do. And where I am destructive to myself or others, change me from the inside out. I pray that you would help me tend to my own soul in healthier ways. In Jesus' name, Amen.*

7.

Redemption

Success is the ability to go from one failure to another with no loss of enthusiasm ... Success is not final; failure is not fatal: it is the courage to continue that counts. [14]
—Popularly attributed to Winston Churchill

To my friend who is full of regret and feels like a failure,

As we've discussed, the feeling of failure is gut-wrenching. You told me, "The feeling of failure stands over me like a ghost I cannot escape." That's profound. That's insightful. That's haunting. When I've walked in your shoes, my feelings of failure have been haunting as well. I want you to know that you are not alone.

We all know how regret feels. Something haunts you that you wish you hadn't done. An addiction you didn't confront. A bad decision you wish you didn't make. Something to keep hidden that you don't want others to know about.

Sometimes our regrets are things we *didn't* do. We *didn't* go back to school. We *didn't* stick it out in that relationship. We *didn't* spend more time with our kids when we had the chance.

A lot of us collect regrets the way kids collect rocks. We keep them somewhere private. And we get them out to look at every now and then, as if we needed reminders of our wrongness, as if we were batteries requiring a charge of regret. Then we put them back in the box and shove them away under the bed where we hope no one else will see them.

Here's the thing: Regret serves as a continual reminder of our *past failures*. But Jesus serves as a continual reminder of our *future hope*. Regret won't let me forget my past. Jesus won't let regret win. What's more, He won't let regret be the only thing we remember. Jesus reminds us of redemption.

I want you to learn to distinguish between failing and failure. *Failing* to achieve a goal is part of the learning process; it doesn't mean you are a failure. *Failure* is giving up entirely.

Do you remember the story in Luke 22 where Peter, after swearing he wouldn't, denied knowing Jesus? It was all predicted there as well. Jesus told Peter it would happen. Three times Peter denies knowing Jesus. Peter swore to Jesus that this would never happen. It did. Standing around a charcoal fire, hiding in the shadows after Jesus was arrested, Peter denies knowing Jesus when confronted about who He really is.

Fast forward. Jesus was crucified. After denying Jesus three times, Peter ran. He was not there when Jesus died on that cross. Jesus was resurrected. Peter was hiding away with the other disciples. After hearing from Mary Magdalene, Peter and John run to see the empty tomb for themselves. Later, they see the resurrected Jesus. But something is still bothering Peter. Peter boasted and bragged that he would never deny Jesus. Then he did. He fled. He denied three times that he knew Jesus. He wasn't there when Jesus died.

Peter likely feels like a disappointment, a failed leader who turned coward when Jesus needed him most. Peter has to wonder how Jesus still feels about him as a person. As a follower. As a leader.

He and some of the disciples were fishing, their jobs in their previous lives. Jesus approaches them from the shore, but they don't recognize Him. He tells them where to catch some fish, and they catch 153. A specific number to go with a big fish story. Peter recognizes Jesus and jumps in the water to swim to shore. When he gets to Jesus, there's a charcoal fire burning. The same kind of fire that was burning when he denied he knew Jesus. If I'm Peter, that smell would trigger my memories of denial and feelings of deep regret.

Jesus is prepared to handle whatever we bring him. He knows we need to process our pain and regret. Sometimes, the deepest soul work happens in nature, around a fire, in the context of a meal, when we finally decide to be honest with ourselves and honest with God about how we really feel.

When they had finished eating, Jesus said to Simon Peter,

> Simon son of John, do you truly love me more than these?" "Yes, Lord," he said, "you know that I love you." Jesus said, "Feed my lambs." Again Jesus said, "Simon son of John, do you truly love me?" He answered, "Yes, Lord, you know that I love you." Jesus said, "Take care of my sheep." The third time he said to him, "Simon son of John, do you love me?" Peter was hurt because Jesus asked him the third time, "Do you love me?" He said, "Lord, you know all things; you know that I love you." Jesus said, "Feed my sheep."
> —John 21:15-17

Do you know how many perfect people there were in the Bible? Jesus. Party of one.

Ever felt like God couldn't, or wouldn't, use you because of your regrets and failures? Welcome to the club. God doesn't call us because we will never fail. Jesus calls us because He is in the business of redemption. Before he called you, God knew every regret you would have. God uses us to minister to others *because* of our brokenness, not *despite* our brokenness. Our lives are a showcase of His grace, love, and relentless pursuit of us even when we are at our worst.

How does Jesus respond when I have failed? Disappointed Him? Hid from God? Run from Him? Jesus responds by seeking us out. We hide. Jesus seeks. God has been seeking hiding sinners since Genesis 3. Jesus will never give up on me, and He will never let me give up on Him. Jesus' grip on my life is stronger than my grip on Him will ever be. He refuses to let my future be defined by my past. This is what redemption is all about. I will be defined by His work in my life.

So, what can you and I do when we are overwhelmed with regret and failure?

Run to Jesus. Stop running away. Stop hiding. In the presence of Jesus, explore the hard questions with total honesty and vulnerability. Jesus asks Peter three times if he loves him more than these. Peter is forced to explore what's going on deep inside.

As I'm processing the pain, the motives, and the regrets in my life, I must learn to let Jesus take them. Let them go. It's not just ignoring them, denying them, or pretending they have gone away. It's surrender. It's laying my regrets, my life, and my future at the feet of Jesus. When I won't let go of such things, I'm telling myself that what Jesus has done for me is not enough. That the death of Jesus on the cross is not sufficient. That I must continue to pay the price for my sins. We must decide once and for all that what Jesus has done is enough. Like Peter, I need to keep my eyes focused on my redeemer. And get back up and start serving.

At some level, my obsession with my collection of regrets is an obsession with me. It's a weight and responsibility I simply cannot handle and do not deserve. Only Jesus deserves to be the obsession of our lives. When I'm focused on my past, my pains, my regrets, my failures, my shortcomings, my plans that didn't happen, my lack of success, who am I obsessing over? ME.

Regret and failure are real. The illusion is our obsession with regret and failure. It's an obsession with ourselves. As Christians, the truth that defines who we are is redemption. It's time we lived like it.

You are redeemed,
Pastor Brian

Jesus, thank you that I am yours and no one can snatch me from your hand. Thank you as well that you bring grace and redemption even when I bring sin and failure. Help me to remember that the measure you are looking for isn't success. It's faithfulness. I'm confessing that I have many regrets that I don't know how to let go of. And I'm running to you. Help me to explore and process why this is. Thank you that you have forgiven me. Help me to forgive others and forgive myself. In Jesus' name, Amen.

MINDSET 2
Embrace your life despite your pain

Magic tricks work because humans have a hardwired process of attention and awareness that is hackable. [15]
—Stephen L. Macknik and Susana Martinez-Conde

Therefore, in order to keep me from becoming conceited, I was given a thorn in my flesh, a messenger of Satan, to torment me. Three times I pleaded with the Lord to take it away from me. But he said to me, "My grace is sufficient for you, for my power is made perfect in weakness." Therefore I will boast all the more gladly about my weaknesses, so that Christ's power may rest on me. That is why, for Christ's sake, I delight in weaknesses, in insults, in hardships, in persecutions, in difficulties. For when I am weak, then I am strong.
—2 Corinthians 12:7-10

I was merely thinking God's thoughts after him. Since we astronomers are priests of the highest God in regard to the book of nature, it benefits us to be thoughtful, not of the glory of our minds, but rather, above all else, of the glory of God. [16]
—Astronomer Johannes Kepler

When you feel pain, the most natural thing to want is *not* to feel pain. Escape comes in a lot of forms. We bury our head in the sand. We drink. We take drugs. We pursue out-of-control lusts to feel something that resembles pleasure. Whether it's gambling, overeating, overspending, hyper-sexual behavior, or something else, we pursue anything that will dilute the pain, if even for a few moments.

In the fictional world of "Star Trek," the "Prime Directive" provides vision, scope, and boundaries regarding how Star Fleet should interact with new cultures. But we've never been told what the Prime Directive actually states.[17] Not so with us and pain. We know *exactly* what the Prime Directive is. Our personal Prime Directive regarding pain is to get out of it. Stop the pain. Find a way to escape it.

And when we embrace escape as our personal "Prime Directive," it becomes the most important thing about us. When I live to escape my pain, my life is increasingly defined by my unhealthy coping mechanisms that I use to escape it. Addiction sets in. Life becomes unmanageable, and we attempt to manage it through more escape. Sure, our coping mechanisms feel good at first, but will cost us more than we are willing to pay down the road. Enter the previously mentioned addictions.

What's more, even healthy things can become unhealthy when they become the escape from our pain-filled life. I've seen people who run from their pain by over-involvement at church, for example.

Why is numbing the pain a bad idea? Most of the time, it makes us insensitive to not only the pain, but to all the other things that do matter in this world. Often, it transfers the pain to someone else. Particularly to those closest to us. Ask the family of any addict. The family and friends know long before the addict because they've been asked to carry the pain.

Oddly enough, when I try to escape my pain and embrace my life, neither tends to happen. When I prioritize escaping pain over every other aspect of my life, my family loses out. God loses out. I lose out. Escaping pain short-circuits the potential growth that would happen in my life because I refused to learn to trust God through this season of my life. Escape short-circuits my growth.

At some level, every single day is a choice between the mission to escape my pain and the need to embrace my life despite that pain. Consciously or unconsciously, I will put my internal energy toward either escaping my pain or embracing my broken yet beautiful life.

I want to appeal to you in the strongest possible terms to embrace your life. All of it. The good and the bad. The better and the worse. The joy and the pain. The sunshine and the rain. All of it. The beautiful and the unbeautiful. The amazing and the ordinary. All of it.

Neuroscience teaches us that there's incredible power in attention. It's natural when we feel pain to shift our attention to the awareness of this sensation. You bite your tongue, literally, a pain so intense that you momentarily ignore everything else. What happens in a moment can become an obsession. We focus all our awareness and attention on the pain. Guess what happens when we do this? We exacerbate our pain and ignore the most important aspects of our lives.

Conversely, we can learn to hijack our attention and shift our awareness—for the good. Magicians do this to us all the time. It's called misdirection. They intentionally work to shift our attention in a way that we are unaware of. Like them, we can learn to become consciously aware of our attention and shift that attention to something better than our pain. There's incredible power in focusing on what is good when we are experiencing what is not good. All this talk about hijacking our attention and shifting our focus has big-picture implications as well. When we shift our focus from escaping pain to embracing life, our experience of life and pain will shift as well. Again, Ambron points out:

> We can flit from one sensation to another very quickly, but we cannot seem to be able to focus on more than one sensation at a time. Pain of course is going to be prioritized over all other sensations because it signifies a threat that might imperil our lives. Consequently, the simple realization above has very important implications for controlling pain because it allows us to propose that painfulness can be diminished by directing our attention to another sensation ... Taken at face value, suffering could be reduced if patients learned to focus their attention elsewhere.[18]

You can hijack your attention and shift your awareness of pain. Create temporary distractions. But what we need to learn are healthier mechanisms to shift our attention and awareness. Less self-destructive. More life-protective and life-productive.

I can read some of your thoughts: "Brian, are you telling me I shouldn't believe in healing or that Jesus won't heal me?" *Not at all.* "Are you telling me to just accept that I will feel this pain forever?" *Definitely not.* "Are you telling me it's wrong to seek medical treatment to reduce my pain?" *Absolutely not.* I am saying that you and I must learn to trust God's grace *while still suffering.*

As long as we are alive on this side of eternity, there is some kind of suffering going on inside of us. Suffering won't end until we're on the other side of this life. But being stuck can end now. Pray for healing? Sure. But trust Jesus whose answers are sometimes "Yes, healing is right now," and sometimes "No, healing will come later, even in eternity."

What's your definition of beauty? Are you swayed more by the awe of the mountain, the rhythm of the ocean, or the painting in the museum? Travel the world looking for beauty. If you open your eyes, the beauty of God is all around you.

> The heavens declare the glory of God; the skies proclaim the work of his hands.
> —*Psalm 19:1*

I've walked through some of the world's biggest museums. Hiked through some of the world's most magnificent mountain ranges. Walked through some of the world's most majestic cathedrals. Is there beauty there? Of course. But have you considered that some of the most beautiful moments of your life come with pain?

Consider childbirth. I know, I know, I'm a guy. I haven't experienced the pain myself. But I served my wife through the sickness of pregnancy and was present for the birth of both our daughters. For sure, she suffered pain to bring our children into the world. But my wife would agree that two of the most beautiful moments of our lives were the births of our daughters, which involved lots of pain. The babies cried. My wife wept in exhaustion and gratitude. We both wept at the beauty of our newborn baby girls.

Consider friendship, marriage, or family. Life's deepest and best relationships are beautiful, but also come with a fair amount of pain. There's no way around it. In fact, pain is sometimes the bond that drives the friendship forward. A friend of mine tells me what really deepened his friendship with his brother-in-law was that brother-in-law losing a son. "I became the 'safe place' for him to share his grief," my friend told me. "That built a new, deeper trust in our relationship." Empathy, compassion, and kindness produce an ever-deepening bond in friendship, yet they are often rooted in a shared painful experience.

Beauty happens when we see what God can do. Take some of the most painful and difficult moments of your life. Lay them at the feet of Jesus. Ask him to bring beauty from ashes. He's been doing it for millennium. Some of the most powerful moments of beauty in your life emerge from the work of God through the moments that were broken, even brutal, just moments before.

I'll bet the deepest moments of your life story involve Jesus doing something transformational amid pain, fear, anxiousness, anger, sadness, depression, or disease. Amid our greatest shame, our worst guilt, our greatest discouragement, Jesus has a way of making everything beautiful in His time.

Living in victory in a pain-filled world is not about escaping pain; it's about embracing life despite it, squeezing out the true meaning of life, and honoring God in the way we live whether we are in moments of pleasure and joy or moments of pain and grief.

You may know the sixties song "Turn, Turn, Turn" that emerged from Ecclesiastes 3, but do you know the power of that chapter?

> He has made everything beautiful in its time. He has also set eternity in the human heart; yet no one can fathom what God has done from beginning to end.
> —*Ecclesiastes 3:11*

Have you watched as God worked a greater good in your impossible situation?

> And we know that in all things God works for the good of those who love him, who have been called according to his purpose.
> —*Romans 8:28*

Have you sat back and admired, after a time, the beauty that God has brought from the ashes of your life (Isaiah 61:1-3)? Maybe you haven't seen the greater good or the beauty from ashes yet. God isn't finished working. Perhaps others see what God is doing with a Him-first perspective while you're struggling with a me-first inability to see Him at work. But we're all works in progress. Be patient with yourself. Be patient with God.

If He is going to make something beautiful out of what is broken in our lives, we might want it done immediately. But God works on no person's timetable. Some things take a while. And some things will take our lifetimes. Have you seen diamonds? Coal isn't beautiful. But give it immense pressure and heat, and it produces mind-numbing beauty—after millions of years.

You say, "I don't want to wait that long." Me either. But neither do I want to be left holding a bag of coal the rest of my life.

I'm not much of an artist; I take pencil and paper and make stick figures at best. But put the pencil of my life in the hands of God and I can see His handiwork and find His masterpiece. Put the clay of your life in the hands of Jesus and you will find immense beauty in what He re-forms with your life. Artists do the same thing. Some take broken pieces of pottery and use them to make something beautiful. This is nothing new. Jesus has been in the beauty business longer than humans can imagine.

Are you familiar with the Japanese art of Kintsugi? Google it. Have you seen the work of the Spanish artist Gaudi? There are many other artists whose work takes the broken or ordinary pieces of life to make beautiful art. If science is thinking God's thoughts after Him, then art is creating God's beauty after Him.

> Kintsugi—which means "join with gold"—is the Japanese art of repairing broken objects, often ceramic pottery or glass. Traditionally, gold lacquer is used to piece shards together again, creating a more beautiful object through the acts of breaking and repair. Kintsugi encourages us to fix rather than discard, thus placing a higher value on the objects we bring into our lives.[19]

God does this with us.

> For it is by grace you have been saved, through faith—and this is not from yourselves, it is the gift of God—not by works, so that no

one can boast. For we are God's handiwork, created in Christ Jesus to do good works, which God prepared in advance for us to do.
—*Ephesians 2:8-10*

The word handiwork is "*poiema.*" It means "that which is made, work, creation."[20]

Or consider this one:

> But we have this treasure in jars of clay to show that this all-surpassing power is from God and not from us. We are hard pressed on every side, but not crushed; perplexed, but not in despair; persecuted, but not abandoned; struck down, but not destroyed. We always carry around in our body the death of Jesus, so that the life of Jesus may also be revealed in our body. For we who are alive are always being given over to death for Jesus' sake, so that his life may also be revealed in our mortal body. So then, death is at work in us, but life is at work in you.
> —*2 Corinthians 4:7-12*

There's a common theme here. Jesus is in the business of redemption, of restoration, of reconciliation, and of bringing beauty from the ashes of our lives. Broken does not equal "not beautiful." And our brokenness does not doom us to lives that cannot bring glory to God. In fact, quite the opposite.

Life can, and must, be embraced despite the pain. What's the alternative? Sulking, pity parties, and endless bouts of escapism. Life can, and must, be embraced in the pain, trusting that Jesus, on His timetable, will take the broken and painful pieces and create something beautiful and unique.

Truthfully, I don't want the pain. And you do not either. But God often does His best and most important work in the context of suffering. It was true in Jesus' life. And it's true in my life and yours. The brutal truth is that if I do not come to admit I am broken, I am far less likely to turn to God. And then, without God, I attempt to create a life of beauty that ends up as a life with pride, pretending, guilt, and shame. When I try to make beauty out of the broken, I'm left with my usual stick-figures messes.

Embracing my life with pain means embracing my life with Jesus in the pain. And it means embracing a life that lives His way of life in suffering. A way of grace, a way of love, and a way of sacrifice. In the Garden of Gethsemane, Jesus prayed.

> My Father, if it is possible, may this cup be taken from me. Yet not as I will, but as you will.
> —*Matthew 26:39b*

Is there anything wrong with wanting to skip the painful parts? Not at all. Later, Paul pleaded three times, *"Please take away this thorn in my flesh."* Jesus asked three times in the Garden if He could skip what was coming. But His prayer embraced God's plan and embraced the good that God would do with His pain and suffering. Yet not my will but yours be done.

Here's one more thing that might be a struggle for you: God created the capacity for pleasure and pain. Both capacities are there for a reason. Weird as it sounds, the same nerves carry the signals of pleasure and pain. As humans, we want the good without what we perceive to be the bad. I say "perceive to be the bad" because we associate all pain as bad. But what if some pain is good for us? What if pain is an indicator of a problem? Among other things, numbing our pain removes our ability to know when something unhealthy is going on because we don't feel anything. Some would say that's the point. To feel nothing. But to feel nothing means: No pleasure. No pain. The result? Numbness.

Honestly, that's no way to live. It's not living. It's merely existing.

Living well despite pain looks like walking with Jesus through the joy and the pain. Living my day-to-day life. Doing the activities I enjoy that I can do. Living well means being present with the people I love. Living well means sharing my journey of brokenness and beauty with others. Worshipping Jesus no matter what life is serving up in the moment. Living with faith even when pain screams not to. Serving God's people and lifting up God's glory, even when it isn't easy.

Living well means embracing my broken, but beautiful, life with Jesus, even when life is brutal.

Dear Jesus, I admit that I never want to choose suffering, but I am suffering. I am asking that you bring healing and take away my pain. But I am here praising you amid it. Not what I will, but what you will for my life. I want to be well, not just physically, but in every way. Help me to honor you mentally, emotionally, spiritually, relationally, and physically. In Jesus' name, Amen.

8.

Peace

Imagine you are on a high cliff and you lose your footing and begin to fall. Just beside you is a branch sticking out of the edge of the cliff. It is your only hope and seems more than strong enough. How can it save you? If you are certain the branch can support you, but you don't actually reach out and grab it, you are lost. If instead your mind is filled with doubts and uncertainty that the branch can hold you, but you reach out and grab it anyway, you will be saved. Why? It's not the strength of your faith but the object of your faith that actually saves you. Strong faith in a weak branch is fatally inferior to weak faith in a strong branch.[21]
—Timothy Keller

To my friend with neuropathy,

It's impossible some days to live with chronic pain and the chronic fatigue that goes with it. I know this is a difficult season for you. I feel your pain. Literally. Neuropathy—whether the sensation of burning, stabbing, or numbness—can be crushing, and if it is accompanied by muscle weakness, can be devastating. I know that this is hard on you.

You've told me how neuropathy has turned your life upside down. You couldn't plan for this, and many days, you're uncertain where life goes from here. It interferes with day-to-day life, and you barely have energy left to get the basics done. As you said, there are many days when you feel like you're caught in one of those car-crusher machines, and you fear what's ahead.

I wish I could tell you that this season will end soon, but the reality is, I don't know. And I understand not knowing is difficult. In contrast, we do know this suffering will end someday. In fact, all our days of pain on this side of eternity point us to that greater reality where there will be no more suffering, no more crying, and no more pain. It's called heaven.

One of the brutal facts of life is that there is no living without pain and suffering. You would be hard-pressed to find one true instance of life that involves no pain. What about the rich and famous? Surely, their lives seem to be insulated from suffering because they are wealthy, right? Are you kidding me? Hollywood and Monaco are filled with people who, on the one hand, possess more money and means than most of us, but on the other hand, can't escape their drug addictions, their empty fame, their family struggles, their egos, their jealousy, and their destructions. The reality for the rich and famous is that richness and fame bring more troubles, not less. Same with the rich and un-famous; if you doubt it, read any book about what happens to people who win lotteries. Few wind up happier; most wind up consumed by their winnings, preyed on by friends and family. Some wind up broke.

It seems obvious to me that we want the quickest and easiest solution to be the obvious solution. This showed up in my life when I wanted my neurologist to prescribe medicine, but I didn't want to try physical therapy for my headaches. It turns out the physical therapy proved to be both helpful as a diagnostic tool and helpful for my pain. Likewise, we pop a pill in hopes that everything will change. We long for a pill to take away the pain, a pill to help us sleep, and a pill to help us feel better about all of it. Some might call that denial.

Don't get me wrong. Medications can be helpful. I take them, and there's nothing wrong with that. But relying solely on a pill to solve all our pain without exploring the deeper physical and emotional sources of pain as well as the broader physical, psychological, emotional, relational, and spiritual solutions can be short-sighted. We give so much power to the insurance companies and medical community and then grow frustrated when they make it complicated or the pills don't work. Bessel Van der Kolk writes:

> The drug revolution that started out with so much promise may in the end have done as much harm as good ... After conducting numerous studies of medications for PTSD, I have come to realize that psychiatric medications have a serious downside, as they may deflect attention from dealing with the underlying issues. The brain-disease model takes control over people's fate out of their own hands and puts doctors and insurance companies in charge of fixing their problems.[22]

It's easy to see that the pharmaceutical solution to pain has been the most relied-upon solution over the last 50 years, but it is also easy to see that this solution by itself is not working. Please don't misunderstand me. I'm asthmatic with severe allergies; I appreciate what the pharmaceutical industry has done for my life. We need better and broader approaches to pain solutions. I'm not saying there are no benefits in medicine. I am saying that in many cases we rely too heavily on pharmaceutical solutions because we rely on medicine alone. It's also easy to see that the pharmaceutical solution is wide open to abuse. Medicines that used to be prescribed in mass are much harder to receive today because of the ease with which addiction develops.

There is a spiritual component that can help us in our physical battles. Not long before he was crucified, Jesus warned the disciples again about what was coming.

> Do not let your hearts be troubled. You believe in God; believe also in me. My Father's house has many rooms; if that were not so, would I have told you that I am going there to prepare a place for you? And if I go and prepare a place for you, I will come back and take you to be with me that you also may be where I am.
> —*John 14:1-3*

This world is full of trouble. There's no escaping it. The very word comes from the Latin root *turbulare* or *turbidare*. It shares its root with words like *disturb, turbo, turbulence,* and *turbine,* where it has the meaning "to stir up." In this sense, the word *trouble* and the word *turbulence* are cousins. You might feel like your life has been stirred up and turned over, resulting in a fair amount of confusion and disorder. Indeed, life is full of trouble. Jesus warned us.

There are moments when all this turbulence and trouble convince you that "You won't make it. You can't do this." You know as well as I do that there are days when you tell Jesus, "I just can't do this anymore," or "I don't know how much longer I can hold on."

While we do our best to manage our daily to-do list when living in chronic pain, I want to remind you to hang on tightly to something Jesus said a little later that same night.

> Peace I leave with you; my peace I give you. I do not give to you as the world gives. Do not let your hearts be troubled and do not be afraid. "You heard me say, 'I am going away and I am coming back to you.' If you loved me, you would be glad that I am going to the Father, for the Father is greater than I.
> —*John 14:27-28*

And again that same night:

> A time is coming and in fact has come when you will be scattered, each to your own home. You will leave me all alone. Yet I am not alone, for my Father is with me. I have told you these things, so that in me you may have peace. In this world you will have trouble. But take heart! I have overcome the world.
> —*John 16:32-33*

Of course, all of this is spoken just hours before the cross and on the night he was arrested. But through the centuries, these words bring comfort to every generation when they face the stirring up and turning upside downs of life.

How can we embrace life despite our troubles?

Jesus offers us great comfort in His peace. Even better, he offers us His peace because He offers Himself. For all the trouble life brings our way, troubled times may have to be endured but don't have to be feared. Jesus knew all of this was coming toward Him and the disciples. And He's not caught off guard regarding our troubles as well. Jesus warned me that trouble is coming. Jesus promises to be with us in our troubles. You are not alone because He is with you. And Jesus overcomes your trouble with peace that was paid for on the cross.

In other words, whatever the world throws at you, Jesus brings something else. Something better. And something even more abundant. His Peace. Jesus' peace is both quantitatively and qualitatively different than any other peace. Biblically speaking, peace is wellness and wholeness. Peace is not the absence of pain. Peace is the presence of Jesus.

His peace is not temporary. His peace will last forever. And His peace brings the ability to face our troubles with our eyes and our faith wide open. We don't have to pretend our troubles are not real. We know they are. But we can face them with our eyes and hearts wide open, knowing that Jesus is present and He himself is our peace. Jesus himself is the overcomer, and with Jesus, you can know beyond a shadow of a doubt that your pain, while chronic, will not be chronic forever.

I wonder why pain is the only thing that gets to be chronic. Why can't peace be chronic? Can anything else be chronic besides pain? What about chronic *gratitude*? What about chronic *hope*? What about chronic *joy*?

I believe they can be chronic. New discoveries in neuroscience suggest that how you think about your pain will heighten or lessen your experience of that pain. It's not a matter of thinking about pain or not thinking about pain. It's a matter of thinking *healthily* about your pain. Richard Ambron states:

> What we have just learned is the almost bewildering number of mental processes that determine the degree of painfulness that we experience. Reward, acceptance, knowledge, and belief can diminish the experience of pain, whereas stress, fear, anxiety, and emotional state can worsen the pain … If dwelling on pain exacerbates the painfulness, then diverting attention away from the pain might remove the hurtfulness.[23]

The bottom line: When surrendered to Jesus, you are stronger than you think you are, because you are stronger in Christ than you think you are. When you have no strength, His never runs out. And He promises He will never leave you nor forsake you. The key is to not attempt to overcome the pain in you but, as Jesus said, to overcome your pain-filled life turned upside down in His Peace.

You are an overcomer in Christ,
Pastor Brian

> *Dear Jesus, thank you for entering our trouble and thank you that you chose not to be immune to it. And thank you for warning us. Even more, thank you that we are not alone and that you provide peace. Help me to walk with you, and with your Spirit, in your peace. Let not my heart be troubled in this world, not because I can overcome my troubles but because you have overcome this world and the trouble in it. Thank you that I have your peace both now and for eternity. In Jesus' name, Amen.*

9.

Hope

You keep track of all my sorrows. You have collected all my tears in your bottle. You have recorded each one in your book.
—Psalm 56:8 (NLT)

To my friend who just lost her husband,

 I feel sorrow with you. I know how much you loved your husband. I don't pretend to understand all your sorrow and grief, but I share in some of it. I understand his loss leaves a gaping hole in your heart and in your family. I get that none of this seems fair. Death is hard. And some days, grief feels impossible. He was your world. Gone too soon. He had a way of lighting up a room, and you lit up at his gigantic smile and deep laughs. I miss those, too.
 You might feel too raw right now, and you might want to wait to read what I am writing in this letter. Or at least lower your expectations. How else can I say this? There is nothing I will say here that will take away your pain. Scripture does provide great comfort in our pain, but the pain of

grief still lingers.

For decades, some have questioned whether psychological pain was real. Of course, it is. Neural imaging studies offer proof that pain, whether physical or psychological, emerges from the same areas of our brains.[24] There's no question that our emotional pain is as real as our physical pain. Of course, this does mean that our comforts and solutions must include those beyond the physical.

Grief, especially for those we love the most, is among the most difficult pains we ever experience in this life. Please don't misunderstand what I am about to say.

Grief can be good. Grief indicates the presence of love. Grief is good in the sense that it is a necessary part of love. If I experienced no grief when someone dies, it means something's lacking. Perhaps my heart is hardened to life and death. Or perhaps there was no love present at all. You are grieving deeply, dear friend, because you loved him deeply.

It's worth understanding that grief and mourning are slightly different from each other. Grief is the experience we have when we have lost something or someone. Grief happens whether we choose it or not, showing up in times and ways we can't control. Mourning, on the other hand, is a choice. Mourning is the intentional expression of deep sorrow after experiencing loss. Mourning is something we intentionally embrace to feel the emotions of our loss. And it is healthy.

Grief, of course, happens when someone we love dies. But it represents more than loss of life. Grief occurs when we experience loss of any kind. Or undergo a substantial change. Consider the grief we all experienced during the COVID-19 pandemic. Many people lost someone they loved. We didn't all lose someone. But we all lost our sense of normality, our sense of control, our sense of dreams, plans, and opportunities that all disappeared because of either COVID-19 or the control measures put in place.

It's natural to want to escape the pain of grief. In fact, denial is often the first stage of the grieving process because we simply can't bring ourselves to admit that the death or loss is happening. But we don't have to escape grief. In fact, we must learn to embrace it.

I take great comfort that Jesus knows what it is like to experience grief. In fact, I think He understands more than anyone else the consequences of death and loss. Do you remember the story of the death of His friend Lazarus? Jesus didn't just feel compassion for Mary and Martha. Jesus felt grief. *Grief is godly. Jesus wept.*

I can learn much from the way Jesus grieved. Jesus grieved because Jesus loved. There's no escaping grief unless I cut off my capacity to love. And that just wouldn't be healthy.

Read John 11. Jesus' friend Lazarus has died, and his sisters Martha and Mary are grieving the loss of their brother.

> "Lord," Martha said to Jesus, "if you had been here, my brother would not have died. But I know that even now God will give you whatever you ask." Jesus said to her, "Your brother will rise again." Martha answered, "I know he will rise again in the resurrection at the last day." Jesus said to her, "I am the resurrection and the life. The one who believes in me will live, even though they die; and whoever lives by believing in me will never die. Do you believe this?" "Yes, Lord," she replied, "I believe that you are the Messiah, the Son of God, who is to come into the world."
>
> *—John 11:21-27*

> When Mary reached the place where Jesus was and saw him, she fell at his feet and said, "Lord, if you had been here, my brother would not have died." When Jesus saw her weeping, and the Jews who had come along with her also weeping, he was deeply moved in spirit and troubled. "Where have you laid him?" he asked. "Come and see, Lord," they replied. Jesus wept.
>
> *—John 11:32-35*

You really should read the rest of the story. Jesus brings Lazarus back to life, but I want to focus on the way Jesus grieved.

Jesus grieved with deep emotion. There's nothing wrong with that. In fact, if your grief doesn't come out through deep emotion, sorrow, and tears, you're missing something. Jesus is compassionate toward Mary, Martha, and the others who are grieving. But more importantly, Jesus is grieving Himself. Death certainly breaks our hearts, but it breaks the heart of God too.

You and I worship a God who weeps. Jesus is not immune to the way sin and death affect us. In fact, Jesus walked to the cross for this very reason. Grief does not make Jesus weak. It makes Him more powerful than we understand. Jesus is, after all, a man of sorrows, acquainted with grief. (Isaiah 53:3)

Jesus' grief and Jesus' love were not cheap. It cost him dearly. To be the resurrection and the life, He had to die. It cost him a crucifixion, death, and all your sin poured out on him. That's how much He loves you, and that's why He grieves.

Jesus' grief was not shallow because His love was not shallow. Like Jesus, we grieve because we love. No love, no grief. After all, life without love is not life. It's existing. Grief is simply love in another form. We worship a God who grieves because we worship a God who loves. If you never want to feel the pain of grief, you will never experience the goodness of love.

> Grief, I've learned, is really just love. It's all the love you want to give but cannot. All that unspent love gathers up in the corners of your eyes the lump in your throat, and in that hollow part of your chest. Grief is just love with no place to go.[25]
> —Jamie Anderson

Jesus is with us in our grief. God is with us in our grief collecting our tears in his bottle. He knows our pain. He is not tired of sadness. In fact, when we have no words to pray, His Spirit is in us, praying for us.

Jesus grieves with you. Jesus ministered to Mary and Martha by grieving with them, not just for them. He comforted his friends through His own grief. God in the flesh, who has unlimited strength, ministers and comforts through grief. Grief is both an opportunity to minister and a means through which we minister by coming alongside a person and grieving with them.

And Jesus grieves with hope.

> Brothers and sisters, we do not want you to be uninformed about those who sleep in death, so that you do not grieve like the rest of mankind, who have no hope. For we believe that Jesus died and rose again, and so we believe that God will bring with Jesus those who have fallen asleep in him. According to the Lord's word, we tell you that we who are still alive, who are left until the coming of the Lord, will certainly not precede those who have fallen asleep. For the Lord himself will come down from heaven, with a loud command, with the voice of the archangel and with the trumpet call of God, and the dead in Christ will rise first. After that, we who are still alive and are left will be caught up together with them in the clouds to meet the Lord in the air. And so we will be with the Lord forever. Therefore encourage one another with these words.
> —1 Thessalonians 4:13-18

Jesus grieved with hope beyond the grave because He is life before the grave. Both sisters pointed out to Jesus that He could have prevented the death of Lazarus had He been present. They had seen these kinds of miracles before. We, too, would prefer a world like that. A world where nobody dies. And a world where all our pains are prevented from ever happening. Of course, there was an option for a paradise like that where nobody dies. Adam and Eve made the wrong choice. As humanity, that's on us. Jesus grieved the loss of His friend, but Jesus also saw through it to His own death and resurrection. Jesus knew the very reason He came was to reestablish the Kingdom of Heaven. Jesus knew that one day, there would be no more death nor mourning nor crying nor pain. Jesus knew there would be no more grief one day because His resurrection was coming.

Likewise, we should grieve this way. Your grief is not only understandable, but predictable, in that you've lost someone you love deeply. As believers in Jesus, we grieve with hope beyond the grave. We grieve with hope in light of the resurrection. We're not asked by God not to grieve. Jesus grieves with us. But our grief is comforted because we know it is not permanent. Death will not ultimately win. Jesus is the resurrection and the life.

We may never stop grieving in this world, but neither will we spend eternity in grief. Our grief truly is longing for the day when Jesus restores paradise on earth and there's no more death. He will wipe every tear from our eyes.

Don't get me wrong. Many people will tell you that when you lose someone you love, grief will fade in time. That time will heal all wounds. That the pain of grief will eventually evaporate, and you will move on. Frankly, such advice sucks. In this life, grief changes, but it doesn't just evaporate. But knowing the one you love will be resurrected in Christ provides great comfort and even greater hope.

You are comforted,
Pastor Brian

> *Jesus, Thank you that you are life. You are the resurrection. Thank you that you are alive. Help me as I am grieving right now. Grieving the loss of my person, my plans, and my dreams and hopes with them. Help me to grieve with deep emotion. To know that I am grieving a lot because I love a lot. But remind me as I grieve to grieve with hope beyond the grave. Please bring comfort to my soul. Help me to have eyes for others, to minister to them in their grief as well. In Jesus' name, Amen.*

10

Providence

And we know that in all things God works for the good of those who love him, who have been called according to his purpose.
—Romans 8:28

To my friend who is angry at God,

Are you angry at God because of your pain? I've been there too. But what if I told you that anger at God is a natural step toward overcoming your pain?

I won't pretend to understand what has happened in your life that brought you to this point. You said, "I'm ready to damn God because I feel like He damned my life." You have this sense that God did something wrong and allowed something unfair. You're convinced that God can no longer be trusted. On your best days, you still trust God, but you are mad at Him anyway. Other days, you're so angry at God that you've stopped believing in Him altogether. Some people end up in a place where their belief about God is "God doesn't exist, and I hate Him because of what

He allowed."

If that's you, and you've given up your faith in God, or maybe you never put faith in God to begin with, this might all seem a little weird to you. What I mean is people who believe in God sometimes stop believing because of anger, and people who don't believe in God sometimes start believing because they need someone to blame.

There will be days where you scream, understandably, "God, where are you? Where are you when I'm in pain?" It's easier to tell you where He is not. He is not immune, and He has not abandoned you.

For most of us, it usually starts like this: Some deeply painful event happens in your life. Sometimes, it's something you did. Sometimes, it's something somebody else did to you. And, sometimes, there are no explanations. There's a difficult diagnosis, or a tragic car accident, or a wildfire caused by lightning that destroys your home. There's no one to blame. You pray. You seek God's healing work, but it doesn't happen. One day, you wake up realizing that all of this sounds unfair, and you are angry. Angry at anyone. Angry at everyone. And, for sure, angry at Jesus.

Many of us blame God when the unthinkable happens. Insurance companies call them "acts of God." Earthquakes, tornadoes, hurricanes. In our world, we also deal with unspeakable tragedies: school shootings, terrorist bombings, and all-out war in which innocent children sometimes die as pawns. Sometimes, the tragedy feels like it's personal between you and God: Your child is born with a disability, or you develop early onset Alzheimer's. Other times, we blame ourselves. It's part of our human nature to want to hold someone, anyone responsible.

It would be nice if Jesus spoke to tragedies like this. Are we to blame? Is He to blame? Who can we blame? In Jesus' time, it was common to believe that your suffering was the direct result of your sin or perhaps your parent's sin. In common belief at the time, you could see how bad of a sinner a person was by looking at their suffering. More sin would equal more suffering. Jesus spoke against this on a couple occasions.

> As he went along, he saw a man blind from birth. His disciples asked him, "Rabbi, who sinned, this man or his parents, that he was born blind?" Neither this man nor his parents sinned," said Jesus, "but this happened so that the works of God might be displayed in him.
>
> —*John 9:1–3*

> Now there were some present at that time who told Jesus about the Galileans whose blood Pilate had mixed with their sacrifices. Jesus answered, "Do you think that these Galileans were worse sinners than all the other Galileans because they suffered this way? I tell you, no! But unless you repent, you too will all perish. Or those eighteen who died when the tower in Siloam fell on them—do you think they were more guilty than all the others living in Jerusalem? I tell you, no! But unless you repent, you too will all perish."
> —*Luke 13:1–5*

Often, there are no good explanations. What we can look for is the good that comes from tragedy. Jesus healed the man born blind.

I lived in Oklahoma at the time of the 1995 Oklahoma City bombing. The response of Oklahomans was a collective good, and the tragedy gave birth to the Oklahoma Standard and its core values: service, honor, and kindness. In the face of tragedy and suffering, we can look for who to blame, or we can look for the good that happens next. As much as suffering is often unimaginable, suffering is sometimes just unexplainable. But we can look for the good that God and others bring from that suffering.

A couple of things I know with certainty. First, you are not the first person to be angry with God. Just read Job in the Old Testament. Second, He can handle your anger. Again, read Job. Or Psalms. Any casual reading of the Bible will reveal these two truths. So, what do we do with that anger?

For starters, realize it's OK to be mad at God about your pain. He's above it. But you don't want to dwell in that anger. Try to see it as a temporary resting place on your journey up the mountain. You don't want to camp there, and you sure don't want to make it the permanent home for your soul.

At the same time, don't confuse the *hands of people* with the *heart of God*. Are you clear about your reasons for anger? Sometimes, we've been angry for so long that we don't remember why. We just know we are. What is it that God did? What is it that God allowed to happen that makes you so angry at Jesus? Be sure not to confuse people with God. Often, we are mad at Jesus for what some human being did or did not do to us.

Just for discussion, let's say someone caused deep trauma in your child's life. If some person did the unimaginable and unthinkable that has caused incredible grief and unspeakable pain in your life and theirs, have you considered that God might feel the same way you do? God might be angry about that as well. I find in my own life that I sometimes blame God for what other people have done. I need to look past their hands to God's hands and God's heart.

I'm often reminded of the story of Joseph in the book of Genesis. One day, he dreams of leading his great family. And the next, he finds himself sold into slavery to an Egyptian by his brothers. From there, he's thrown into prison for something he didn't do. And he's basically forgotten for thirteen years. A perfect recipe for bitterness, resentment, anger, and hatred. Not only toward his brothers, but toward God.

Of course, God had not forgotten about Joseph. God took what his brothers meant for evil and used it for good. God moved Joseph into a place of leadership in Egypt. God used Joseph to prepare the Egyptians for an incredible famine and, in turn, used Joseph to save the very brothers who sold him into slavery. Do you remember the moment Joseph revealed himself to his brothers?

> Then Joseph said to his brothers, "Come close to me." When they had done so, he said, "I am your brother Joseph, the one you sold into Egypt! And now, do not be distressed and do not be angry with yourselves for selling me here, because it was to save lives that God sent me ahead of you. For two years now there has been famine in the land, and for the next five years there will be no plowing and reaping. But God sent me ahead of you to preserve for you a remnant on earth and to save your lives by a great deliverance. "So then, it was not you who sent me here, but God. He made me father to Pharaoh, lord of his entire household and ruler of all Egypt.
> —*Genesis 45:4-8*

When their father died, Joseph's brothers were overwhelmed with worry about whether Joseph would take this moment to exact revenge.

> When Joseph's brothers saw that their father was dead, they said, "What if Joseph holds a grudge against us and pays us back for all the wrongs we did to him?" ... His brothers then came and threw themselves down before him. "We are your slaves," they said. But Joseph said to them, "Don't be afraid. Am I in the place of God? You intended to harm me, but God intended it for good to accomplish what is now being done, the saving of many lives.
> —*Genesis 50:15, 18-20*

Here's what I'm getting at: Anger is a key part of grief. Whatever it is that someone else did, whatever it is that you think God allowed to happen, it has caused incredible pain and loss in your life. Anger is a part of grief. Somewhere between trauma and acceptance are anger and grief. So, grieve. Be angry about what happened or what didn't happen. But do your grieving and your anger processing *with* Jesus, not *without* Him, not in defiance of Him. If you're grieving, the question is not whether you are going to be angry. The question is whether you are going to be angry *with* Jesus or be angry *without* Jesus. Being angry without Jesus often leads to us being angry at Jesus.

Being angry at God is common. But *staying* angry at God forces me away from dependence on God and toward dependence on myself to solve the pain and the puzzle of life.

On the other hand, being angry in the presence of Jesus is beneficial. Tell Jesus about the pain and unfairness of it all. Yell if you need to. Remember, He can handle it. Release your hurt to the heart of Jesus. Weep if you need to. Joseph did so on at least seven occasions. Walk with Jesus through your pain and through your anger. Lean into the heart of Jesus about your trauma. Make sure you include Jesus in the story you tell about the trauma. You will repeat this story over and over in your mind long before you repeat it to others. Make sure you look for what Jesus is doing in this story.

Did something bad happen? Yes. But will you open your heart to Jesus to help you interpret that event? Joseph's brothers meant it for evil, but God meant it for good. Trust Jesus, and lean into His providence. Look for the heart of Jesus in what happens from here. How is Jesus working to bring good in a situation full of evil?

I need to learn to trust the heart of Jesus when I don't understand the plan of Jesus. If you are struggling with doing any of this, look at that cross most of all. On it hung God in the flesh, doing everything He possibly could to overcome sin and suffering in our world. Jesus entered our suffering and died to end it. This is what our faith is all about.

Sometimes, we've bought into the not-so-Christian belief that God's only goal is to relieve us from our suffering. We minimize our sin, thinking, "Yes, he came to save us from our sins, but the relief I really want is from my suffering." Ultimately, he will save us from suffering. Our earthly and eternal suffering. But our sin is the ultimate cause of all that suffering. He's dealing with the macro big-picture solution, and we're down here just wanting our own personal pain to go away.

God's answer to all the sin in the world, all the suffering in the world, all the evil in this world might not make sense to us. But God's answer was a cross for His one and only Son. A cross I honestly deserved, by the way. The cross is the ultimate bad thing happening to the world's only truly good person. Jesus is not immune to our pain and suffering. I love what Tim Keller says about this.

> Let's see where this has brought us. If we ask again the questions: "Why does God allow evil and suffering to continue?" And we look at the cross of Jesus, we still do not know what the answer is. However, we now know what the answer isn't. It can't be that he (God) doesn't love us. It can't be that he is indifferent or detached from our condition. God takes our misery and suffering so seriously that he was willing to take it on himself.[26]

If you feel abandoned by God, come back here often. God didn't abandon you in your pain. He entered into it. Before you were ever born, God chose to enter your pain. The pain of this world. God didn't abandon you. Jesus suffers with you. In fact, Jesus suffers for you! Jesus is not immune to our suffering because He plunged headfirst into it. He is God incarnate. Think about that: I am not alone. He suffered spiritual death so that I won't have to.

The bedrock truth is that God is faithful more than He is fair. In fact, Jesus is better than fair. Jesus is gracious. If I got what I deserved, it wouldn't be what I'd really like to receive. Life is not always good. Life is not fair. But Jesus is good, and Jesus is faithful. I can trust Jesus precisely because He offers me something much better than fair. He offers me Himself.

God has a way of taking the pains of our lives and using them for our good and His glory. Does that mean that God caused all your pain and mine? I don't think so. But it does mean that there are no wasted lives and there are no wasted pains in God's kingdom.

I'm sure you've wondered about what your life would be like if the trauma never happened. On one hand, how much greater would, or could, your life be if you were not limited by the trauma of your troubles? This question is completely understandable. I've asked it myself hundreds of times. But this question should be asked with its correlating alternative: what would be lost from my life if the pain never came? In what ways would I be more isolated from others? In what ways would I be more self-sufficient rather than Jesus-dependent because I did not feel the need to turn to Jesus in the first place?

One last thing. I've said elsewhere in this book: Look ahead to the end. Root your faith here. One day, all the suffering will end. There is coming a day when ...

> He will wipe every tear from their eyes. There will be no more death or mourning or crying or pain, for the old order of things has passed away.
> —Revelation 21:4

On this side is the old way ... the way of grief and death and pain. On the other side is the way of comfort, the way of life, the way of love.

Friend, I don't have all the answers. Like you, in my own pain and sometimes my own anger, I'm looking up to the one who does.

You are not alone,
Pastor Brian

Jesus, I need to be honest. I'm angry at you because ... Through my anger and even my tears, I want to see you. I want to see your heart. I want to see your hand at work. Please forgive my avoidance of you because of my need to hold you responsible when I don't know who to hold responsible. Show me and give me your heart for what has happened. And bring your goodness to my impossible circumstance. Thank you that died to end this kind of suffering. Stretch my faith in you during this season and help my faith in you to become stronger day by day. Thanks for loving me even when I don't feel very loveable. In Jesus' name, Amen.

11.

Lament

Ministry is a series of ungrieved losses.[27]
—Terry Wardle

Blessed are those who mourn, for they will be comforted.
—Matthew 5:4

See to it that no one falls short of the grace of God and that no bitter root grows up to cause trouble and defile many.
—Hebrews 12:15

To my pastor friend who is suppressing the hurt and trauma that come from leading a church,

Your job is demanding. Sunday recurs every seven days, whether you are ready or not. People call with great needs. And you're there whether it's your day off or the middle of the night. Sometimes, they don't call, and then they're mad you didn't come to see them in the hospital. Other times, your best isn't deep enough, short enough, or relatable enough. As you said, "It's not one thing or another. It's everything all at once that gets overwhelming."

Most pastors experience primary and secondary trauma. Like you, I've struggled with the overwhelming feelings of burnout. In fact, recent studies indicate that you and I might be at least as likely to be affected by PTSD as combat veterans, police officers, firefighters, and disaster recovery workers.[28] (Not that I equate my job with the physical courage theirs do!) I want you to know that there is never shame in seeking help for this.

If you're not a pastor, please read this letter anyway. It will give you great insight into one of your pastor's greatest struggles. I guarantee it. And most likely, if you were to substitute your work for the word pastor, you would find that a lot of it still applies.

> Pastors live under relentless pressure to be "on-target." And it's not good enough to be "on-target" once. Pastors face daily demands of hitting targets of success in every area of life—for the long haul. How are pastors ever supposed to finish well?[29]
> —*Marissa Postell Sullivan*

Under this ongoing pressure, pastors walk away from ministry all the time. Some pastors refuse to burn out, but they fill their lives with sinful behavior to drown out the pain of ministry. Some pastors spend every Monday wishing they were somewhere else. Ministry hurts. This is one thing I can tell you from personal experience. Whether it's the ups and downs, the stresses of declining attendance patterns, the pressure to figure out how to navigate the COVID pandemic without angering everybody and pleasing nobody, or the loss of real friendship because of ministry decisions—ministry hurts. And often, we don't handle that hurt very well.

If you've been a pastor for even five minutes, you know that it hurts to lead. People who believe in you will leave. Some will move away, and others will walk away. It's painful because the people you lead will sometimes say the ugliest things about you or to you. The people you serve will love you as long as you are making them feel good about their life and spirituality. Some of those same people will turn on you, reject you, and publicly say awful things about you to others. I had a pastor friend tell me his life was threatened physically by a deacon in his church.

Ministry is hard because everyone has expectations of you. You're supposed to be just like Jesus, but with a bigger following. Jesus has billions of followers today, but a very small following when He walked the earth. Bigger budgets. More baptisms. Larger buildings. And no character flaws. Oh, and don't forget: your family has to be picture-perfect as well.

All of that said, let's be brutally honest for a moment. The person with the greatest expectations of me is ... me. Not only are there a lot of real hurts in my life that still sting, but there are also all the failed expectations of bigger, stronger, faster, and better that come from me. Add to that the battle with pride. Being in the spotlight increases the temptations of pride, and its twin, insecurity.

My friend and mentor Joe Chambers likes to say, "I don't care how big or how small your church is, how big or small your staff is, how big or small your budget is. What I want to know: How are you and where are your hurts?"

A few of you reading this may pastor larger churches, but few pastors experience fame. Your pastor probably lives in great anonymity. Those of us who pastor "smaller churches" often beat ourselves up because our church isn't as big as XYZ church down the road. Truthfully, "smaller churches" are normal-sized churches. Not only is there nothing wrong with that, but there is something very right about it. Neighborhood churches provide better community than megachurches. Those of us who pastor "larger churches" feel even more pressure to be bigger and better. Our denominations often imply that if you do your job well enough, your church will automatically grow larger and bigger as well as give more. We're all left with *the feeling that our best is never good enough.*

Might I remind you at this point that serving Jesus was never about you being good enough or great enough? In fact, your value to the King and the kingdom is not about the size of your church at all. You can easily see how our insecurity can be driven by pride in our hearts—and a culture that defaults to bigger is better. Truthfully, ministry is not about you at all. And it will always require more of you than you have to give.

Being a pastor is hard. So is being a teacher. So is being a nurse. So is being a firefighter or an accountant. "It's hard" is no excuse for pride. No excuse for sin. No excuse for treating poorly the people we are called to serve with love and grace. Ministry is also a privilege. Let's never lose sight of the fact that throughout history and around the world, most pastors received less than many of us do today for the same work.

Trust is hard in ministry precisely because we've been hurt countless times. Many of us become so hardened by the hurt and trauma that we refuse to trust anyone else we lead, taking control and often manipulating those we work with to ensure that our hearts feel safe. Resentment is never good for the soul nor for the relationship we have with our families and our spiritual family. Broken trust often leads to broken hearts, and when we don't process our pain, broken hearts become hard hearts.

So, what do we do? What do we need?

As Terry Wardle wrote, I agree that ministry is a long series of ungrieved losses. And there are many.

Ungrieved losses. That's a short way of saying that the hurts pile up faster than you can process them. *You're so busy helping other people through their hurts that you don't make the time to process your own. Or at least that's what you tell yourself. Truthfully, processing them hurts.* It brings us to a place where we feel like giving up. So, we deny, bury, escape, and numb the pain just like a lot of the people we serve. Maybe with the same vices they use to numb and escape their own pain.

For a century now, therapists have known that we must learn to process the feelings we would rather escape. Bessel Van Der Kolk explains:

> Semrad taught us that most human suffering is related to love and loss and that the job of therapists is to help people "acknowledge, experience, and bear" the reality of life—with all its pleasures and heartbreak. "The greatest sources of our suffering are the lies we tell ourselves," he'd say, urging us to be honest with ourselves about every facet of our experience. He often said that people can never get better without knowing what they know and feeling what they feel.[30]

It's an easy slide from the early naïve years of ministry to the hardened, burnt-out years. It works like this: We refuse to process the deepest hurts because it's too painful. We'd rather not feel those emotions, and we'd rather not be honest with ourselves about those feelings. So, we avoid them, deny them, and numb them just like everyone else. But that's no way to live, and it's certainly not healthy—especially for people who, fair or not, are supposed to be living standards for others. Despite our preaching about truth, we prefer denial to facing reality. When we've been hurt long enough, we harden our hearts, refuse to trust, and, in some cases, hurt others so they cannot hurt us. It's easier to feel nothing than it is to be hurt by the people we trust. It's even easier to become the person causing the hurt than to be the person receiving it. It's Sin Nature 101. If we are not intentional about processing our hurts, we become the monster that someone else was to us. This is the ugly side of ministry.

Here's a harsh reality: Denial doesn't work. Denial may or may not delay our experience of suffering, but it will not allow us to actually skip it. Escape doesn't work. Anyone who has worked with addicts knows this to be true. And so do those who work with trauma patients. Neuroscience indicates that your brain can send stress chemicals to your body while your mind pretends that everything is OK. And the price paid by your body is enormous. Bessel Van der Kolk says:

> We now know that there is another possible response to threat, which our scans aren't yet capable of measuring. Some people simply go into denial: Their bodies register the threat, but their conscious minds go on as if nothing has happened. However, even though the mind may learn to ignore the messages from the emotional brain, the alarm signals don't stop. The emotional brain keeps working, and stress hormones keep sending signals to the muscles to tense for action or immobilize in collapse. The physical effects on the organs go on unabated until they demand notice when they are expressed as illness. Medications, drugs, and alcohol can also temporarily dull or obliterate unbearable sensations and feelings. But the body continues to keep the score.[31]

To embrace life, you must allow yourself to feel the pain, explore the emotions, and surrender the pain to Jesus. Ministry, like life, will be full of brokenness, but brokenness does not mean that ministry and life cannot be beautiful as well. For those of us who've been deeply hurt in ministry by the very people we serve, I have several big suggestions.

1. Slow down long enough to grieve the ungrieved losses and hurts.

If you have not done that in a long time, this process will take a while. Get a mentor, a counselor, or a spiritual director. Attend a soul care retreat. Unearth the hurts. Process them one by one. If you are used to keeping short accounts, learn to grieve as you go. Process the pain. Be honest about your role in it. Make things right where you can. Forgive what feels unforgiveable. Prioritize the processing of your grief and the embrace of your weakness, an opportunity to practice the very grace you preach every single Sunday. Funny thing about being a preacher. It's easier to preach grace and forgiveness than it is to practice it.

Grieve the losses. Feel the pain. Forgive the hurt. Let me add one thing, one *important* thing: If you are being abused by other leadership in your church, have the hard conversations and, if necessary, for the sake of your mental health and your family, walk away from that church. There are others who need honest, healthy leaders. We need to learn emotional intelligence skills.

We need to learn to feel our emotions, not suppress them. We need to learn to sit with them, not run from them. We need to learn to legitimize them, not minimize them. We need to learn to process them, not ignore them. And we need to learn to understand them and even learn from them, not pretend they do not exist. Suppression creates a place where the soul will be stuck. Processing sets us free to embrace the emotion of the next season.

This is called lament. It's biblical.

No one would deny the difficult impact that trauma has on the body and mind. Neuroscience is discovering just how significant that trauma can be. In fact, neuroscience teaches us that experiences can change the brain and the nervous system. Trauma might shift our entire nervous system toward survival of the trauma rather than engagement with our lives. Solutions for trauma survivors, including those with PTSD, must treat the entire person: mind, body, and soul. One last time, Bessel Van der Kolk teaches us:

> After trauma the world is experienced with a different nervous system. The survivor's energy now becomes focused on suppressing inner chaos, at the expense of spontaneous involvement in their life. These attempts to maintain control over unbearable physiological reactions can result in a whole range of physical symptoms, including fibromyalgia, chronic fatigue, and other autoimmune diseases. This explains why it is critical for trauma treatment to engage the entire organism, body, mind, and brain.[32]

2. Remember your calling.

Let's be honest. It's easier to be jaded than it is to practice grace. It's helpful to remember where we were when God first called us to ministry. What is the simple calling you have long since forgotten? Can I just remind you that when you began:

- The gravitas of your church was grace, not you, and not your strengths. Not the quality of your preaching. Not your influence. Not your platform.
- Preaching was a privilege you looked forward to with fear and excitement.
- The goal was pleasing Jesus, not pleasing people.
- Love looked like treating people the way that Jesus would.
- Ministry looked like serving others, not being served by others.
- The affirmation you wanted to hear would come from God: *Well done, good and faithful servant.*

If you've lost these things, the place to begin searching for them might be the mirror.

3. Spend some time asking yourself: Could Jesus say to me, "Well done, good and faithful servant?"

If you're not sure you can answer this question with brutal honesty, ask someone who is close enough to your ministry to do so. If you don't think Jesus would say that, make the adjustments necessary. It's incredibly easy to be caught up in metrics that stoke our ego. We must embrace servanthood over ego and serve Jesus without regard for what is in it for us. Maybe it's time to return to those simpler times and simpler expectations.

- Be faithful. This always matters more than "success."
- Preach the Gospel. It's the only real power to change lives.
- Love people. Especially when they don't deserve it.
- Serve your community. God is watching, and so are your neighbors.
- And wait for the affirmation of the King of Kings: "Well done, good and faithful servant."

Jesus never promised it would be easy. In fact, he promised the opposite. Read Matthew 28 again. What did he promise? He would be there. And it would change the world.

You are called,
Pastor Brian

> *Jesus, help me to live from your love for me, knowing that my identity is not defined by what other people think or what other people say about me. I confess that I've allowed the hurts, distrust, and insecurity to take my eyes off you. Please forgive me. Give me the space and the strength to process my hurts. And give me the grace to forgive those who have hurt me deeply, including myself. Remind me of my calling. Help me to experience your love in fresh ways today. And give me the wisdom and strength to serve others out of your love, not just my own. In Jesus' name, Amen.*

12.

Gratitude

Finally, brothers and sisters, whatever is true, whatever is noble, whatever is right, whatever is pure, whatever is lovely, whatever is admirable—if anything is excellent or praiseworthy—think about such things. Whatever you have learned or received or heard from me, or seen in me—put it into practice. And the God of peace will be with you.
—Philippians 4:8-9

Give thanks in all circumstances; for this is God's will for you in Christ Jesus.
—1 Thessalonians 5:18

To my friend who's trapped in the vortex of complaining and negativity,

We've talked about how when we're complaining, we don't see it. You told me that when you hear other people complain, it gets under your skin, and you think, "I don't want to be like that. I don't want that kind of negativity in my life. I have enough of my own to put up with." We don't like complaining when others do it, but tend to think it's more than justified when we do. It's one of the more subtle illusions of this life. Of course, it's not just looking backward that gets us in trouble. Your pain makes it easy to expect everything to go wrong in the future as well.

It's so easy to find yourself trapped in such a cycle. A long time ago, I challenged our church to go an entire week without complaining. A friend and I went to a baseball game, and by the final out, I was right back to negativity and complaining. My friend set a trap to see if I would complain. I walked right into it.

Complaining is a habit, albeit a very self-focused habit. Some of us have been practicing this habit for decades. Also, like yawning, complaining is contagious. Hang out with complainers, and you will find yourself complaining. Complaining subtracts joy from my life. When I complain, I'm throwing my chances of joy and gratitude right out the window.

Neuroscience has revealed that your experience of pain is helped or hindered by your expectations, stress levels, and emotions. Pain catastrophizing will only increase your experience of pain. Expectations work both directions. Negativity about our pain worsens our experience, while positive expectations work to our advantage. Expect the best, and you just might experience it. Expect the worst, and you'll probably get the worst. Some people call it luck.

What if it's just the power of expectations? And what if, as believers in Jesus, we have something better than expectations and luck? We have hope—the confident belief that God will achieve all He intends in His time. We have faith—the trust that Jesus is real and working. We have love—the willingness to lay down our lives because Jesus laid down His. All of this should produce real gratitude, and gratitude will only help, not hurt. Richard Ambron sums it up well:

> Studies have shown that anticipating pain increases ... and exacerbates painfulness ... Another important factor in the experience of pain is our emotional state, with negative emotions enhancing pain-evoked activity ... Senses are heightened and relaxation becomes difficult. Being in pain for long periods is obviously very stressful, and there are many reasons to believe that the suffering experienced by patients with persistent or chronic pain is enhanced due to a fear of the pain and the stress that it places on the quality of their lives. In fact, the psychological term for it, pain catastrophizing, encapsulates many of the negative emotions that contribute to the experience of pain.[33]

This reminds me of what Paul told the Philippian church in Philippians 2:14

> Do everything without grumbling or arguing.
> —*Philippians 2:14*

Everything is comprehensive. It includes, well, everything. All circumstances. The word grumbling is *goggusmos*. It means a complaint uttered in a low and indistinct tone. It's the same as murmuring under our breath. The ancient Hebrews had a word for complaining and murmuring: *lun*. It means to camp out. When I murmur and complain, I've decided to put down my tent stakes in this place and stay a while. I've pitched my tent next to something I think is unfair, and I've decided to stay. I camp out on negative island. But I eventually find out this camping spot has become stuck in my heart and this sense of negativity creeps inside of me like bed bugs. Neurology would tell us that once our brains have built this connection, it just becomes a habit. And the longer we live in the habit, the harder it is to change.

So, what's a person to do?

It sounds simpler than it really is for most of us. *My life will be filled with grumbling or gratitude. Pain makes it very easy to choose grumbling. God provides the perspective. I need to choose gratitude.* In fact, the sin nature in all of us chooses grumbling naturally, instinctively, and reactively. Whether grumbling or gratitude camps out in my heart is up to me. It's all a choice. In fact, neurologically speaking, I need to replace grumbling with gratitude. If I want more joy in my life, I need to destroy the habit of complaining before the habit of complaining destroys me.

It starts with the admission that I have a problem. Admit it to myself and to others close to me. I need to embrace the idea that God knows what He is doing. Maybe even return to a posture of childlike faith. Trust that God is good. Look for the hand of the Father when things get difficult.

I need to learn to practice delayed gratification. We're so used to getting what we want as soon as we want it that any delay is an opportunity to complain and grumble. Overcoming this negative attitude in my life will require an intentional decision to embrace my faith by waiting on God to work.

We rarely practice gratitude because it will cost us time, focus, and energy. But if you think about it, not practicing gratitude still costs us time and energy because our time and energy get sucked up with grumbling and complaining. It's so easy for today's gratitude to become tomorrow's expectations. And today's expectations become tomorrow's complaints. So, we must learn to develop the habit of frequent gratitude.

If I am going to embrace life, including all the painful parts that I really don't like, I'm going to have to spend a lot of energy building deep roots in gratitude. Gratitude might be inconvenient, but it is incredibly soul-cleansing and soul-changing. Gratitude might be the single greatest habit that can change your experience with pain because it can change your experience with God.

It's hard to change your thinking, but it's harder for you *not to*. As we've discovered, the more we focus our awareness and our attention on our pain, the greater our sensation and experience of pain. Thinking these thoughts repeatedly creates a habit of focusing on pain. Those habits can be changed. Thinking the same thoughts repeatedly forms habits. If we want to change our experience of pain, we must learn new mental habits. We can learn to tune our brain into the benefits. We can learn to acknowledge our pain without obsessing over it. We can learn to shift our awareness away from pain and back to life. We can learn to meditate on what God is doing in the moment. We can learn to choose gratitude for what God is doing rather than obsessing over what God isn't. Changing our thinking is hard, *but not changing our thinking is harder.* Neuroscience teaches us about a process called neuroplasticity. Our brains change as we think new thoughts and reinforce those thoughts. Richard Ambron explains this concept:

> The brain is constantly changing with experience, which explains why a nurturing environment in early childhood is especially important. We actively direct some of these changes when we learn to hit a golf ball or do a summersault. In these cases, we are reinforcing circuits to learn a skill, and the more we practice, the more skilled we become and the more the circuits are strengthened ... Moreover, just as learning to execute a tennis serve, is it possible with sufficient training that our brains could be rewired to greatly extend the duration of diminished pain?[34]

Gratitude is good for the soul because gratitude is an expression of grace. We literally can change our brains as we practice this concept.

In the New Testament, the word for grace is *charis*, and the verb for gratitude is *eucharisteo*. You can see the word *charis* or grace right there in the middle. To give gratitude is to give good grace. This is precisely why we say that we say "grace" before our meals. It's a practice of gratitude. In the Latin languages, it's easy to see the connection between gratitude and grace. In Italian, it's *grazi*. In Spanish, it's *gracias*. In French, it's *merci*. And you'll probably recognize the English usage of eucharist as Communion, Mass, or the Lord's Supper. This most important religious observance is an expression of gratitude and grace.

What do I have to thank God for in the pain? He is there. He comforts. He is compassionate about my pain. He is powerful. He is the ultimate healer. He loves me. He hasn't abandoned me. He will end my pain in eternity. The list goes on.

So right now, slow down. Take time. Give focus and attention. Don't just be thankful for Jesus. Express your thanks to Jesus. You just might find that embracing life with gratitude, despite your pain, helps lessen the pain, lighten the load, and reduce your stress. And, frankly, God deserves our worship and gratitude.

You are blessed with the goodness of Jesus,
Pastor Brian

> *Jesus, please fill me with gratitude, not grumbling. Forgive me for being so me-focused and impatient. Help me to change my bad habit of complaining. And help me to choose joy and choose gratitude daily. When I camp out and put down tent stakes in my heart, help me to do so by your goodness. Help me to choose to be content because I have you. Give me the persistence to make gratitude a new daily rhythm in my life. In Jesus' name, Amen.*

MINDSET 3
Finding a new power source

People who struggle with pride and defensiveness tend to:

- *Cover their feelings of sorrow and confusion in front of others—out of concern for what others think.*
- *Refuse to fall apart, always modeling strong faith and vision, especially in front of others.*
- *Seldom appear needy.*
- *Stand tall, being decisive and unwavering, so that others can lean on them.*

People courageous enough to embrace weakness and vulnerability:

- *Allow themselves to be sorrowful and troubled in front of others.*
- *Admit to their team when they are feeling overwhelmed.*
- *Are quick to ask for help and prayer from others.*
- *Have no problem falling face down on the ground in front of others when they struggle to submit themselves to the will of the Father.*[35]

—Peter Scazzero (Paraphrased)

It's natural to want to be self-reliant. It's easy and automatic when life is comfortable. It's human to want our lives, thoughts, answers, experiences, and strengths to be enough. Ever since we were about two years old, we learned that we like to do it all by ourselves. And it's normal to pretend to others that we are strong when we know we aren't.

When I was a kid, I would pretend to be Superman. I was fast. I was strong. I could fly. I liked to pretend. In truth, I still like to pretend to be Superman. And so do you. We pretend.

The older we get, the more we know we are not a superhero. But we like to pretend that we don't have limitations anyway.

Of course, our strength is not infinite. The problem is not that we are not superman or superwoman. The problem is that we *actually attempt to be* superman or superwoman. We rush through our days as though our speed is no problem. We put our heads down, push through problems, and ignore issues causing real detriment to our families. We leap from experience to experience, chasing a high that never seems to last.

The reality is that we would prefer to have near-infinite strength. We'd prefer for all the pains of life to just bounce off us. But life doesn't work like that.

Interestingly, Jesus is a superman, and yet he embraced weakness, and He challenges you and me to do the same.

In the meantime, many of us galivant around the world doing the best we can to make other people think we are strong. We masquerade ourselves as stronger than everyone else because we want to pretend we are strong. And if I can fool others into thinking I am strong, then maybe I can fool myself into believing the same.

One of life's greatest questions relates to where we find our source of strength.

In many ways, it's a paradox. The stronger I try to be on my own, the weaker I truly become. Faking strength only weakens my soul and body. The more I fake strength, the less strong I am.

In some very real sense, it takes an incredible amount of personal strength in the form of humility to admit that I am not strong enough to face this life on my own, not strong enough to carry the overwhelming weight of my personal sins, and not strong enough to face the pains in this world by myself. I need strength I simply do not have. I am nothing like a superman or superwoman. And I need help and strength I simply do not possess on my own. But life is not hopeless.

Life is full of moments where we tell ourselves, "I have to be strong." That's what this book is about. The truth is "I have to be strong" is rooted in my pride and often means "I have to *look* strong."

Before we talk about where strength is truly found, we must

slow down long enough to admit to ourselves where strength is not found. Strength is not found in ignoring my problems. *That's denial.* Strength is not found in pretending to be strong. *That's faking it—hypocrisy.* Strength is not found in posing for others as though I am superman when I am not. *That's posturing.*

The path of real strength is found in learning to embrace my weaknesses, my limits, and my life with pain because it is this very life that reminds me to depend upon the Almighty. It's my sins, weaknesses, limits, and pain that remind me that I am not even mighty, much less *al*mighty.

The truth is that I am inadequate. I come up short. I'm trying to do on my own what is impossible to do on my own. I am not the almighty, but I like to pretend I am Him.

While we are at it, I also like to pretend to be all-knowing, all-good, and all-present. Not one of those things is true.

If real strength is not found in pretending and posturing, where do I find the strength I need to embrace my life with pain?

Real strength is found in admitting my weakness and learning to lean on Jesus! For those of us who have been doing this a while, this seems like "no duh." But for the person who has resisted God their entire life, this changing of the guard in our minds is enormous.

Soul care must acknowledge the real pain inside of us. Christians sometimes feel the need to fake that everything is OK when it isn't. I generally consider myself a hopeful person, but positivity that's rooted in "social pressure" and "faking it" is toxic positivity.

Real strength is found in leaning on Christ when my soul has nothing to offer. God's power is best displayed in my weakness. Just as stars shine against a night sky, as good shines against evil, as love wins over hate, as flavor explodes against the bland, God's power shines brightest against the backdrop of my weakness.

This is just the problem: I'm too busy pretending to be strong to admit that I am so weak and incapable that I truly need Jesus.

Pride is the character flaw that often traps me in The Pity Vortex. Pride is a character flaw that we all struggle through. More than not, pride is the sin that prevents the power of God in my life.

This all reminds me of something Jesus said:

> I am the vine; you are the branches. If you remain in me and I in you, you will bear much fruit; apart from me you can do nothing.
> —*John 15:5*

The key to the Christian living a life amid pain is Christ living in the Christian. Jesus living through me. That's what Paul is saying in 2 Corinthians 12. It's what Jesus is saying in John 15. The reality, whether we admit it or not, is that every single human being lives their life dependent on something. Even atheists and agnostics live dependent on something. Christians are people who choose to live in Jesus and depend upon Jesus for everything. We dwell in Him. Can we admit something to ourselves? When your life is painful, and you need strength from Jesus, "casual" won't cut it. To find strength, we need to shift our relationship with Jesus from casual to "essential."

Every single day is an invitation from Jesus to live like my entire life depends on my connection to Him because it does.

If I am going to dwell in Christ daily and find my source of life, strength, holiness, and so much more in Jesus, I am going to need to accept the invitations outlined by Jesus in this incredible passage from the Bible.

> I am the true vine, and my Father is the gardener. He cuts off every branch in me that bears no fruit, while every branch that does bear fruit he prunes so that it will be even more fruitful. You are already clean because of the word I have spoken to you. Remain in me, as I also remain in you. No branch can bear fruit by itself; it must remain in the vine. Neither can you bear fruit unless you remain in me. "I am the vine; you are the branches. If you remain in me and I in you, you will bear much fruit; apart from me you can do nothing. If you do not remain in me, you are like a branch that is thrown away and withers; such branches are picked up, thrown into the fire and burned. If you remain in me and my words remain in you, ask whatever you wish, and it will be done for you. This is to my Father's glory, that you bear much fruit, showing yourselves to be my disciples.
> —*John 15:1-8*

Invitation #1—To live with abundant clarity regarding who is God and who is not.

Jesus is the true vine. His Father is the Gardener. I am neither the vine nor the gardener. I am not the source, and I am not God. And I am not the one who tends to the source. Again, we like to pretend we are the vine or the vine dresser, but that's all baloney. We like to take God's place. That's not possible.

Invitation #2—To learn to trust God's pruning.

There's no dwelling in Christ without pruning. There's no finding strength in Jesus without pruning. To sign up for the Jesus way of life is to sign up for Pruning 101. Let's be honest. Pruning hurts. It's no fun.

You're walking along one day in your life at the corner of Vine and Gardener Sreet. When you look down, you see all these pruned-up branches and clippings everywhere, and it hurts. It sucks. It's painful. You weep at your losses. You feel the hurt and feel the pain, and you argue with the gardener. Let's take a hypothetical exchange between you and Him:

>**You:** "What's with all this pain? What's with all this loss? What's with all this grief?"
>**Him:** "I am doing it for your good. I am doing it because I know what is coming, and you need this."
>**You:** "But I don't like this. I don't like change. I don't want this. This doesn't make me feel very good."
>**Him:** "I understand. But what's coming is more of what is so good for you. What is coming is more of Me in your life. What's coming is more of My work in your life. What's coming is more of My love in your life and more love for others in your life. What's coming is more grace in your life. What's coming is more strength in your life. Don't you want that?"
>**You:** "I guess so."
>**Him:** "This is what it means to have My favor in your life. For the life of Jesus to flow through you and in you. So much so that fruit is produced, great fruit—fruit that I, as the Gardener, want to produce

in you and through your life. Having My favor isn't about you. It's about Me and what I want to do in you and through you."

Jesus says, "Apart from me, you can do nothing." Do you believe that? A stronger Life. A better Life. A more fruitful life is found in all the pruned and cut-up branches on the ground at the corner of Vine and Gardener Street. The pruning is an invitation to lean into Jesus and find more of His strength in my life and yours.

The invitation to dwell in Jesus always includes the pruning God wants to do in my life. Pruning is painful, but trusting the pruning trusts what God cuts back in my life and trusts what God allows life to cut back in me.

Without God's pruning, there are no deeper roots and, therefore, no greater fruits in my life. I must learn to trust God in the pains of my life. Either way, I am going to be cut by the vine dresser. I will be pruned or cut off. Trust the pruning.

By the way, never is the vine dresser closer to you than when He is pruning. Pruning moments provided the opportunity to lean on the nearness of God. To be deeply aware of his presence and lean on that presence for strength.

Can we address one more thing? Not all loss, not all grief, is God's pruning. Some of our loss is caused by our own poor decisions. Or by the poor decisions of others. Some are unexplained. No, I don't believe that God takes your loved ones, your babies, or your siblings because He is pruning. Nonetheless, those moments are incredible moments to lean into my connection to Christ and find strength in Him.

You've heard the phrase "No pain, no gain." Did you know that there is neuroscience to back up the idea that your brain can suppress your experience of pain by embracing the benefit of the pain? What this means for us is that we must learn to see past the pain to the meaning, growth, and connections that will arise from the pain. When we can embrace the fact that pain is part of this world, and when we can embrace the faith that God uses our pain to do good in our lives and others, we can change our perception of our pain. When we see the pruning as beneficial, we can find reasons to endure the pain.

Richard Ambron reminds us:

> Relating this to our own lives, we might be willing to accept pain from, say, lifting weights during training, or sprinting to the finish line if we believe the race has great value. Sometimes the decision has to be made very quickly. If we pick up a very hot cup, we will drop it to avoid being burned. However, if the cup is part of a very valuable set, then we will bear the pain and gently put the cup on its saucer. In this case the reward might be to avoid embarrassment or to be proud that we saved the cup ... Nowhere is the connection between acceptance and belief more important than in the role of suffering in religion.[36]

A word of caution: We're always tempted to trust the need more than the "need-meter." The provision rather than the provider. The protection more than the protector. The strength we already have more than the one who provides the power we need. Let's not be more in love with what God can do for us than we are with Jesus himself.

What happens when I live like my entire life truly depends on Jesus?

When I've allowed God to mature my thinking, to strengthen my soul, to grow my heart in grace, someday I'll stroll down the road, and I will look down and see all these pruned branches of my life on the ground, and it will be oh so painful but ... I will smile, too, because I know what's coming and who is coming on the corner of Vine and Gardener Street.

Dear Jesus, I confess that I often confuse my role in this world with yours. Forgive me for playing God. I also confess that I'd rather skip the pruning. But I want all the fruit. Forgive me for preferring shortcuts. Since there are none, please add to my life what needs to be added, and please remove from my life what needs to be removed. Strengthen me through my trials, pains, and problems. Through it all, help me to live like my entire life depends on you because I now know it does. In Jesus' name, Amen.

13.

Weakness

God is our refuge and strength, an ever-present help in trouble.
—Psalm 46:1

Do you not know? Have you not heard? The LORD is the everlasting God, the Creator of the ends of the earth. He will not grow tired or weary, and his understanding no one can fathom. He gives strength to the weary and increases the power of the weak. Even youths grow tired and weary, and young men stumble and fall; but those who hope in the LORD will renew their strength. They will soar on wings like eagles; they will run and not grow weary, they will walk and not be faint.
—Isaiah 40:28-31

To my friend with no energy left in the tank,

During the COVID-19 pandemic, every one of us, on multiple occasions, thought to ourselves, "I'm fed up. I'm done. I don't know how much longer I can do this. When the next domino falls, I don't know how I will react." That was a season for most of us, but you feel the same way during everyday life. You're at the proverbial end of your rope.

Remember? You texted me to say, "I'm running on fumes, and I'm not sure what to do next. What do I do when my tank is empty?"

For the young and healthy, just getting up every day isn't such a pain. For you, it often is and yet you do. You endure more than most just getting through the day. When you are not feeling insecure on the inside, you know this to be true. You're living through a season that could be described as "walking while feeling faint."

You need to find a way to refill your tank more frequently because living in chronic pain is like living with a tank that has sprung a leak. Someone will tell you, "You just need to find the leak and fix it." Like you and your medical team haven't already thought of that.

Emotional fatigue can make you feel dull, drained, discouraged, depressed, or even defeated. That sucks. It's common to feel stuck in this place, where you feel like you just can't get past empty. Chronic fatigue is often the result of chronic pain.

As you and I both know, the two can be debilitating when experienced together. You long for an easy solution. Unfortunately, life doesn't have an on-off switch for more energy—regardless of what the energy-drink people may think.

In Ephesians, our relationship with Jesus is described as a walk (Ephesians 4:1, 4:17, 5:1, 5:8, and 5:15). The word "walk" is sometimes also translated as "live," but it is "walk" in the original language.

> Follow God's example, therefore, as dearly loved children and walk in the way of love, just as Christ loved us and gave himself up for us as a fragrant offering and sacrifice to God.

—*Ephesians 5:1-2*

If you are struggling to understand how this works out daily, or if you struggle to understand prayer as a way of finding strength, think of you and Jesus going for a walk. That's what prayer is—an ongoing conversation as you walk together. In fact, I often pray when I am walking alone. I find that walking helps my mind focus. I hope you realize that prayer doesn't require you to always have your eyes closed.

My wife and I go for a lot of walks. We talk a lot about our day, our struggles, our frustrations, and our lives. Funny thing is sometimes she's moving faster and occasionally I'm moving faster, but we're always together. It's not her on one side of the street and me on the other. Walking with Jesus is the same. He is there every step of the way for the conversation.

Some find it beneficial to pray with their palms down or their palms up. Palms down is a posture of releasing. Palms up is a posture of receiving and embracing.

While you are walking with Jesus through chronic pain and fatigue, there's much to let go of and much to embrace. Release:

- Knowing how everything will turn out.
- Being able to control the outcomes.
- The emotions and tears that overwhelm.
- The feeling that you must pretend.
- The frustration of feeling weak.
- The need to appear "strong" in other people's eyes.
- Anything that smells of self-reliance and self-sufficiency.
- The pity, escapism, and illusions of The Pity Vortex.

Once your heart and your hands have released the wrong things, here's what to lean into. Embrace:

- That your weaknesses are real and beneficial because they remind you that when you are weak, He is strong.
- A dependence on Jesus, who already knows and can handle the outcomes.
- The hope rooted in the eternal reality that today's pains will not last forever.
- The power that belongs to Jesus to sustain you and carry you through this season.
- The life you have, knowing that despite your pain, the goodness of God and the grace of God are at work in your body and soul right now.
- The next step, and only the next step, you need to take on your journey of recovery and healing.

You've already endured a lot, and you often forget that. You have a source of strength that is more powerful than most understand because we tend not to rely on Jesus for strength until relying on Jesus is the only choice we have. No matter how overwhelming your pain is, Jesus is stronger.

We are all pushed beyond our limits at some point. That's the moment we find out that Jesus really is stronger. The moment where what we know in theory becomes what we know by experience.

When I had my spinal fusion surgery in 2016, my family gave me a little plaque that says, "You never know how strong you are until being strong is the only choice you have." I like the sentiment of the plaque, and I completely appreciate the encouragement I received from my family, but I would like to modify it just a bit: "You never know how strong Jesus is until being strong in Jesus is the only choice you have." In my humanness, I wish it didn't work that way.

But years of experience and observation of our common human nature convince me that we don't rely on the strength of Jesus until our strength runs out. *I have to hit the bottom of my own strength to admit I need His.* Have you noticed that about people? If you don't believe in Jesus, but you've come this far, I'm asking you to seriously consider where else you will find a source of strength when yours runs out.

When the rug is pulled out from under you, when life slaps you down, and when you really are out of strength, life's not about you finding a way for you alone to stay strong enough. It's about relying on Jesus, who already is strong enough because He is God in the flesh.

The question really becomes: how do I find strength in Jesus when I have no strength left? The answer is outlined clearly in Ephesians 6.

> Finally, be strong in the Lord and in his mighty power. Put on the full armor of God, so that you can take your stand against the devil's schemes. For our struggle is not against flesh and blood, but against the rulers, against the authorities, against the powers of this dark world and against the spiritual forces of evil in the heavenly realms. Therefore put on the full armor of God, so that when the day of evil comes, you may be able to stand your ground, and after you have done everything, to stand. Stand firm then, with the belt of truth buckled around your waist, with the breastplate of righteousness in place, and with your feet fitted with the readiness that comes from the Gospel of peace. In addition to all this, take up the shield of faith, with which you can extinguish all the flaming arrows of the evil one. Take the helmet of salvation and the sword of the Spirit, which is the word of God. And pray in the Spirit on all occasions with all kinds of prayers and requests. With this in

mind, be alert and always keep on praying for all the Lord's people.
—*Ephesians 6:10-18*

Ephesians 6:10 literally says, "Be strengthened in the Lord and in his mighty power." I want to be clear about this. The world says, "Be strong." Period. Pull yourself up by your bootstraps. Jesus says, "Be strengthened." To be strengthened is to put on the strength of Jesus. It is described as putting on the armor of Jesus. Think of it like getting dressed in the morning. We put on the armor one piece at a time, and we need to do it every single day.

To put on the armor is to become more like Jesus. It's to put Jesus in my mind, heart, hands, and feet. Daily strength when I'm on empty is found in the daily application of Jesus' life to mine.

Here's what we need to know about this: It's not a pick-and-choose buffet where I take the parts I like and leave out the parts I don't. It's not a compartmentalized process where what I do on Sundays is enough, and the rest of the week doesn't matter. It's a relationship lived out day by day and moment by moment. When life is so overwhelming that the strength of Jesus is the only hope I have, it's not just day by day. It's moment by moment. We need to put on the full armor. It is not enough to put on the helmet but not take up the shield or leave the sword sitting on the coffee table. The pieces of the armor are not decorations or accessories. We need the complete ensemble. Life is a battle. Jesus is essential.

The armor is more about defense than offense. Think through the pieces. This is more about the security of protection that comes from Jesus than it is about slaying my enemies. In fact, Jesus taught us to love our enemies. Truth, righteousness, peace, faith, salvation, and the Word all protect me and provide great security. I'm firmly held in the grip of Jesus.

If you think deeply about it, my armor is Jesus himself. Truthfully. Jesus is my truth. Jesus is my righteousness. Jesus is my peace. Jesus is my faith. Jesus is my salvation. Jesus is My word made flesh. Jesus is my strength. Consider these verses:

Jesus is Truth. Is Jesus the center that holds my life together?

> Jesus answered, "I am the way and the truth and the life. No one comes to the Father except through me.
> —*John 14:6*

Jesus is Righteousness. Am I trusting in my own ability to be right or the rightness of Jesus in my life?

> God made him who had no sin to be sin for us, so that in him we might become the righteousness of God.
> —*2 Corinthians 5:21*

Jesus is Peace. Does peace guide my relationship with others?

> For he himself is our peace, who has made the two groups one and has destroyed the barrier, the dividing wall of hostility.
> —*Ephesians 2:14*

Jesus is my Faith. Is faith in Jesus my greatest protection?

> I have been crucified with Christ and I no longer live, but Christ lives in me. The life I now live in the body, I live by faith in the Son of God, who loved me and gave himself for me.
> —*Galatians 2:20*

Jesus is Salvation. Do I dwell in the security of Jesus' grip on my salvation?

> Salvation is found in no one else, for there is no other name under heaven given to mankind by which we must be saved."
> —*Acts 4:12*

Jesus is The Word. Do I allow the Word of God to speak to what is unhealthy or sinful in my life?

> In the beginning was the Word, and the Word was with God, and the Word was God ... The Word became flesh and made his dwelling among us. We have seen his glory, the glory of the one and only Son, who came from the Father, full of grace and truth.
> —*John 1:1, 14*

Jesus is my Access to Prayer. Are there occasions where I need to spend more time connecting with Jesus?

> Therefore, brothers and sisters, since we have confidence to enter the

Most Holy Place by the blood of Jesus, by a new and living way opened for us through the curtain, that is, his body.
—*Hebrews 10:19-20*

Putting on the armor is living with daily spiritual habits that are intentional to drive me back to Jesus repeatedly. It's turning to Jesus because there's nowhere else I'd rather turn. It's relying on Jesus to resolve my impossible circumstances that make me weak. It's relying on Jesus to help me bear up under the load and find perseverance. It's falling on Jesus when my life is falling apart. It's leaning on Jesus.

When I'm out of strength, and my mental, emotional, and spiritual tanks are empty, Jesus is stronger. Walking with Him provides greater perseverance and strength for my battles. And not just mine, but for yours.

You are stronger when walking with Him,
Pastor Brian

> *Dear Jesus, I thank you for being both my protection and my strength in this world. As I fight the battles of life, remind me daily that you are my armor. Help me to become more like you every single day. Give me the wisdom to make the choices you would make. Jesus, I lean into you, and I cast the pain of my beautiful but broken life upon you. In Jesus' name, Amen.*

14.

Self-Honesty

Therefore, since we are surrounded by such a great cloud of witnesses, let us throw off everything that hinders and the sin that so easily entangles. And let us run with perseverance the race marked out for us, fixing our eyes on Jesus, the pioneer and perfecter of faith. For the joy set before him he endured the cross, scorning its shame, and sat down at the right hand of the throne of God. Consider him who endured such opposition from sinners, so that you will not grow weary and lose heart.
—Hebrews 12:1-3

To my friend who hit the wall,

Some days, you are strong. Stronger than you know. Other days, you crash.

You reached out to me, saying, "I hit the wall. My emotions are all over the map. I don't think I can do another thing this week. What should I do?" For a bit, the answer might be nothing. Eventually, you must do some evaluation.

Your fatigue is more than physical. It's emotional, even spiritual.

When I find myself in this place, one of the greatest steps I can take is to honestly answer two questions: *How did I get here?* And: *How do I get out of here?*

In 1 Kings 17-18, Elijah announced that a great drought was coming. Two-plus years passed. There's a wicked king married to an even more wicked woman. They worship Baal, the supposed god of rain and lightning. He's the god of the weather and, therefore, the supposed god of prosperity. A great showdown takes place between Elijah and the 850 prophets of the king and queen. Elijah calls on God to send fire from heaven. And boom. It happens.

On the heels of great victory, Elijah discovers the crash that follows the high of victory. Everything was stacked against Elijah, except he had God. God won. The queen promises to have Elijah killed. And now, with even more stacked against him, in fatigue, Elijah runs for his life and, in his fatigue, seems to forget about God. By the way, the distance between Mt. Carmel and Beersheba is more than 100 miles—just under four marathons.

> Elijah was afraid and ran for his life. When he came to Beersheba in Judah, he left his servant there, while he himself went a day's journey into the wilderness. He came to a broom bush, sat down under it and prayed that he might die. "I have had enough, Lord," he said. "Take my life; I am no better than my ancestors."
>
> —*1 Kings 19:3-4*

Elijah experienced the crash that follows the big win, and we would be wise to learn to anticipate the same after the spiritual highs in our lives. There's a crash that follows the intense season of God working. I've experienced this adrenaline crash on many occasions. Most pastors will tell you that they experience some version of this adrenaline crash every Monday morning.

Here's when I'm likely to experience the same crash:

- When I've been through a spiritually intense season of victory.
- When I'm dealing with difficult people and difficult situations for extended periods.
- When I'm physically depleted.
- When I'm living in caregiver mode while neglecting the care of my

own soul.
- When I've been running on adrenaline for a season.
- When I'm living in fight or flight mode that can be triggered by chronic pain.
- When I'm feeling isolation, fear, and anxiety.

Then Elijah travels for 40 days and 40 nights to Horeb, the mountain of God, another 200 miles or so. And Elijah threw himself a bit of a pity party—a sure sign that He had taken his eyes off the Lord and put them on himself.

This is what emotional fatigue does to us. In exhaustion, we put the focus on ourselves.

After all this running, notice what God did not do to Elijah. God's prophet is out of strength and hope. God *did not* lecture Elijah. Emotionally beat him up. Shame him. Reject him. Or grant his request to die.

So, what did God do? Check out the exact sequence of steps that God pursued on behalf of Elijah. God started with Elijah's physical needs. Food. Rest. Exercise.

We would be wise to do the same.

> Then he lay down under the bush and fell asleep. All at once an angel touched him and said, "Get up and eat." He looked around, and there by his head was some bread baked over hot coals, and a jar of water. He ate and drank and then lay down again. The angel of the Lord came back a second time and touched him and said, "Get up and eat, for the journey is too much for you." So he got up and ate and drank. Strengthened by that food, he traveled forty days and forty nights until he reached Horeb, the mountain of God.
>
> —*1 Kings 19:5-8*

God asked Elijah a pointed question.

> There he went into a cave and spent the night. And the word of the Lord came to him: "What are you doing here, Elijah?" He replied, "I have been very zealous for the Lord God Almighty. The Israelites have rejected your covenant, torn down your altars, and put your prophets to death with the sword. I am the only one left, and now they are trying to kill me too."
>
> —*1 Kings 19:9-10*

God provided his presence and counseled Elijah with grace.

> The Lord said, "Go out and stand on the mountain in the presence of the Lord, for the Lord is about to pass by." Then a great and powerful wind tore the mountains apart and shattered the rocks before the Lord, but the Lord was not in the wind. After the wind there was an earthquake, but the Lord was not in the earthquake. After the earthquake came a fire, but the Lord was not in the fire. And after the fire came a gentle whisper. When Elijah heard it, he pulled his cloak over his face and went out and stood at the mouth of the cave. Then a voice said to him, "What are you doing here, Elijah?" He replied, "I have been very zealous for the Lord God Almighty. The Israelites have rejected your covenant, torn down your altars, and put your prophets to death with the sword. I am the only one left, and now they are trying to kill me too."
> —*1 Kings 19:11-14*

God gave Elijah next steps and purpose. In 1 Kings 19: 15-17, we read that the Lord said to him:

> "Go back the way you came, and go to the Desert of Damascus. When you get there, anoint Hazael king over Aram. Also, anoint Jehu son of Nimshi king over Israel, and anoint Elisha son of Shaphat from Abel Meholah to succeed you as prophet. Jehu will put to death any who escape the sword of Hazael, and Elisha will put to death any who escape the sword of Jehu."

God reminded Elijah that he wasn't alone.

> Yet I reserve seven thousand in Israel—all whose knees have not bowed down to Baal and whose mouths have not kissed him." So Elijah went from there and found Elisha son of Shaphat. He was plowing with twelve yoke of oxen, and he himself was driving the twelfth pair. Elijah went up to him and threw his cloak around him.
> —*1 Kings 19:18-19*

In the middle of this experience, *Elijah has an emotionally honest conversation with God. This is the part we usually skip. We don't want to give God honest answers because that would mean admitting the truth not only to God but to ourselves.* Read verses 9-14 again.

So, when I'm fed up, what can I do to help me move forward? How can I find strength in the Lord? How can I learn to rely on God for strength when I have none?

1. Start with my physical needs.

Food, rest, and exercise. In church world, we so often skip these physical solutions in favor of spiritual solutions: prayer, time in the Word, and community. While those are good things, what we often need is more basic. Habits that ensure physical self-care and rest. Both are biblical and recommended.

At some level, after any crisis, if you are wrestling with a sense of constant tiredness, you need to assess:

- Am I tired? Tired can be remedied with rest.
- Am I fatigued? Fatigue can be remedied with self-care, but it can take a long time.
- Am I exhausted? Exhaustion and weariness can take even longer to recover from.
- Am I weary? Weary begins to feel hopeless. But it doesn't have to be.

2. Ask and answer hard questions with complete honesty.

How did I get here? Recently, I attended a soul-care retreat. We were asked to bring something symbolic that represents where we are internally and emotionally in the moment. I'm not the most creative guy. I brought Scrabble tiles that spelled T.I.R.E.D. I told my story, sharing how the constant juggling of pain, struggle, work, and leadership had me on empty. When the retreat was almost over, someone re-ordered my Scrabble tiles to spell T.R.I.E.D. Most of us who are soul-tired have been through soul-trials. Until we are honest with ourselves, and with Jesus, about the exact nature of our trials and tiredness, we're not going to get anywhere. It's time to have an honest conversation with myself so that I can have an emotionally honest conversation with God.

3. Start an emotionally honest conversation with God that becomes an ongoing daily practice.

I say start because, truthfully, you want this to become a normal part of your prayer life. You might want to write it out. You might want to go for a drive to the middle of nowhere. You might want to lock yourself in your room alone. Yell at God if you need to. Tell Jesus that you are fed up. I read somewhere that "being angry at God is a dangerous thing, but telling God you are angry is called prayer." Dig deeper into what God is saying. What is it you need to admit to yourself and to God? Two questions might help:

- First, what in my life has God allowed that I am unwilling to accept? Talk that out loud to God. He is listening, and He can handle it.
- Second, what am I believing that isn't true?

Elijah needed to answer both. And so do you and me.

4. Expect my honest conversation with Jesus to correct my vision and my "I" problems.

You might have noticed. Elijah has a prepared and rehearsed speech for God. Take note now of how many times Elijah used the words "I" or "me" in his self-defense speech to God. Count them. Often, when I'm weary, exhausted, and overwhelmed with fatigue, I'm too focused on myself. You and I need to let Jesus correct that flaw.

Let's think this through. What if meditation, prayer, Bible reading, faith, and hope provide something superior to a pill ... *an actual relationship with the God of the universe who can do something greater than heal your physical pain? He can heal your soul.* And what if the greater healing comes not through the magical snap of Jesus' fingers but through the outpouring of our faith, hope, and love? What if our connection to each other, particularly to those who've been through what we are going through, is more powerful than we realize, and yet we cut off our connection to those very people because we see the church as problematic? It turns out that pharmaceutical solutions have been around for a long time. But faith has been practiced far longer. And Jesus? He's been around forever. An eternal solution is right in front of us, if only we will embrace it. ... if only we will replace our "what ifs" with "why nots?" Neuroscience demonstrates the value of faith, meditation, and prayer. Richard Ambron states:

> Eastern societies took a different route to manage pain with the introduction of meditation, and its practitioners have claimed for thousands of

years that training the mind can attenuate pain ... recent studies have shown that meditation has a firm foundation in neuroscience and that the ability of practitioners to willfully modulate pain provides an important alternative to drugs for the treatment of chronic pain.[37] In essence, we can learn to use the mind to distract our attention from the pain, as occurs via hypnosis, a placebo, or meditation ... As of this writing, mindfulness-based meditation is the best nonpharmacological treatment for chronic pain because it can benefit the greatest number of patients, is low risk, and is inexpensive, although it does require training.[38]

Of course, the story of Elijah moves on. He finds Elisha and moves forward. Ten more years of ministering and prophesying pass by. God was not done with Elijah. And when the time comes for Elijah to die and be taken to heaven, he doesn't die. Do you remember the story? It's in 2 Kings 2. God sends a chariot of fire and whirlwind to pick Elijah up and deliver him to heaven. I bet Elijah was glad that God didn't let him die when he asked him ten years before. He needed to get through what he was going through. And the strength for all of it was not found in himself, but in honest conversation with the Lord.

> You are stronger when honest with Jesus,
> Pastor Brian

> *Dear Jesus, I'm so tired. And so tired of being tired that I'm fed up. I haven't been totally honest with myself or with you. Forgive me. What I'm afraid to tell you is ... Show me where to start—is it my diet, rest, or maybe exercise? Help me to be in your Word to hear your voice in these emotionally honest conversations. Take my eyes off me and put them back on you where they belong. In Jesus' name, Amen.*

15.

Resurrection

You must face this pain together. The pain is her legacy to you both. It's proof that she was here. And I have experience with this, this sort of pain, and you can't escape it by building walls around your heart, or by breaking the universe, or by vengeance.[39]
—On the TV show "Fringe," Walter Bishop speaking to his son and daughter-in-law after the loss of their daughter.

Resurrection means that the worst thing is never the last thing.[40]
—Fredrick Buechner

To my friends who lost their child,

There are no words. You're living every parent's worst nightmare. And I'm not going to pretend that my words will change your grief, but I do hope they encourage you. I can express my empathy and grief for you, but there are no words that help. I understand that. I ache with you and for you. I also understand that there are a lot of words that don't help.

I see your loss, and I acknowledge that losing your child is life-altering. So much so that this loss will color everything—how you see yourself, each other, and God. Everything.

While this is a pain I have not personally experienced, I've walked with many different friends and church members through the loss of babies or children.

People say the stupidest things sometimes. To be fair, most of the time, people do not know what to say, and so they say nothing. Other times, people, with all the best of intentions, say things that are hurtful:

- "It's not a big deal." This is heartless to say to someone grieving the loss of their baby.
- "Don't you know that this increases the likelihood you will get a divorce?" While the trauma of losing a child is an understandable strain on any marriage, you need comfort and care. Any person who thinks offering such a warning represents caring or comforting needs to have their heart checked.
- "God needed your child more than you do." I hear this one a lot. It's unhelpful and theologically harmful. It implies that if somehow you needed your child more than God, you would still have them. And it implicitly states that God needs them. God doesn't need any of us, but He chooses us anyway.
- In the case of a miscarriage: "At least they weren't born yet." Grief is not somehow lessened by the baby's presence inside the womb instead of outside the body. Your baby is your baby, whether that baby was three months premature or three days old. There's always grief when losing a baby.
- After time has passed following the death: "Don't you think it's been long enough? Don't you think it's time to get over this?" People say similar sentiments to grieving widows and widowers. It's not helpful. Grief is most overwhelming in its earliest days, but grief can hit you out of nowhere on any given day and at any given time.
- "Time heals all wounds." Not true, period. It'd be nice, sure, but time does not heal all wounds.
- "When I lost my baby …." or the person avoids your pain while focusing on their own. When done rightly, it can be comforting to hear from someone who has been through what you are going

through. But, sometimes, we relate to others through the lens of our own experience, and often, when we share that experience with someone, we like to talk about ourselves. Sometimes, too much. Some of us just like to hear ourselves talk. The obvious challenge is that when you lose your baby, your grief is about you, not about them.

Often, when couples first find out they are pregnant, they don't tell others because they want to make sure everyone is healthy. This often means that when babies are lost in the earliest days of a pregnancy, we suffer alone because no one ever knew we were pregnant.

Many of us never tell anyone we lost a baby. One of the reasons we don't is because we don't want their attention. Another reason is the insensitive things that people say, even if they're said with all the best of intentions. Some are simply cruel. A friend of a friend lost a 19-year-old son to cancer. "I know how you feel," a guy at church told him. "We recently lost our cocker spaniel after twenty years." No words.

Losing a child must be the hardest of all other kinds of grief. Please don't misunderstand. I know there are many forms of grief that feel impossible. Grief is hard for every person. And it's not a comparison. But I also recognize that there's something particularly painful about losing your child. I'll never forget the time my grandmother told me, after my uncle died, that "grief is so hard because you're just not supposed to bury your kids. Your kids are supposed to bury you." When we lose our parents, it can be somewhat expected. I'm not minimizing that grief. That grief is hard, too, but it is different. Losing a child, whether pre-born, in childhood, or even as an adult, is a loss like no other.

Where is God in all of this? What is God's perspective?

I don't pretend to have all the answers to your questions. Why did this happen? Why did God spare their child and not spare ours? Why did we lose the baby? How could God allow my 3-year-old to become so sick? These are impossible questions to answer. We want answers, but answers won't help. It's not like our grief will go away with answers. *God rarely gives us answers. He gives us something far better—Himself. God gives us Himself in our grief. He can because He is the resurrection and the life.*

Here's a question I believe we can be certain about: when babies die, do they go to heaven? I believe they do 100%. A seminary professor, Dr. Stan

Nelson, taught me years ago, "Babies aren't saved. They are safe in the hand of God." I believe with all my heart that babies are safe in the hands of God. This equally applies to those with mental disabilities. There are several places in Scripture that speak to God's perspective on babies and children.

When David lost a child:

> But now that he is dead, why should I go on fasting? Can I bring him back again? I will go to him, but he will not return to me."
> —*2 Samuel 12:23*

When the disciples wouldn't let people bring their children to Jesus:

> People were bringing little children to Jesus for him to place his hands on them, but the disciples rebuked them. When Jesus saw this, he was indignant. He said to them, "Let the little children come to me, and do not hinder them, for the kingdom of God belongs to such as these. Truly I tell you, anyone who will not receive the kingdom of God like a little child will never enter it." And he took the children in his arms, placed his hands on them and blessed them.
> —*Mark 10:13-16*

God will always *recognize* the life of your baby, born or unborn. God will always *value* the life of your child, born or unborn. God will always *understand* your grief. You will be the parent of that child for eternity.

I don't want to take the illustration too far, but God knows something about losing a son. Let me be clear: God is not asking you to sacrifice your child the way that He sacrificed His. But throughout the Bible, I think you can see God's understanding, comfort, love, and strength offered to those who have lost a child. The pages of the Bible are colored by the death of sons and daughters, and the very essence of the teaching of Scripture revolves around the death of God's Son.

The opening pages of the Bible involve the loss of a son. In fact, one son was killed by the other son. (Cain and Abel.) How must Adam and Eve have felt and must have wished they could continue to walk with God in the Garden after that loss. Abraham is asked to sacrifice his son. Bathsheba lost her baby because of David's sin. The pages of the Bible are covered with parents losing their children.

Here's an astonishing truth: The very reason God sacrificed His Son is so that we wouldn't be lost from His Son nor our sons and daughters for eternity. He took our sins, conquered death, and lives to remake eternity so that we can enjoy His Son and our sons and daughters forever.

His resurrection is the guarantee of our future resurrection.

> But Christ has indeed been raised from the dead, the first fruits of those who have fallen asleep. For since death came through a man, the resurrection of the dead comes also through a man. For as in Adam all die, so in Christ all will be made alive. But each in turn: Christ, the first fruits; then, when he comes, those who belong to him. Then the end will come, when he hands over the kingdom to God the Father after he has destroyed all dominion, authority and power. For he must reign until he has put all his enemies under his feet. The last enemy to be destroyed is death.
> —*1 Corinthians 15:20-26*

There really is hope after we've lost our kids, and real hope for our grief. I hope to encourage your soul with these words from 1 Thessalonians 4.

> Brothers and sisters, we do not want you to be uninformed about those who sleep in death, so that you do not grieve like the rest of mankind, who have no hope. For we believe that Jesus died and rose again, and so we believe that God will bring with Jesus those who have fallen asleep in him. According to the Lord's word, we tell you that we who are still alive, who are left until the coming of the Lord, will certainly not precede those who have fallen asleep. For the Lord himself will come down from heaven, with a loud command, with the voice of the archangel and with the trumpet call of God, and the dead in Christ will rise first. After that, we who are still alive and are left will be caught up together with them in the clouds to meet the Lord in the air. And so we will be with the Lord forever. Therefore encourage one another with these words.
> —*1 Thessalonians 4:13-18*

As people who believe that Jesus was raised from the dead and that there will be a time when we will be resurrected as well, we can live with faith that we will one day physically hold our children in our arms again. While the age that any of us will be after the resurrection is open to both mystery and discussion, it is more than apparent from these Bible verses that not only will we be able to be held physically by the resurrected Jesus, but we will also be able to physically hold one another.

Death is overwhelming. Grief is deafening. But death does not get the final word.

I love the Fredrick Buechner quote at the top of this letter. *Losing a child must be the worst thing. But thanks to the resurrection, it isn't the last thing.*

The Bible tells us that there is nothing wrong with grieving. In fact, grief is a recognition that someone who died was loved. The Bible affirms us in our grief, but also gently reminds us that death and grief do not get the final word.

Your grief is unimaginable. Your grief is deeply sorrowful. And your grief is understandable. But, thanks to Jesus, your grief can point you toward hope, resurrection, and eternity with your child and His Son. In that, there is comfort, strength, and peace that passes all understanding.

You are held in His arms,
Pastor Brian

> *Dear Jesus, I bring you my grief, my anger, my sadness, and all my questions. While I realize there may never be any answers this side of heaven, I'm thankful that I have you. I thank you for eternity, and I ask for your comfort in my grief and your hope in my soul. Give me the strength to find a safe person to talk with about the weight of this loss. Thank you that you personally understand my tears, and that you sent your Son so that those very tears can be wiped from my eyes. In Jesus' name, Amen.*

16.

Waiting

But he said to me, "My grace is sufficient for you, for my power is made perfect in weakness." Therefore I will boast all the more gladly about my weaknesses, so that Christ's power may rest on me.
—2 Corinthians 12:9

To my friend who is struggling with discouragement and disappointment,

You've felt like giving up countless times. You and your doctors have tried solution after solution. Treatment after treatment. As you've said, "Every time I get my hopes up—and then disappointment. I'm starting to believe I will never be well."

You're facing so much temptation to give in or give up. But you haven't. You're still doing the right thing. I'm so proud of you for not giving up when you've grown weary.

We've talked about how tired you are from not making any progress and how it seems harder than ever to muster the energy to take another step because it takes all your energy to just keep moving through daily life. A lot of us feel like we spend all our energy treading water in the mundane things, but not making any progress in what makes a difference. It sucks to feel stuck.

One of the Greek words in the Bible often translated as perseverance or endurance is *"hupomone."* It means to "be steadfast, to bear up under." It's used in a great prayer about strength found in Colossians 1:11, where it is translated as endurance. It's my prayer for you.

> For this reason, since the day we heard about you, we have not stopped praying for you. We continually ask God to fill you with the knowledge of his will through all the wisdom and understanding that the Spirit gives, so that you may live a life worthy of the Lord and please him in every way: bearing fruit in every good work, growing in the knowledge of God, being strengthened with all power according to his glorious might so that you may have great endurance and patience, and giving joyful thanks to the Father, who has qualified you to share in the inheritance of his holy people in the kingdom of light.
> —*Colossians 1:9-12*

Discouragement and disappointment are difficult, especially when you've been stuck in them for a season or more. Every athlete faces a slump. Every author faces writer's block. Every parent reaches a breaking point. It's a whole different thing to dwell in discouragement and disappointment because you have come to expect them.

Discouragement is a feeling of disheartenment, a lack of courage to face the day. I like what Charles Stanley said years ago, *"Disappointment is inevitable, but to become discouraged, there's a choice I make."*[41] Discouragement is an emptying feeling. It empties me of energy. It magnifies my fears. It cripples my confidence in God. And when I live it in long enough, it hardens my heart. All of that magnifies my pain.

> Let us not become weary in doing good, for at the proper time we will reap a harvest if we do not give up.
> —*Galatians 6:9*

If you feel like no one else understands, I'd like to remind you of a couple of important people in the Bible who faced discouragement. Arguably, the greatest prophet in the Old Testament, Elijah, faced incredible discouragement. We've already talked about that. And the greatest prophet in the New Testament, John the Baptist, was discouraged when Jesus wasn't doing what John expected him to do.

Expectations can form an illusion in our minds. Often, we expect others to do something to help us, even if they might not know what we're going through. Mentally, we live in the illusion that something is happening or will happen. We do this with Jesus. We place expectations on the Son of God, and when He doesn't do what we want, we are disappointed, if not discouraged.

Expectations are powerful. You've probably heard of the placebo effect; did you know that in some studies, as many as 33% of patients can find relief from pain in a sugar pill? The power is not simply in the pill. The power is in the trust of the doctor, which leads to expectations that the pill will be beneficial. This has two powerful implications for us:

First, our trust or distrust of God is significant in our experience of pain.

Second, our expectation of God's faithfulness to work in our pain to bring relief, meaning, or healing plays an increasing role in our experience of God's strength in our pain. In other words, if we don't expect God to work, there are consequences to that belief. And if we do expect God to work, there are benefits to those expectations. Neuroscience confirms that expectations matter. Richard Ambron writes:

> A much more profound and clinically valuable example of how the mind controls pain is the placebo effect, which is a fascinating phenomenon that occurs when pain is relieved by a sham treatment ... It turns out that whether or not a placebo is successful in attenuating pain depends on many factors, including who is giving the placebo, such as a doctor or a stranger, knowledge of the treatment, verbal encouragement, and mood. In general, a placebo is much more likely to relieve pain if the patient believes that the treatment will be successful. Thus, if a patient has been taking a pill that eliminates his pain, the pain will continue to be relieved if the patient is unknowingly given a pill that looks the same but is a placebo. In contrast, if the patient is skeptical of the success of the treatment, the placebo is much less likely to be successful. Success then is linked to the patient's knowing that the pill worked in the past and an expectation that the pain will be relieved.[42]

Longer-term discouragement is a good indicator that I have taken my eyes off Jesus and put them on my expectations. When discouraged, the greatest step of soul care I can take is to shift my focus from my expectations that I perceive aren't being met back to Jesus and the work He is actually doing. False expectations are my illusions. What Jesus is doing today, that is the truth.

We all have expectations of God that go unfulfilled. Sometimes, I'm discouraged because my expectations aren't being met. Sometimes, I'm discouraged because the timing I hoped for isn't meshing with God's plan. And sometimes, I'm discouraged because God is not working in the way that I asked Him to. While I am working to move God toward my agenda, God is always working to move me toward His.

So, I can find strength to overcome discouragement when I shift my focus from my expectations to the work that Jesus is actually doing today. This is what Jesus told John the Baptist when John was full of doubt:

> John's disciples told him about all these things. Calling two of them, he sent them to the Lord to ask, "Are you the one who is to come, or should we expect someone else?" When the men came to Jesus, they said, "John the Baptist sent us to you to ask, 'Are you the one who is to come, or should we expect someone else?' " At that very time Jesus cured many who had diseases, sicknesses and evil spirits, and gave sight to many who were blind. So he replied to the messengers, "Go back and report to John what you have seen and heard: The blind receive sight, the lame walk, those who have leprosy are cleansed, the deaf hear, the dead are raised, and the good news is proclaimed to the poor. Blessed is anyone who does not stumble on account of me."
> —Luke 7:18-23

Strength comes from focusing on the work of Jesus in my life today—work that has been promised by the Word of God. So, practically speaking, what does my faith need? To:

1. Focus on the actual work of Jesus today.

There is always good news because Jesus is always working. I'm often not paying attention to what Jesus is doing because I'm so focused on what I want done. Again, it's very easy, often without realizing it, to focus my gaze upon myself and miss Jesus.

2. Bend my expectations to the work of Jesus in the here and now.

I need to be fluid and flexible. I need to bend my life to Jesus rather than trying to bend Jesus to my expectations. What is Jesus actually doing today? What did He do yesterday? What gratitude do I need to choose? How can I join Jesus in what He is doing right now?

3. Slow down.

This is largely about God's timing, which is a mystery. Be willing to wait in the gap between what Jesus has promised and what Jesus has finished. Jesus does not march to the beat of anyone's drum. He listens to the Father, who has His own timeline. Some things will be finished down the road.

Some things will be finished when we are transformed in heaven. All our life is a gap between what Jesus has started and what He has finished so far. We are all waiting for that time when there will be no more disease or sickness, death or grieving, sorrow or pain. This waiting points me to that greater reality in the future when Jesus will finish all that He started.

Overcoming discouragement can be a long-term battle. We must give God time. Actually, whether we give it to Him or not, it will take as long as it takes. Time is not something you and I can control.

We need to be patient with our recovery. Patient with ourselves, patient with others, and patient with God. People say you shouldn't pray for patience. I see it the exact opposite. I must pray for patience. It's something I desperately need, and life requires it of me, whether I pray for it or not.

We often give up way too early on God—and on ourselves. Our least favorite thing to do is to wait. And our least favorite of God's answers to our prayers is to wait.

But when I give up too early based on incomplete information about what Jesus is going to do in the days ahead, I short-circuit the healing process and the strengthening process. When I wait on Jesus to work with great expectation, I'm given something incredibly valuable: hope.

Patiently keeping our focus on Jesus resets our priorities in the only place where real strength is found: Him.

You can expect Jesus to work,
Pastor Brian

> *Jesus, I confess that discouragement is overpowering, and I need your encouragement. Fill my heart with your undeniable presence. Fill my soul with your unlimited strength. Fill my life with your unfailing love. Fill my future with your unending work. In Jesus' name. Amen*

17.

Confidence

Three times I pleaded with the Lord to take it away from me. But he said to me, "My grace is sufficient for you, for my power is made perfect in weakness." Therefore I will boast all the more gladly about my weaknesses, so that Christ's power may rest on me. That is why, for Christ's sake, I delight in weaknesses, in insults, in hardships, in persecutions, in difficulties. For when I am weak, then I am strong.
—2 Corinthians 12:8-10

To my friend who feels like life is a perpetual crisis,

Since the stroke, your daily life has changed so much. I would never pretend to understand how you feel or what you are going through. After the stroke, you told me that many days feel impossible. The key word is "feel." As I've watched you wrestle through this for years now, you have endured. You've done more than you thought you could do. Yes, you've had to let go of many dreams. But you've chosen a courageous path. I see in you what you may not see in yourself: the courage to face each day.

When we are experiencing crisis, we often long for answers. However, explanations often don't help. The truth is, even if God gave us the explanations we long for, it wouldn't change much. Sometimes, there are no explanations. On the TV show M*A*S*H, after B.J., a doctor, loses a patient, Radar questions why the soldier died, suggesting it was unfair. "I could give you a lot of medical reasons," says B.J., "but understanding doesn't make it less painful."[43] So true.

At some point, you said something to me like, "What good is faith when I've lost so much?"

I realize that there's no pretending that life's all good. Living life with God means that we walk with Him through the good times and the sorrowful times. It's OK to be sorrowful about what you've lost. What good is our relationship with God if we can't be honest with Him about our grief and what we've lost?

I know you've lost a lot. There's real grief in what you've lost. Walking with God isn't pretending that all the loss and pain aren't there. Walking with God is walking with him through the sorrow, through the chaos, and through the grief.

It would be easy to pull away from God because of the sorrow and grief. I want to encourage you to do the opposite. Lean in and be honest with Him about what's there. We just want things to go back to normal. There's no going back. Only going forward.

I want to encourage you with a verse from the book of Philippians that I hope instills courage in you.

> Being confident of this, that he who began a good work in you will carry it on to completion until the day of Christ Jesus.
> —Philippians 1:6

God has not forgotten about you. When your crisis began, it was natural to ask good questions like, *Why is this happening?* And, *Why me?* Somewhere along the way, you and I talked about feeling forgotten or abandoned by God. You're not alone.

Lots of people feel abandoned by God when they receive life-altering news. The Bible says that's just not the case. God has not abandoned you. God has not forgotten about you.

Many Christians take a verse like this for granted. We think, *I can be confident in Jesus when I need to.* It's almost like Jesus is a get-out-of-jail-free card we can play when we need Him, but until then, "I'm OK. I'm glad I have Him. But I'm confident in this moment without Him."

What's implied is that I don't always need to find my confidence in Him. You, however, don't have that luxury. As difficult as it is to admit, you can't find courage in *your* unhindered ability to finish what you have started in your life.

Based on this verse, my best encouragement to you would be to *rebuild your life from here by rebuilding your confidence on God's unhindered ability to work through your chaos. Jesus' unhindered ability to finish what He started. The Spirit's unhindered ability to work through doctor appointments and physical therapy and one step forward and two steps back.*

What you're experiencing these days is unpredictable. Your life has been shaken to the core. You're hindered in more ways than one. God is not. Your life has been shaken. God's work in your life is unshaken.

You and I need to shorten our focus to tune into the moment by moment care of God. Remember the prayer, "Give us this day our daily bread." Daily. The bread of God's Word reminds us that even in crisis, God is sovereign. And we must come back to that every time where we worry that He is not.

I particularly like the emphasis overall in the book of Philippians. Paul's desire is to take the Gospel to far-reaching places that have never heard it. Yet he's in Rome under house arrest. He is hindered in his ability to do the very thing he wants to be able to do. He doesn't know if he will live or die. And yet he writes more about joy in the book of Philippians than any of his other writings.

I find that amazing. Even more, this letter about joy has traveled the world over and over again.

Why can he choose joy in his circumstances despite the chaos in his life? His confidence is not found in achieving the circumstances he wants. His confidence is not in his grasp of this world.

Rather, his confidence is found in God's ability to achieve what God wants. Truth is, when I find my confidence in me and my hands and my grip on my circumstances, it's a false confidence. It's an illusion. Confidence is not truly found in my ability to achieve my desired outcomes. Confidence is found in God's unhindered ability to achieve His.

Think of what Paul is really arguing through all the book of Philippians

God Finishes What He Starts

> Being confident of this, that he who began a good work in you will carry it on to completion until the day of Christ Jesus.
> —*Philippians 1:6*

God Always Works to Accomplishes What He Intends

> Therefore, my dear friends, as you have always obeyed—not only in my presence, but now much more in my absence—continue to work out your salvation with fear and trembling, for it is God who works in you to will and to act in order to fulfill his good purpose.
> —*Philippians 2:12-13*

God Moves Me Forward

> Not that I have already obtained all this, or have already arrived at my goal, but I press on to take hold of that for which Christ Jesus took hold of me. Brothers and sisters, I do not consider myself yet to have taken hold of it. But one thing I do: Forgetting what is behind and straining toward what is ahead, I press on toward the goal to win the prize for which God has called me heavenward in Christ Jesus.
> —*Philippians 3:12-14*

God Can Bring His Peace to My Anxiety

> Do not be anxious about anything, but in every situation, by prayer and petition, with thanksgiving, present your requests to God. And the peace of God, which transcends all understanding, will guard your hearts and your minds in Christ Jesus.
> —*Philippians 4:6-7*

God Gives Me Strength I Can't Find in Myself

> I can do all this through him who gives me strength.
> —*Philippians 4:13*

God Meets My Needs When I Live Generously for the Kingdom

> And my God will meet all your needs according to the riches of his glory in Christ Jesus.
> —*Philippians 4:19*

Philippians 2:12 does not say to work *for* my salvation or, work *toward* my salvation, or even work *at* my salvation. It says to *work out my salvation with fear and trembling*. When it says fear and trembling, think awe, respect, and wonder. I am working out the salvation that I already possess in my inner life into my outer life. God's role is to work salvation in me toward His good purpose. My role is to work out the implications of that salvation in my life today. I can identify with a workout. I know what a workout looks like, even if I don't always feel like exercising. It's good for me.

I need to do the particular work by choosing joy—the mood of Jesus. Read all four chapters of Philippians in one sitting. It won't take long. Choosing joy is the workout. I need to do the work out of obedience. Of dependence. Of releasing my circumstances and embracing the work of Jesus in them. I need to rebuild my confidence on Jesus, and His work in my life, in my pain, in my relationships, and in my outcomes. Doing this will transfer my reliance for strength from myself to Jesus, who is willing and able to provide the strength we need.

I need to do the work of rest and recovery. One of the best things I can do when I am experiencing crisis fatigue is nothing. Let me repeat that because it might have clanged with your sense that smacks of the lazy way out of this. Again: One of the best things I can do when I am experiencing crisis fatigue is nothing. Simply rest. I need to acknowledge my limits. Rest and Sabbath are an act of faith to trust that God is working when we are not. Acknowledge His sovereignty and my lack of control over anything. And rest in the goodness of the salvation He is giving me.

Let's be practical. Here are four tools God will use as you work out:

- God will use his Word to reshape me.
- God will use his Spirit to empower me.
- God will use my circumstances as His laboratory.
- God will use rest to replenish me.

When life is good, it's easy to let what's going on in our circumstances dictate what will go on in our heads. Our thinking and mindset waffle and wriggle like a fish out of water. It may be difficult to see it this way, but you don't have that luxury. Life's circumstances require you to keep your focus on God's work in your circumstances. Lean into that day by day, moment by moment.

Remember, when I embrace my weakness, I'm finally in the place where His grace is sufficient for me. I'm finally in the place where I can be *strong in Him*, specifically because *I am weak in me.*

All of us wrestle with this. It's a conscious choice. I will either let my circumstances or God's work in my circumstances dictate my headspace. You and I need to choose to see life through the lens of God's work, not the lens of our own work in this life. This provides hope, strength, perspective, and the ability to let go of what I cannot control and trust God for strength one moment, one breath, and one day at a time.

Every single day, life is a choice between Jesus' work in your life or your work in your life. Like you, I'm going with Jesus.

You are guarded by grace,
Pastor Brian

> *Dear Jesus, When I look at my own life and my own strength, it's easy to run out of hope. Please take my eyes off me and help me to keep them fixed on you. It's hard to thank you for my weakness, but I've arrived at the end of what I can do on my own. Weakness is a pretty good word to describe where I'm at. I ask for your unlimited strength and your unending grace. Help me to focus on your unhindered work in my life and my future. Show me my next step forward. In Jesus' name, Amen.*

MINDSET 4
Choose a better support network

Two are better than one, because they have a good return for their labor: If either of them falls down, one can help the other up. But pity anyone who falls and has no one to help them up. Also, if two lie down together, they will keep warm. But how can one keep warm alone? Though one may be overpowered, two can defend themselves. A cord of three strands is not quickly broken.
—Ecclesiastes 4:9-12

What's more natural for you when you face difficulty? To reach out for support, or to retreat into your shell and hide? We have lots of sayings, but do we practice them?

- "We're in this together."
- "Two are better than one."
- "Teamwork makes the dream work."

It doesn't matter how you say it. It does matter how you practice it. Our lives are stronger when we are not alone.

Christianity was never meant to be a solo experience. Life is not meant to be lived in isolation. Yet The Pity Vortex pulls us in the direction of not only self-reliance, but self-isolation. The life of pretending feels so lonely because no one is allowed to see the real me. Hiding the real me from others not only isolates me physically, it isolates me emotionally, even when I'm in a room full of people I consider friends. Once I've decided that I must escape my pain at any cost, and once I've decided to rely on myself and myself alone for strength, I've committed myself to a direction that pushes and pulls me away from the people I most need in my life.

Here's what I can tell you beyond a shadow of doubt: When life gets overwhelming, the temptation will always be to pull away from others, to pull back in my shell, to isolate myself from others because I think that they don't truly understand what I am going through. *But if I am going to get through what I am going through, I cannot do it without the encouragement, support, and accountability of community. Specifically, God's community of faith.*

When the pain grows out of control like a wildfire, we're afraid of how the fire inside of us might overflow to hurt others. But what if they are the very people we need to get the fire under control?

Early in 2 Corinthians, Paul writes:

> Praise be to the God and Father of our Lord Jesus Christ, the Father of compassion and the God of all comfort, who comforts us in all our troubles, so that we can comfort those in any trouble with the comfort we ourselves receive from God. For just as we share abundantly in the sufferings of Christ, so also our comfort abounds through Christ. If we are distressed, it is for your comfort and salvation; if we are comforted, it is for your comfort, which produces in you patient endurance of the same sufferings we suffer. And our hope for you is firm, because we know that just as you share in our sufferings, so also you share in our comfort. We do not want you to be uninformed, brothers and sisters, about the troubles we experienced in the province of Asia. We were under great pressure, far beyond our ability to endure, so that we despaired of life itself. Indeed, we felt we had received the sentence of death. But this happened that we might not rely on ourselves but on God, who raises the dead.
> —*2 Corinthians 1:3-9*

In many ways, Paul outlines the same principles that show up later in the book. God didn't cause our pain, but He wants to work through our pain to both strengthen us and encourage others as well. When difficulty comes, God is in the business of sustaining, not explaining. These things happened that we might not rely upon ourselves but on God.

Paul describes the pains he experienced with a variety of words. Words like trouble, suffering, distress, pressure, despair, death, and peril. But there are other words that show up over and over in this passage—words like comfort, deliverance, and hope. The word comfort is repeated nine times in this passage.

We want the choice to be to suffer or not to suffer. That's not reality.

There are three clear truths I want to make sure we hold onto:

1. God wants to work in my life through my troubles.

God is the God of all comfort. And the God of all comfort wants to comfort me. I think of all the times when my daughters were babies. Something upset them. When they could not console themselves back to sleep, my wife or I would get up in the middle of the night, hold them, and comfort them, providing a soothing touch and gentle consolation. God does the same with us if we let Him.

Paul assures us that our sufferings, as painful as they are in this realm, can never outdistance God's comfort because He is the God of all comfort. Paul repeats the word "comfort" in one form or another nine times in five verses.

The words "affliction" and "comfort" stand out in this text. Whether it's sleepless nights, daily stress, a gnawing feeling in our gut, or an unending pressure to perform, we all feel affliction regularly. These feelings are an opportunity to experience God and His comfort regularly as well.

God not only offers me comfort, but God offers me strength and hope.

We believe the only two choices in life are "I can suffer or "I can not suffer." But, actually, the two choices are: "I can suffer alone, or I can suffer with God and His comfort." Like it or not, suffering is a given. But going it alone is not.

2. God wants to work in my life through other people's troubles.

God comforts me through Christ. God empties me of self-reliance. And God comforts me through other people because of the troubles they have endured. We often think that no one understands what we are going through. That's not entirely true. Someone else has been through what I am going through. And they've found comfort and can offer me comfort. In fact, if you think about it, God uses troubles to connect people. Like the raised bumps on Legos, the bumps of life connect us to other people. We need each other. The real question is: Will I let into my life the people who can comfort me?

Have you ever noticed it takes a veteran to help a veteran? An addict to help an addict? Why? Because they've been there. Because they understand. God uses people who've been through the same troubles we've been through to bring His comfort and their comfort to our lives. As C.S. Lewis said: "Friendship ... is born at the moment when one [person] says to another 'What! You too? I thought that nobody but myself ... .'"[44]

The real truth: I can suffer alone, or I can suffer with the people of God.

3. God wants to work in other people's lives through my troubles.

Not only does God use the troubles of other people to provide me comfort, but He wants to use my troubles to comfort other people. My suffering can be pointless, or I can allow God to bring good from my suffering. Pain, trouble, and tribulation break me so that I can see those around me with God's eyes. Who needs comfort and consoling from me? When I think about the times I've been used as a pastor to comfort others, it's usually because of my *troubles*, not because of my *answers*.

The real truth: My suffering can be meaningless, or my suffering can be redeemed.

We are all wounded healers. We are all wounded with the pains, burdens, failures, and troubles of this life. God has committed the very ministry of sharing burdens and the ministry of providing comfort to all of us who have wounds. God doesn't waste your pain. Pain will provide an opportunity to grow closer to Jesus and His people, especially when it becomes a means to minister to others. Also, I would suggest our evangelism is far more effective when we reach out to others in their pains and share with them the comfort and hope we have received.

God gives us a mission in this world. As we grow in maturity, we want to help others become stronger by learning from our experiences of pain, weakness, and strength. That mission involves reaching other people and extending His grace to them. As we grow closer to Christ, maturity demands that we become people who share more grace with more people. As we become stronger in Christ, we want to help others become stronger in Christ as well.

The church has often been described as a hospital for sinners, not a country club for seasoned saints. We only achieve this potential when we take off the masks, share our wounds, and allow God to heal us together.

This will never take place in "pseudo-community," a term coined by Scott Peck referring to the earliest stages or pretense of community building.[45] To move beyond pseudo-community, a group must begin to live vulnerably, risk conflict, and resolve to love beyond their differences. This will require ever-growing amounts of emotional maturity among those of us who want to live in true community. An article describing Peck's approach says:

> Pseudo Community is the front porch of Community in Peck's model. It is dominated by convention, orderliness, superficial communication, and a search for similarities. In this stage, interactions are typically very polite—exchanging business cards and avoiding difficult issues. Trust is shallow. However, it is shallow not because members are untrustworthy but because they are untested. The circumstances are uncertain and nothing much has happened to the group to reveal how members will behave under pressure. Rather than step into this uncertainty, members mostly keep to safe ground—and "talk about the weather." [46]

Do you and I need God to work in our lives? Of course, but we also need other people to support, encourage, strengthen, and hold us accountable as we go through the turmoil and turbulence of life. As long as we remain in isolation mode, we leave ourselves vulnerable to the suction of The Pity Vortex. Health comes when we receive grace from others. And health remains as we share grace with others. In fact, this very mission to help others through their pain often provides the strength, even the motivation we need to keep going in addressing our own pains and troubles. Strength comes as we experience the community of The Perseverance Revolution.

We aren't created for loneliness, isolation, judgmentalism, tribalism, alienation, or seclusion. Now, I'm not arguing that everyone should be extroverted; generally, introverts are better at deep friendship than extroverts. I'm saying that we're created for community, and our troubles and trials bond us together in ways that our self-isolating does not. Solitaire is good for cards but not for enduring life's difficulties or celebrating life's wins.

> *Dear Jesus, thank you for giving me the grace gift of your people who are meant to be a haven of love, truth, and grace. Help me to lean on them for support, community, comfort, encouragement, friendship, and accountability. And grow me so that I can provide the same to the people you put in my life. In Jesus' name, Amen.*

18.

Vulnerability

I lift up my eyes to the mountains—where does my help come from? My help comes from the Lord, the Maker of heaven and earth. He will not let your foot slip—he who watches over you will not slumber; indeed, he who watches over Israel will neither slumber nor sleep.
—Psalm 121:1-4

To my friend who is freaking out but doesn't want anyone to know,

Life is overwhelming for all of us. You're freaking out on the inside while playing cool on the outside. You wouldn't want anyone to know. You sometimes feel like you are on the verge of a breakdown, especially when you hold these feelings in without talking about them. You've said that you just want someone to be there—to know that you are still loved, and everything will be OK. I understand that feeling. Like you, I've thought to myself, *If everyone knew I was this anxious, they would think I am a fraud.* The truth is that everyone experiences anxiety, but not everyone knows what to do with it.

Christians are funny about this. We tend to believe that since we are people of faith, we should never be fearful. So, it is common to see Christians bury their anxiety deep within, hoping that nobody notices their "lack of faith." We don't want to be criticized. And we tend to believe that any of our solutions must be spiritual. So, we pray, which is a good thing. But, if the anxiety doesn't fade away through prayer, we bury it even deeper so that no one knows we are "failures" at this thing called faith. You are not a failure.

I want you to notice what we have just done. We engage our pain but put ourselves in isolation. We pretend to others that we are something we are not. We deny the truth, embrace the illusion, and remove our real selves from the people we need the most. Furthermore, we let what other people think about us drive our decision-making rather than resting in an identity that is settled as a child of God. And, in many cases, when we embrace the need to hide our true feelings, we take no other steps toward wholeness.

All of this leaves you feeling invisible, afraid, and disconnected. You're at coffee with a friend. They ask how you are. "I'm good." Which can be a code for "I don't want to talk about it." In small group, you give the right Bible answers, but don't engage the difficult "feeling" questions. You don't have any interest in the "touchy-feely" stuff. At home, after a long day, you spend your evening in an endless Netflix marathon and scrolling through Instagram. Safer to explore the pretend life of others than to open up about your own fearful reality.

Anxiety tricks the brain into acting as if there is real danger when there is little physical danger ahead. Anxiety may come for a lot of reasons. It may be that we're suffering through real circumstances that produce fear. That we're struggling through perceived circumstances that trigger our fight or flight mechanism. Or that we have a chemical imbalance in our brains that keeps us stuck in fight or flight.

Sometimes, our anxiety is an attempt to control circumstances or people that can't be controlled. We want certain outcomes, and we cannot guarantee those outcomes. So, we worry and feel anxious about it. We can't control it, so we control what we can—our reactions. And our reaction is anxiety, which can be an attempt to control the uncontrollable.

At some level, anxiety is a faith or fear kind of issue. Anxiety is an indicator that I'm trusting in my ability to control circumstances rather than trusting in the control and sovereignty of Jesus. You're not the only person to try to control the uncontrollable. In this very real sense, my anxiety is an opportunity to trust Jesus and others with my fears. Not to ignore my fear. But to acknowledge my fear to Jesus and trust Him with the outcome. It's an opportunity to learn to trust others as well.

It all reminds me of the story in Mark 4, where Jesus and the disciples are crossing a lake on a boat. Jesus falls asleep in the stern. An intense storm arises, and the disciples fear they will drown with Jesus asleep on the boat. What do they do? The same thing you and I would probably do. Wake Jesus up. When we wrestle with anxiety and can't sleep, we often talk to Jesus. I think sometimes we just want to make sure Jesus is awake and paying attention to our storm.

> Leaving the crowd behind, they took him along, just as he was, in the boat. There were also other boats with him. A furious squall came up, and the waves broke over the boat, so that it was nearly swamped. Jesus was in the stern, sleeping on a cushion. The disciples woke him and said to him, "Teacher, don't you care if we drown?" He got up, rebuked the wind and said to the waves, "Quiet! Be still!" Then the wind died down and it was completely calm. He said to his disciples, "Why are you so afraid? Do you still have no faith?" They were terrified and asked each other, "Who is this? Even the wind and the waves obey him!"
>
> —*Mark 4:36-41*

How does faith become stronger, deeper, richer? By walking through the storms and learning to trust Him with my anxiety. To discover more about this man who can speak to the weather and the waves, and they obey him.

For those who teach that our faith can lead to a storm-free life, I must confront that false teaching. Jesus led the disciples across the lake and right into this storm. Jesus also led the disciples right into the storm of the crucifixion. Sometimes, obedience will lead me out of a storm, and sometimes, obeying Jesus takes me right into the eye of life's hurricanes. I must learn to see it as an opportunity to stretch my faith in my Creator, who is also the Wind Whisperer.

Up to this point, I'm just reinforcing what we've already talked about regarding our need to choose between self-sufficiency and Jesus-dependence. If we can't learn to be honest with God about our fears, we won't find the courage to do what comes next.

Take notice that there were "other boats" with them on this journey through the storm. Others got to discover more about Jesus as they did life with Jesus and the twelve disciples. I'm sure they experienced some fear and anxiety as well. When we do life with others, sometimes there is collateral damage when our fear burns out of control. Those closest to us often reap the worst. But there's also the opportunity for collateral hope when others see Jesus' work in our fear and anxiety. And, quite honestly, *we need each other. We need others to see the real us. We need to drop the pretending and let them see our fears, our anxieties, and our worries. When we are real, other people have permission to be real as well. Together, we find collataral hope.*

It's powerful when we let others inside to see not only our anxiousness, but our trust in Jesus through that anxiety. What we tend to "see" as a weakness—vulnerability—is often a strength. The disciples were all in the same boat together. This was a shared experience. Certainly, there was a bond as they looked back on this moment. Not just among the disciples, but among all those on the other boats. It turns out that the bonds of collateral faith and collateral hope are powerful reminders that Jesus is indeed stronger. This is what the community of faith called the church is all about.

Churches get a bad rap. Everyone has had a bad experience at one. Of course, churches are gatherings and communities of broken, sinful people. That said, healthy churches provide a safe environment to be real about your struggles, not just your faith.

One more thing about life's storms: They tend to clarify what panic and anxiety can't do. For all the fear of the disciples, it didn't calm the storm; it triggered a calming of their hearts—when they reached out to Jesus. Not only can He calm storms, but He can calm our hearts. This is a lesson they learned together. Sometimes, Jesus speaks to the waves and wind and calms the storm. Sometimes, Jesus speaks to our fear, panic, worry, lack of control, and anxiety—and calms the storm going on within us. And sometimes, Jesus reminds us that He is present in the storm, and He simply walks with us through it. Whatever the case, we must learn to trust His answers together.

Often, our storm, and the anxiety we bring to Jesus, form not only an opportunity to grow but a testimony that will encourage others. What if they kept it hidden and Mark didn't record the story for us? What if they ignored the storm and their panic? What if they drank it away or "numbed it" away? By engaging their life and their panic with Jesus, they grew stronger. And because they shared their story with us, so do we. This is the model for real community, and it starts with vulnerability.

> You are stronger when vulnerable,
> Pastor Brian

Dear Jesus, my storm, anxiety, and fears are real. My perceived need to control and real lack of control are real. More than anything, thank you that you are real, and my faith in you is real. Thank you that there are people just like me who understand because they struggle in just the same ways I do. Together, help us discover how powerful shared faith in you can really be. Give me the courage to practice vulnerability with your people. In Jesus' name, Amen.

19.

Reaching Out

NOTE: If you, or someone you know, is considering suicide, please reach out for help, which can be found by calling the National Suicide and Crisis Lifeline: 988. Or going online to 988lifeline.org

To my friend who is thinking about suicide,

When you asked to meet, I didn't know what to expect. You said, "I've been thinking seriously about suicide. Life has become too much pressure and offers too many choices and an overwhelming amount of stress and sadness that I'm not sure how to handle." I cried. You cried. I was so taken with emotion I'm not sure exactly what we talked about in the rest of that conversation. But I can say I'm deeply thankful you reached out.

I'm heartbroken for you.

Let me start with what I won't do:

- I won't tell you that your pain isn't real. It is.
- I won't tell you that I can fix everything. I can't.
- I won't tell you that faith in God makes pain and depression go away. That would be a lie.

Being a Christian does not make you immune to pain, despair, or depression any more than it makes you immune to disease or physical death.

Do Christians struggle with despair? Yes. Next time you open the Bible, read it for emotion. Jeremiah was known as the weeping prophet. Paul admitted he was in despair. Depression is clear in many of the Psalms. Job was an emotional wreck, and rightly so.

It's OK to not be OK. It's OK to feel like you are at the end of your strength.

I want to gently remind you that you are loved and cared about. I want you to know that there is someone who will help you process your pain and discover that there is something greater in your life than pain.

No matter how strong something inside of you is screaming that nobody cares and nobody loves you, that's just not true. There is someone who will listen.

If you cannot think of one safe family member or friend who will listen right now, please call 988—the National Suicide and Crisis Lifeline.

As a person who believes in Jesus, I want you to know that Jesus will always listen, but for now, I want you to have a real flesh and blood person to talk to. Isolation convinces us that no one listens, and no one cares. That's just not true.

Here are a couple of verses in the Bible that really help me remember that I am not the only one to feel despair about life.

> We do not want you to be uninformed, brothers and sisters, about the troubles we experienced in the province of Asia. We were under great pressure, far beyond our ability to endure, so that we despaired of life itself. Indeed, we felt we had received the sentence of death. But this happened that we might not rely on ourselves but on God, who raises the dead.
> —*2 Corinthians 1:8-9*

While I don't think Paul is saying he was suicidal, I do think he was saying that he needed help from God to save his life. He said he despaired of life itself. The word despair means to completely fall apart, to lose it emotionally, or to be in difficulty, doubt, and embarrassment. I do find in this simple couple of verses the help and hope we need.

He felt great pressure far beyond his ability to endure. That probably sounds familiar to you.

Suicide might be tempting when:

- Our pain is high, and our strength is low.
- Our problems are big, and our hearts are empty.
- Life feels shaken beyond our capacity to handle.
- The troubles outweigh the good we had planned.
- The pressures outweigh our ability to endure.
- The despair outweighs the reasons to live.
- The troubles of the moment outweigh our strength in the moment.
- The consequences outweigh our ability to face them.

Suicide sometimes seems like the only way out of pain and is often about escaping pain. Suicide, more than not, is an escape from current pain (our problems) or future pain (consequences or pain that is coming). It's a heavy juxtaposition in the mind, a wrong supposition that our only hope is to abandon hope and take our own life.

There are several examples of this in the Bible, including Saul in the Old Testament and Judas in the New Testament.

Yes, suicide can be about ending pain. But it is also about taking control of something—pain—that we cannot control.

I'm begging you to take control of your pain in a healthier way.

Here's what I really want you to know:

It's healthy to be honest enough with myself
to admit to myself
that I need to reach for help beyond myself.

It's healthy to admit that I need help from outside of me. Do this as soon as possible. Sooner is better than later.

It's beneficial to come to the place where I admit that I do not have strength and that I need help from someone else, whether Jesus or another human being.

When you break it down, there are three aspects to this:

- A *perspective*—be completely honest with myself.
- A *decision*—to admit to myself.
- An *action*—I need to reach for help beyond myself.

There are some in the Christian community who imply, or even directly state, that you need help from God and that other people are not necessary. While I agree that help from Jesus is good, needed, and always available, help from another human being is necessary now.

Anyone who wants you to believe that to be a person of faith, it all must be between you and God and not involve doctors, therapists, counselors, pastors, friends, and family members is not giving you good advice. Whether the person's intentions are good or not, telling someone who is considering suicide that they should pray, and trust God alone, is not enough. Telling a person that you will pray for them and trust God for them is not enough.

Right now, if you are tempted to end your own life, you need compassion in human form. You need someone who will listen. You need someone to see and enter your pain, and advocate for your life, because you feel too empty to advocate for your own life. You need to reach out and open up to someone who can do what 2 Corinthians 1:8-9 is talking about—bring you back to life.

There's nothing wrong with praying. I would encourage you to do that. In fact, if you have the strength, take out a paper and pen and write a note to Jesus right now. I think you will find it helpful.

But if you don't believe in God, or you don't have the strength, I would encourage you to reach out to someone safe. Someone who will walk with you and advocate for you.

If you are still thinking of suicide, I want you to know:

1. There is someone who cares.

Someone with real flesh and blood in your life who cares enough to hold onto your life and not let go. Someone who will stay with you until you get the help you need. Someone who will reach out for help on your behalf if you cannot reach out yourself. Someone who will make a life-and-death difference.

2. There is someone whose primary skill is listening who can help.

I am talking about counselors and therapists. They have training and tools to help. If you need someone right now, and there is nowhere else to turn, walk into an emergency room. Help will be made available. Therapists can help you develop a safety plan and give you tools and training with healthy coping mechanisms. They will listen and provide comfort. They will help you develop a plan for safety rather than a plan for death. They will help you understand your feelings, find beauty, and develop strength. They will help you learn healthy coping skills so that you have options when life is overwhelming.

3. There is someone who can help you embrace your beautiful but broken life.

Yes, our lives are broken. Sometimes, life is brutal. But that does not mean that your life isn't beautiful. You matter. Your life matters. And despite all the pain you feel right now, your life can be beautiful again.

At some level, I'm going to suggest that Jesus can do all these. Jesus is full of compassion, and I believe that Jesus sees suicide and thoughts of suicide as a tragedy. Jesus always cares. Jesus will always listen. Jesus will strengthen you. Jesus will help you cope. Jesus will help you embrace your broken but beautiful life.

Yes, Jesus is the giver and restorer of life. Jesus can bring us back to the idea of living rather than dying. Jesus stands lovingly, compassionately, willingly able to help. But, right now, I want you to have flesh and blood people in the here and now who can do that for you.

So, right now, I want you to reach out to someone who stands ready to help.

I would caution any church that would say, "a person should rely on God alone for help." We are never told in the Bible that relying on God means never relying on other human beings.

Rather, we are told that we are created for community, that we are to love one another, comfort one another, and encourage one another. Biblically, the bottom line is we need each other in times when life is overwhelming.

Pain sucks, but you're not alone. Many of us are here to help.

Your life matters,
Pastor Brian

P.S. Here are some questions everyone wonders about suicide but are afraid to ask:

1. Is suicide a sin?

This is a common but difficult question—and there are no easy answers. Theologians have debated for centuries whether suicide is sinful. On one hand, as hard as it is to think about, suicide is murder—self-murder. On the other hand, suicide does not determine a person's eternal destiny. Whether suicide is a sin or not, our relationship with Jesus determines our final destiny. And Jesus is the most compassionate human ever.

2. Is suicide forgivable? Is it unpardonable? Does suicide mean a person is not a Christian?

This is just like asking, "Is sin forgivable?" Yes. Absolutely. It's why Jesus died. Is it pardonable? Absolutely. Is it hard for us to work through forgiveness when someone we love commits suicide because there's a lot of pain involved? Yes. No doubt. But is suicide forgivable? Yes.

3. What does God think of suicide?

Just as I wrote in this letter, I believe that God will always see suicide as a tragedy. Jesus is compassionate. The enemy longs for death, but Jesus is the giver and restorer of life. Jesus roots for life. Jesus brings life. Jesus will always bring compassion, grace, truth, love, life, and His Spirit to any sinner who reaches out for help. He is the way, the truth, and the life. Like Him, we're encouraged to pray Psalm 31:5:

> Into your hands I commit my spirit;
>   deliver me, Lord, my faithful God.

And Psalm 31:15:

> My times are in your hands;
>   deliver me from the hands of my enemies,
>   from those who pursue me.

Dear Jesus, thank you that you are with me. I'm asking right now, as clearly as I can, that you bring me back to life, back to living, and back to the strength to go on. Let me see that there is hope. Whatever it is that I want to escape, help me see that escape is not the answer. Please give me the strength to reach out to someone right now. To another human being. Put their name in my head. Please use them to save my life. In Jesus' name, Amen.

20.

Forgiveness

See to it that no one falls short of the grace of God and that no bitter root grows up to cause trouble and defile many.
—Hebrews 12:15

To forgive is to set a prisoner free and discover that the prisoner was you.[47]
—Lewis Smedes

Life is short even in its longest days.
—John Cougar Mellencamp

To my friend who is bitter,

A conversation with my brother changed everything, but before I get there, I want to tell you about my dad.

Over the years, Mom taught me the value of integrity and hard work. Mom and Dad taught me the importance of character and the value of showing up for your kids at their life events. Dad taught me to play baseball, to love my country, to appreciate the outdoors, to tell the truth even when it hurts, and to make sacrifices for my family. I grew up loving my mom and dad.

But, in my teenage years, a wedge of misunderstanding split my father and me from each other. For one, I knew everything. I was a teenager, and Dad could no longer teach me anything. When I was fifteen, I became a Christian. Dad grew up as a Methodist pastor's kid. He didn't have the best experience with other denominations, or for that matter, the way his Dad was treated by his own denomination back then. Today, I get that, but back then, I did not.

Dad didn't discourage my going to church, but he wasn't all that encouraging either. When I began to feel the call to be a pastor, Dad knew how hard that would be. I didn't, and it led to several arguments where I misunderstood his heart. I thought we were arguing about Christianity, my choice to be a pastor, my choice of where to go to college, etc. We were really arguing about the different ways he saw life and his desire to protect me. Back then, I didn't know that.

Fast-forward a few years. I got married, finished college, moved to Colorado, and completed my master's degree. I talked to Dad in those years, but there was a definite strain on our relationship.

At some basic level, I felt rejected—not loved, not supported, and not encouraged regarding my faith, my marriage, my ministry, and my future.

Have you ever gone through that with a parent, sibling, or friend? You were so sure they didn't have your back.

Over time, I began to recognize that I was angry at Dad. Some of it was his fault. And some of it was my fault. But I was bitter.

My brother and I were talking one day, and I shared with him how I felt. He said, "Oh, things aren't as bad as you think. Dad still loves you." But I protested. I explained the problems and told him that I didn't feel loved or supported. And he could tell I was angry at Dad.

My brother said, "Don't block Dad out. Don't assume the worst. *How would you feel if something happened to Dad tomorrow?*" Those words were a turning point for me. I realized I couldn't take Dad for granted. Dad and I began to talk more. Eventually, he visited the church I started and realized I wasn't my father's "kind of negative Christian." And we began to rebuild our relationship. I realized that I had to forgive him. And I needed his forgiveness.

My wife gave birth to our first daughter. Dad was so proud of another grandbaby.

A year later, she and I were visiting Dad and my stepmom. He had a cough that wouldn't go away, and told us that the doctors found a spot on his lungs in an X-ray. They were going to run some more tests. Turned out, it was lung cancer.

We had just begun to rebuild our relationship. I thought, *Why now?* Then I realized, Dad and I had a chance to make it right. I made several trips to see Dad in the coming months. He battled the cancer bravely. Chemotherapy. Radiation. Experimental treatments. Doctors threw everything they had at the cancer.

In the last months of his life, I tried as often as we talked to say, "I love you." And he said it back. Growing up in a family that didn't express love verbally often, this meant the world to me. In fact, Dad expressed love to me more in those last few years than he had in the previous twenty-plus years combined.

While Dad was battling cancer, we found out that my wife was pregnant with our second daughter. Dad really tried to hang on long enough to meet her. I made several trips back to Oklahoma City during that last year of his life. I made a final trip knowing that I wouldn't be able to travel again until after our daughter was born. Dad was not in good shape, but he was trying hard to hang on long enough to meet the new grandbaby. I wept a lot on that trip. Time was short, and he knew it. So did I. We said our goodbyes, and I left thinking I would not see him alive again.

My brother made a trip to see Dad and how he was doing. The answer: Not good. He called 911, then me. Dad was admitted to a hospital.

My wife was due in a few days. I couldn't travel. I talked to Dad on the phone that night.

"I love you," I said for the final time.

He was pretty out of it but managed to respond.

"I ... love ... you ... too," he said.

I told him it was OK to let go. He did. A few hours later, Dad died.

Thirty-six hours later, our daughter was born. Somehow, I believed I could see him in her eyes. Mike and the Mechanics knew what they were talking about in their song "The Living Years."

I hopped on a plane for Oklahoma City to spend time mourning with family and perform Dad's funeral. My emotions were all over the map.

Two extremes marked by love, not bitterness.

I want you to learn from what I went through.

Bitterness can damage and destroy any relationship. In fact, my bitterness toward others will destroy my relationship with myself, with others, and my relationship with God, even if I am not bitter with God himself.

Bitterness is like a guided missile that will seek out and destroy your motivation, your relationships, your energy, and your life. It can damage your relationship with God and hurt those you love the most, your family and friends. But the greatest cost of bitterness is what it does to you. Instead of putting others in prison, it puts the prison in your heart.

Bitterness turns us into the victim. This victim mentality puts control of your life in someone else's hands. Bitterness plays into the hands of the enemy and keeps us trapped in The Pity Vortex.

So, what do you do with your bitterness? How do you let go of bitterness when you've held onto it so long? When it feels as if the bitterness won't let go of you?

When the hurt runs deep, we often run through various stages with the idea of forgiveness. How long this process takes depends on the depth of the hurt and our willingness to listen to God when it comes to forgiving the unforgivable.

- The *feelings*—I don't want to forgive them. I want them to suffer the way I have.
- The *right thing to do*—I know I should forgive, but I'm not feeling it yet.
- The *decision*—I've made the decision to forgive, but I'm still feeling hurt.
- The *process*—I'm working on letting go of the pain and resentment.
- The *freedom*—I've decided to forgive, and I have let go of the pain and resentment.

I want to challenge you with something. What do you gain by hanging onto resentment? Is your life better because you've hung onto the pain? Likewise, what do you have to lose by letting go of the resentment? Much.

St Augustine is credited with saying, *"Resentment is like drinking poison and waiting for the other person to die."*[48] Holding onto a grudge only poisons our own souls. In turn, when we regularly drink from that poison, we pass it on to others as well.

The issue is not how long the bitterness has been present in your life. Time is short. The issue is how long you have left to soften hearts, offer forgiveness, and work on the relationship. My point is that you don't know how much time you, or the person you're bitter with, has left. Tomorrow is never guaranteed. Don't wait.

I find that when I'm struggling to forgive, I need more Bible work in my soul. Here's some to dwell on and in.

> And forgive us our debts, as we also have forgiven our debtors. And lead us not into temptation, but deliver us from the evil one.' For if you forgive other people when they sin against you, your heavenly Father will also forgive you. But if you do not forgive others their sins, your Father will not forgive your sins.
> —*Matthew 6:12-15*

> Get rid of all bitterness, rage and anger, brawling and slander, along with every form of malice. Be kind and compassionate to one another, forgiving each other, just as in Christ God forgave you. Follow God's example, therefore, as dearly loved children and walk in the way of love, just as Christ loved us and gave himself up for us as a fragrant offering and sacrifice to God.
> —*Ephesians 4:31-5:2*

Forgiveness is always possible when Jesus is at the table. Offer forgiveness today. Release the hurt and bitterness today. It's not worth the poison that it's inflicting on your life.

I find that it's easier to think of these as replacements instead of subtractions. Let me explain: Just letting go of bitterness and anger when they run so deep seems impossible. What you and I need is to replace these. Replace malice with kindness. Replace bitterness and anger with forgiveness. Replace brawling and malice with compassion. All of it motivated by the love of Jesus.

This was written to the church, which means that bitterness and anger happen in churches too. For our churches to be healthy and for community to achieve what God intends, we must learn to practice kindness, forgiveness, and compassion in the community of faith.

Let's be honest. Sometimes, we struggle with forgiveness because we don't know how. But more than not, we struggle with forgiveness because we just don't want to. We know how. We just don't want to forgive because our wounds and pains are real. Perhaps we're a little afraid that if we don't hold onto those hurts and pains, no one will, and those hurts and pains will be meaningless. That's not the case. Forgiveness doesn't ignore the real hurt, pain, and trauma. Forgiveness acknowledges that those pains are very real, and that's just the reason Jesus came and died. Forgiveness does not mean that all the negative emotions will disappear instantly.

There's real and present danger in my tendency to want to *receive* forgiveness but not *give* forgiveness. *I need to name what I don't want to forgive.*

Pride says you haven't earned my forgiveness. You aren't good enough for my forgiveness. I am better than you, and I deserve to hang onto my anger, and you deserve to pay the price for your sins. I can be angry and bitter all I want and neither of those will damage my life or relationships. But that's not what Jesus says.

It's human to be stuck in this place. It's very easy to feel complacent, even stagnant, when it comes to our need to forgive. But it's sinful to hurt someone because they hurt us. The hurts we need to forgive run deep. We want the pain to haunt them. It haunts us instead.

What if you've already lost the person toward whom you feel bitter? This kind of bitterness often haunts us, but it's not beneficial to hang onto. What do you do? I suggest you find a way to tell the person what you need to tell them even though they are not alive. Write them a letter. Be completely honest. Talk it over with a safe friend. Then do something to symbolize forgiveness: throw a rock in the ocean, cast leaves into the wind, anything to help you mark this moment of letting go of your bitterness.

What if the person doesn't deserve forgiveness? Who does? It's not about deserving. I forgive because Jesus forgave me, not because someone deserves it. Regrets aren't worth it.

One more thing: Make the decision. Pray. Ask Jesus to help you release the debt. Trust Jesus through the process. Remember how much He has forgiven you. Forgiveness does not mean that trust has been reestablished. Trust and forgiveness are two different things.

What do you have to lose? Stress. Anger. Bitterness. Pain. Addiction. Poison. What do you have to gain? Perspective. Freedom. Grace. Love.

You are forgiven and can be forgiving,
Pastor Brian

> *Jesus, I've held onto my bitterness for so long that it seems like a friend, not an enemy. Help me to see the damage done to my life. Remind me that I don't deserve your forgiveness, but you forgave me anyway. Work forgiveness in my soul today, and tomorrow, and every day that I need to release this bitterness that is destroying my life. Where possible, show me how reconciliation works and bring what you want to my relationships. In Jesus' name, Amen.*

21.

Community

A new command I give you: Love one another. As I have loved you, so you must love one another. By this everyone will know that you are my disciples, if you love one another.
—John 13:34—35

Greater love has no one than this: to lay down one's life for one's friends.
—John 15:13

To my friend whose stomach is sick of religion gone bad and is ready to give up on church,

You've been hurt by a church. I'm not surprised. When I ask people in our congregation how many of them have been hurt by a church, every hand goes up every time I ask. We've all been hurt by Christian people.

Someone meant well, but they betrayed your trust by sharing

something private about you with another person without your permission. Others were manipulative. They shared that message with the whole church, badmouthed you to others behind your back, and gaslit you along the way. Your boiling frustration is completely understandable.

The trauma of church hurt lingers deeply in our soul. It might even be an indicator that you need to find a different place to worship. But being hurt by a church is no excuse for giving up on the Church.

Jesus was hurt by very religious people. In fact, He was killed by them. Religion can easily be twisted for poor motives. But so can everything else in life. I've had some bad experiences with doctors. I still go to see doctors. I've experienced poor customer service in restaurants and have even experienced food poisoning. I still go out to eat. I've been to movies that were awful. I still go to see the next blockbuster. I've been hurt by friends. I still have friends. Having been hurt by religious people is no excuse for giving up on the community of faith.

Jesus spent a significant amount of energy confronting "religion gone bad." There are numerous stories in the Gospels that show us how Jesus was opposed to twisted religion. Jesus stood in opposition to manipulative religious leaders on many occasions. We often associate the name of Jesus with religion. But the truth is that Jesus didn't come to start a religion; He came to correct one.

Let me say it another way: Jesus didn't come to start a religion, but to start a relationship with us. Jesus came to start a relationship, by the way, that would change all our other relationships. He called 12 disciples to follow Him from radically different backgrounds, and then taught them to love one another. One of the disciples was a tax collector. Another one hated and wanted to kill tax collectors. His teaching to love one another was not theoretical; it was boot camp for a war against hatred. So, He sent the disciples into the world to launch the church and build communities who would live the way He taught them. It's easy to miss this aspect of the church.

I recently had the chance to see several cathedrals in Europe. It's easy to see the beauty of the cathedral. Cathedrals are magnificent. When you walk in, you're overwhelmed with beauty and awe. You feel small, and consequently, God feels big. This was intentional. The acoustics in these buildings are beyond anything we attempt to emulate through technology today. Since these buildings are centuries old, you feel the connection to previous generations who worshipped God in these places.

It's worth recognizing, however, that these cathedrals are not the church itself. The church is the people. Cathedrals are buildings. In fact, many of these cathedrals across Europe are more like museums than centers of community and worship. While I was there, cathedrals were full of tourists, but not necessarily worshippers.

Contrast the cathedral with the community of the neighborhood church. It's just as magnificent. Sure, no one is lining up to tour the architecture of your local neighborhood church. But people show up week in and week out to worship God and build community. There's Bible teaching by someone who knows your name and your story. There's someone who cares about your soul and checks in to see how you are with God. I'm not just talking about the pastor. There are friends who walk with you through life's ups and downs. And, together, you and the community of faith work to serve your neighbors, your neighborhood school, and the many needs of the people of your neighborhood. When you walk into the building of your neighborhood church, God might not feel big in the building, but your experience with God is big among your friends as you live out the faith together. There's real beauty in community.

Neuroscience teaches us that isolation exacerbates not only our feelings of loneliness, but also our experience of pain. Our relationships will either hurt or help when we are in pain. Bessel Van der Kolk explains:

> Our capacity to destroy one another is matched by our capacity to heal one another. Restoring relationships and community is central to restoring well-being. [49]

So, all of this raises a question for you and me: How deep is your relationship with your faith community? I often hear people who've been burned by the church say something like, "I don't need church, but I believe in Jesus." The truth is that the Jesus we put our faith in started the church because we need it. The church is His bride. Yes, we need Jesus, but we also need each other. We need the support and encouragement provided by the faith community. We need people to hold us up when we're out of strength and pray for us when we don't know which way to go. We need the accountability provided by the faith community. I find it's common in the American church for people to want the friendship of the community of faith but not the accountability that comes with it.

The "one anothers" of the New Testament seem abundantly clear: we need each other.

Love *one another*. Encourage *one another*. Honor *one another* above yourselves. Show hospitality to *one another*. Live in harmony with *one another*. Welcome *one another*. Be kind to *one another*. Forgive *one another*. Bear with *one another*. Comfort *one another*. Confess your sins to *one another*. Pray for *one another*. Build up *one another*. Teach *one another*. Serve *one another*.

These are literally quotes from the New Testament, and the list goes on. One of the primary ways we grow in faith is deeply connected to how we relate to one another. How do you practice these one anothers of the faith when you abandon the church and try to live your faith on your own?

One of the great discoveries of neuroscience concerns something called mirror neurons, which remind us how powerful relational connections can be. And that we need each other. There are numerous ways we hurt each other, but think about what is lost when we refuse to connect with those who can understand our pain because they have been through it. Neurologist Bessel Van der Kolk explains:

> One of the truly sensational discoveries of modern neuroscience took place in 1994, when in a lucky accident a group of Italian scientists identified specialized cells in the cortex that came to be known as mirror neurons ... it soon became clear that mirror neurons explained many previously unexplainable aspects of the mind, such as empathy, imitation, synchrony, and even the development of language. One writer compared mirror neurons to "neural WiFi" we pick up not only in another person's movement but in her emotional state and intentions as well. When people are in sync with each other, they tend to stand or sit in similar ways, and their voices take on the same rhythms. But our mirror neurons also make us vulnerable to others' negativity, so that we respond to their anger with fury or are dragged down by their depression ... trauma almost invariably involves not being seen, not being mirrored, and not being taken into account. Treatment needs to reactivate the capacity to safely mirror, and be mirrored, by others, but also to resist being hijacked by others' negative emotions.[50]

To heal, we need each other.

> Carry each other's burdens, and in this way you will fulfill the law of Christ. If anyone thinks they are something when they are not, they deceive

themselves. Each one should test their own actions. Then they can take pride in themselves alone, without comparing themselves to someone else, for each one should carry their own load.
—*Galatians 6:2-5*

Carry each other's burdens. The greater the pain, the harder it is to carry that burden alone. Trying to carry it alone proves not only exhausting, but impossible, and leaves a person feeling lonely. We need other people to help carry our burdens.

Of course, there's a warning that comes with this passage. We are to carry our own load. This seems confusing at first glance but is cleared up as we look at the difference between the words "burdens" and "load." The word "burdens" means "a heavy, crushing weight," and the word "load" means "a pack carried by a marching soldier." We're each to carry our own responsibilities. *Sometimes, we need others to help carry burdens that would crush us if carried alone. And, sometimes, we need the accountability of being reminded to carry our own responsibilities. Community offers both.*

Jesus gave us the church as a gift. We are literally God's gift to each other. Who in your church plays that role in your life? And who in your church do you carry burdens for? It's got to work both ways, or it doesn't work at all.

You are created to care and be cared for,
Pastor Brian

> *Dear Jesus, I confess that there are times when I want you but not your people. In truth, you're easier to relate to because your people are so human, like me. I also confess that I don't want and don't like to feel alone. So, put me in the community of faith where you want me. Help me to love others the way you love them. Help me to both give and receive from the rhythms of grace in community. In Jesus' name, Amen.*

22.

Love

*I am so tired of waiting.
Aren't you,
for the world to become good
and beautiful and kind?
Let us take a knife
and cut the world in two—
and see what worms are eating
at the rind.*[51]
—Langston Hughes

To my bi-racial friends who have experienced racism in the church,

Your kids have been called awful names at school, on the playground, and at camp. One of those names is so repugnant that I refuse to use it here, but I'm certain every reader knows the word I am talking about. In one of our appointments, you shared the looks you received in one church after another. Worse than the looks are the words spoken to you, incredulous though they may be: "You aren't welcome here because you're bi-racial." This is infuriating, and never should be.

I'm so, so sorry. I feel deep sorrow for the pain caused by brothers and sisters in Christ. I would never pretend that I completely understand what you know by experience: racism sucks, hurts, and is wrong. Deeply wrong. Obviously, this is painful, and I want you to know that somebody sees your pain. God sees your pain. Jesus sees your pain. And, as a pastor, I see your pain.

Jesus loves everyone. When the church of Jesus Christ, which should be the safest place on earth for anyone, embraces the harsh, ugly judgment of prejudice and racism, it is stomach-turning not just for us but for God. The reality is that many American churches are still as segregated as the 1950s. In America, we often think of racism as something that happens toward black people, but racism and prejudice are more than a black-and-white thing. Racism and prejudice happen toward all ethnic groups.

Our world is brutal. It's ugly when it should be beautiful, evil when it should be good, and rude when it should be kind. What's worse is not that the world is this way; it's that the church is sometimes ugly when it should be beautiful, evil when it should be good, and rude when it should be kind.

It's time for the church to admit where we have been wrong, repent, and change. *Christian love means treating every human being the way that Jesus has treated me.*

Most churches preach that the Gospel is for everyone. Believe the Good News needs to be shared with people everywhere. And celebrate and fund missionaries who take the Gospel to other ethnic groups. But most churches only *preach* that the Gospel is for everyone, whereas healthy churches actually *live and practice it* in their neighborhoods. It's toxic for a church to preach that the Gospel is for everyone but not practice it when someone from a different background walks into their community. Healthy churches put the Gospel into practice by loving and building community among people from every tribe, tongue, and nation. As Revelation 7:9 says:

> After this I looked, and there before me was a great multitude that no one could count, from every nation, tribe, people and language, standing before the throne and before the Lamb. They were wearing white robes and were holding palm branches in their hands.

I know I can't change the pain you feel. But I am here, acknowledging your pain. I stand with you, and I sit with you. And if it is OK with you, I'd like to change the direction of this letter just a bit and appeal to the rest of my friends in the Christian community to be the solution the world will never be. Racism is often seen as a political problem that needs a political solution. Politics has been trying to solve this pain for decades. Politics can change policies, but what's necessary is changed hearts.

I'm not looking for humanistic solutions to real justice problems. Jesus has provided biblical solutions. Can I be honest? We don't live His solutions in the American church. Politics tends to stoke the fires of division that create fear, and fear motivates votes. Our world thrives on division, hate, and apathy at best. *The Church has the answer in the love and grace of Jesus if we will only live it.*

Jesus is the answer we need. After all, He knows something about the pain that results from rejection and hate, and He taught us a lot about the power of loving our enemies. He didn't just teach it. He lived it. The Bible is abundantly clear that we are to love one another. The Gospel has the power to change hearts if only we will live it.

Consider Colossians 3:9-15:

> Do not lie to each other, since you have taken off your old self with its practices and have put on the new self, which is being renewed in knowledge in the image of its Creator. Here there is no Gentile or Jew, circumcised or uncircumcised, barbarian, Scythian, slave or free, but Christ is all, and is in all. Therefore, as God's chosen people, holy and dearly loved, clothe yourselves with compassion, kindness, humility, gentleness and patience. Bear with each other and forgive one another if any of you has a grievance against someone. Forgive as the Lord forgave you. And over all these virtues put on love, which binds them all together in perfect unity. Let the peace of Christ rule in your hearts, since as members of one body you were called to peace. And be thankful.

It's saying some pretty meaty stuff:

- Here there is no Gentile or Jew. The word for Gentile here can be translated Greek, meaning this is about ethnicity. Ethnic prejudice is not biblical.
- No circumcised or uncircumcised. This is about religion but has some ethnic meaning to it as well. A literal translation of the word

uncircumcised would be "foreskins." No circumcised or "foreskins." Neither ethnic prejudice nor religious prejudice is biblical.
- No Barbarians, no Scythians. Both words were sometimes used by Greek speakers in the Roman world as slants against foreigners. Racial prejudice is not biblical.
- No slave nor free. Slavery is wrong. We all agree on that. In that day and time, many of the poor had to sell themselves as slaves to make ends meet. Socio-economic prejudice is not biblical.

While we are on the subject, there's nothing biblical about sexism as well. Yes, there is a difference between male and female, but sexual prejudice is wrong. The bottom line: for people who follow Jesus and embrace Him as Savior, prejudice in any form is wrong.

Real love destroys prejudice. The Gospel breaks down man-made barriers. Christ is in everyone who has put faith in Him. This is our new identity, and this should drive everything about how we treat one another. The Gospel shatters any "us" vs. "them" thinking that exists inside ourselves. Only Jesus is supreme and only Jesus deserves supremacy. All other ethnic supremacy is based in pride, does not represent Jesus, and is sinful.

How, then, are we to treat one another inside and outside the local church across racial, ethnic, and socio-economic differences? Compassion, kindness, humility, gentleness, patience, bearing with, forgiveness, and love. That's a direct command of the Bible. The love of Jesus is powerful if we will just live it in community.

Jesus is the path not just to reconciliation with God, but also with each other. Here's what turns my stomach: the idea that we can love Jesus but not love brothers and sisters in Christ of different ethnicities. When I became a believer in Jesus and His way of life, I turned from isolation to community. He provides His church to give me encouragement, support, accountability, and purpose. In the process, He turns us, the church, into a community that is inclusive, not exclusive.

So, let's get practical for a moment. What can any church do to become the solution? Here's what we're doing to overcome the pains of racism in the church I lead:

- Do a serious study of the Bible about race, ethnicity, grace, and justice. Start with the Greek word *ethnos*. Look back to study how Abraham and his descendants were supposed to bless the nations. Dig into the book of Revelation, where we understand that heaven will be made up of people from every tribe, tongue, and nation. Read the book of Acts and study how the Gospel moved from Jewish believers to Gentile (*ethnos*) unbelievers.

- Do what love would lead you to do. Our interactions should ooze Jesus. Love. Compassion. Empathy. Care. Sacrifice.

- Embrace people as friends rather than as groups. Get to know someone different from you ethnically, different from you socio-economically, and even different from you politically. Get to know them as real people. Stop with the stereotypes and caricatures. Make real friends out of people who are different than you.

- Learn to have loving conversations, even if they might be uncomfortable. Sometimes, these are difficult conversations. Listen to one another. What's the other person's perspective? Listen to understand, not just to be understood.

- Value and celebrate our differences while staying unified in the Gospel. Does this mean we just live colorblind? Absolutely not. Love goes far beyond colorblind. Colossians 3:11 does not mean that we stop being Jew, Gentile, Barbarian, or Scythian. It means that we start loving Jew, Gentile, Barbarian, Scythian, slave, and free for who Jesus made them to be. Jesus is not colorblind. He created us all.

- Practice honest and humble self-evaluation about hurts and motives. Many of you have been legitimately hurt. Let Jesus into that pain in your life and ask Him to bring about healing. Some of you are truly uncomfortable about any of this because of experiences, trauma, or feelings buried deep inside of you. Let the love and forgiveness of Jesus transform those hidden places in your soul. And learn to share the depth of Jesus' forgiveness as we practice forgiveness with one another in the church. Likewise, some of us have real regrets about how we treated others in the past. We need to practice offering forgiveness in such cases and receiving forgiveness. Our world desperately needs to see this practice of giving and receiving forgiveness.

- Learn to practice collective lament and mourning with people we love. When a friend of mine loses someone that they love, I empathize and mourn with them. When we see racism raise its ugly, prideful head, declare it wrong, and mourn with those who mourn. Grieving, mourning, and lament are helpful and encouraged.

Let's be like the early church. It's right in front of us in our Bibles, but we just don't see it. Let's start living the way of love and grace now!

You are seen,
Pastor Brian

> *Jesus, forgive us for any roots of pride, prejudice, or racism that do not reflect your heart and your love for all people. Help me to live the Gospel, not just preach it. May we, your church, be characterized by your love and grace for everyone. Help us to embrace unity, but not uniformity. As a part of your Church, I commit to embrace our differences, and ask you to help me learn from my brothers and sisters who are different than me. May we, in your love and grace, be a witness to our community when we see hate, apathy, and division. In Jesus' name, Amen.*

MINDSET 5
Experiencing growth

The mere opportunity to escape does not necessarily make traumatized animals, or people, take the road to freedom. Like Maier and Seligman's dogs, many traumatized people simply give up. Rather than risk experimenting with new options they stay stuck in the fear they know.[52]
—Bessel Van der Kolk

Do not merely listen to the word, and so deceive yourselves. Do what it says.
—James 1:22

When we're overwhelmed with our trouble and pain, moving forward can feel like running in the wrong direction up the escalator. Lots of movement, but all the energy is moving backwards. When I'm overwhelmed with my headaches, I feel as if I'm running on a treadmill. Lots of energy and exercise, but I'm not going anywhere. If we're honest, that's not only exhausting. It's discouraging.

So, what do we do to move forward? Take one more step.

You're familiar, I am sure, with the Apollo 11 Mission. On July 20, 1969, on the moon, Neil Armstrong took "one small step for a man, and one giant leap for mankind." Certainly, that one small step for a man was the result of a billion other steps, risks, and leaps taken by many others.

It seemed impossible in 1962 when President John F. Kennedy challenged America to go to the moon. Armstrong took that impossible step because President Kennedy, as well as countless other men and women, took amazing steps to move forward.

When pain overwhelms our lives, what feels like one small step for everyone else feels like one giant leap for us. A lot of people, especially those who are not walking in our shoes, don't understand that.

When our lives are overwhelmed with pain, even taking the smallest step feels like a giant leap. And we stay stuck.

We can be certain of this. Knowing what to do is a completely different thing than doing what we know we need to do. Add chronic pain, overwhelming grief, unimaginable loss, and understandable anger to the mix, and you have a strong recipe for doing nothing. The reality is that pain is all-consuming. It takes all the energy we have and asks for more. So, when it comes to taking action that will create change for us, all the momentum works against you. You're stuck. Even worse. You're sinking. It's like pain combined with The Pity Vortex creates a gravity that paralyzes the energy in you that is needed for change.

It's just plain easier to do nothing. In many cases, it is more comfortable to do nothing, even when we know we need to change. In fact, this loss of momentum is what often keeps us trapped in our current pain and circumstances. Making the next doctor appointment, adding a soul-care strategy like reading the Bible daily, or reaching out to find out more information about a grief support group can all feel as difficult as lifting a rocket off the launchpad and into space. All the gravity is moving the wrong direction. In fact, when we're overwhelmed with pain of various types, whatever next step we need to take can feel exactly like rocket science, and therefore, feel impossible.

Once we've taken that rocket-launching next step, there's always another step waiting that feels just as heavy. All of this keeps us paralyzed and traps us in the victimization cycle of The Pity Vortex. Stagnation is hard to overcome.

So, what do we do? Ask Jesus for strength, seek out encouragement and accountability from others, and take the right next step. You've probably heard the old saying about how to eat an elephant—one bite at a time. I don't know about you, but I don't eat elephants. But I do get overwhelmed about processes and appointments and insurance approvals and the complexity of pain management.

The best encouragement I can give your soul is this: the greatest difference maker in the next stage of your life with pain is your answer to this question. *What will I do about what I know?* It's not always easy to know what to do, but once I do know what I need to do, the largest question circling my life is, will I do it? Will I put that next step into practice? *Taking these pivotal steps works like compound interest working in my favor. Ignoring these steps and living stagnant works like compound interest as well, leaving a mountain of debt I owe myself.*

Of course, this applies to more than recovery, pain management, and medical diagnoses. It's a fundamental principle of discipleship. Jesus said it this way:

> Therefore everyone who hears these words of mine and puts them into practice is like a wise man who built his house on the rock. The rain came down, the streams rose, and the winds blew and beat against that house; yet it did not fall, because it had its foundation on the rock. But everyone who hears these words of mine and does not put them into practice is like a foolish man who built his house on sand. The rain came down, the streams rose, and the winds blew and beat against that house, and it fell with a great crash.
> —Matthew 7:24-27

There are similarities between the wise and foolish builders. Both experienced the storms. Both heard the Words of the Lord. Both had the same opportunity. What was the primary difference? The wise man put the Words of the Lord into practice, and the foolish man did not.

My future doesn't hinge upon what I know, but rather, on what I do about what I know in the Gospel. And what I do about what I know in my circumstances.

Next-step opportunities abound.

Medical

- Go to the doctor's appointment.
- Schedule the test.
- Get a second opinion.

- Call the insurance company.
- Do your physical therapy.
- Take the medicine.
- Do your own research.
- Seek alternative options.
- Use the resources at your clinic: more information, support groups, social workers, and case workers.

Emotional

- Spend some time in meditation.
- Call a friend.
- Talk to a counselor.
- Reach out to a therapist for help.
- Take the medication.
- Take a nap.
- Search for a support group.
- Be present.
- If it comes to this, call the suicide hotline: 988.

Spiritual

- Pray again about your circumstances.
- Confess your weakness and embrace humility.
- Find a doable Bible reading plan.
- Read your Bible today.
- Go to church.
- Worship—find songs that speak to your soul and dwell on them.
- Meet a friend for a meal or coffee.
- Keep your small group at church.
- Meditate on the promises of God.
- Take a sabbatical.
- Get involved in serving your community through your church.

Relational

- Have a talk with your family.
- Go to another person's celebration.
- Attend a gathering for a friend.
- Share your grief.
- Call your sponsor.
- If you are extroverted, spend time alone.
- If you are introverted, spend time with others.
- Say yes when invited to spend time with someone.

Physical

- Get out of bed.
- Get dressed for the day.
- Eat healthy meals.
- Sleep 7-8 hours a night.
- Walk 20 minutes a day.
- Get on a doable exercise plan.
- Laugh. Watch *What About Bob?*, a comedy starring Bill Murray whose theme mirrors the very theme I'm addressing: baby steps.

It's important to keep taking steps forward. When the big picture is overwhelming, shrink the steps and shrink the sequence. Ask for help and accountability. Look to Jesus for direction and strength. And then take that one step forward.

To be honest? One of the greatest reasons we don't take that first step is fear. Fear about the test results. Fear about whether the treatment will work. Fear about what other people will think. Fear about whether we can really handle it. Fear about whether we might fail again. This is frankly why I need Jesus. He is bigger and better than all my fears.

Sometimes, the biggest difference maker between victim and overcomer is the space between stagnation and implementation, between inaction and action. Sometimes, the difference between real change and real momentum toward overcoming our challenges lies in whether I will take one more step. One faith filled leap for those of us in pain. One small step for the rest of humankind.

> *Dear Jesus, thank you that you're not stuck when I feel like I am. Right now, I'm asking for hope and help to move forward. I confess my discouragement and I ask that you fill me with hope so that I can take one more step. I confess my weakness, and I ask that you show me the right step forward. Bring momentum from each step I take. In Jesus' name, Amen.*

23.

Transformation

If we cannot find a way to make our wounds into sacred wounds, we invariably become cynical, negative, or bitter ... If we do not transform our pain, we will most assuredly transmit it—usually to those closest to us: our family, our neighbors, our co-workers, and, invariably, the most vulnerable, our children.[53]
—Richard Rohr

To my friend who is passing on the pain to his family,

Passing on the pain is easy. Yet it's hard to admit to yourself that this is happening. We give ourselves the benefit of the doubt. In some unintentional sense, all of us hurt those we love. Passing on the pain is natural, but it shouldn't be so easy.

I saw the devastation in your child's eyes, longing for approval and love from you. She just wants some attention and encouragement from her dad. Watching the agony in your wife's face when experiencing your disengagement moved my heart to have a conversation with you. At Christmas and on birthdays, she doesn't just want presents for her and the kids. She wants you *to be present every day.*

I need to be clear about something: Abuse is never OK. If you are not safe in your own home, please leave and reach out to someone for help. There is never religious justification for abuse.

For those of us who have experienced significant trauma, it's common to pass on the pain. For some, it is the unintentional consequence of deep wounds. For others, it is intentional. Somewhere in our subconscious, it seems like we believe that if others are hurting, then our pain is somehow lessened. Internally, we don't think of it as hurting others. We justify our behaviors as something we cannot control. We hurt those we love and console ourselves with the fact that those around us are experiencing pain too. We find strange comfort in the fact that we are not the only ones in pain.

Sometimes we pass on the pain through:

- Our mouths in the form of yelling, guilt, blaming, gaslighting, and shaming.
- Our eyes in the form of glares and disapproval.
- Our ears in the form of a refusal to listen to the pain we're causing in others.
- Our hearts in the form of neglect.
- Our body language in the form of silence.
- Our feet in the form of walking out.
- Our relationships in the form of avoidance.

Your fallen nature and mine are reactive. We react to the hurt caused by someone else by hurting someone else. *Hurting people hurt other people.* In our selfishness, we don't want to hurt anymore. We hate the pain we are feeling, and often, we hate ourselves for it. When someone hurts us, we want to hurt back. When they're not available to hurt back, often we hurt someone else instead.

Usually, our escapes are rooted here. We don't want to live with the pain anymore. The irony is our willingness to cause others the same pain we so desperately want to numb away.

The bottom line: We're not very good at responding to hurt with grace. It's natural to hurt back. Choosing grace when we've been hurt is not. Sometimes, the person we hurt back is the person who hurt us. Sometimes, the person we hurt back is someone else. And, sometimes, the person we hurt back is the one we see in the mirror.

At some level, hurting others because of our pain is obvious. When we are hurt, we feel:

- Bitter
- Wrathful
- Resentful
- Angry
- Vengeful
- Prideful
- Self-consumed
- Wicked
- Contentious

Yet the Old Testament says:

A gentle answer turns away wrath, but a harsh word stirs up anger.
—*Proverbs 15:1*

The words of the reckless pierce like swords, but the tongue of the wise brings healing.
—*Proverbs 12:18*

Think about many of the family stories in the Bible. Hurt for hurt started in the beginning. Cain kills Abel. We don't even really understand why. Absolom kills Amnon. Abimelech killed all his brothers—69 of them. Solomon killed Adonijah. It's family we often hurt the most. Remember the older brother in the parable of the prodigal son? The older brother who refused to acknowledge his younger brother, much less celebrate his return? How often has that story played out in your family? We're often so self-consumed that we willfully hurt those we are supposed to love the most.

Of course, there are also stories in our Bible of people who did not retaliate when they were hurt by someone else. There's Jesus. I can hear you now: "Uh, I'm not Jesus." Neither am I. There's Joseph after his brothers sold him into slavery, and he had the perfect opportunity for revenge. And there's Stephen, who, when martyred, prayed, "Lord, do not hold this sin against them."

Just because we are hurt does not mean we should hurt back. We need to change. And *change only happens when we take first steps and next steps. Staying the same might be normal, but it isn't helpful. Jesus propels us toward transformation when we do not resist Him.*

Let's simplify this. The people we tend to pass on the pain to most is our family. Not always, but much of the time. Let's fast-forward about 15 to 20 years. Picture your children and their children. The thought of our kids and grandkids is a beautiful thought. Now, picture the hurt you often refuse to deal with in your life. Picture the pain you are burying deep inside your soul. Picture the trauma that you are doing everything you can to escape. And picture your kids passing on that same pain to your future grandkids. That's not a pretty picture at all. In fact, you're probably mad at me for making you think that through. Alas, generational trauma is real.

So, we have a choice: Rely on our nature, and pass on the hurt, or allow God to transform the trauma and pain so our reflex becomes a reflection of His heart and His grace. For that to happen, we have to face the roots of our pain and the consequences of our behaviors.

How does bitterness become grace? How does hurt become forgiveness? How does revenge transform into blessing? How does anger transform into kindness?

Jesus. That's not to say that there isn't a lot of hard work we have to do to excavate and face the trauma buried deep inside of us. I must allow Jesus in to transform what I cannot transform on my own. I'm not overstating this. It requires a miracle for you and me to respond to hurt with forgiveness, kindness, grace, and blessing. But this is what the Bible asks of us. And it is impossible on our own. But, with God, all things are possible.

If we are not intentional about finding healing for the pain in our souls, we will, intentionally or unintentionally, pass on the pain to our kids, who will pass on the pain to their kids. Even when we know it isn't right, we do it thinking it will console our own pain. When spoken to you, hurtful words stick to the soul like tree sap on your fingers. You cannot unhear what you've heard when it's traumatic. It's true for you. It's true for your kids.

When the trauma runs deep, it's not something we can face, process, and transform on our own. What you can do is seek the help needed to allow grace to transform the pain, trauma, and sin in your soul. The help you need might come through a counselor, pastor, social worker, doctor, or psychiatrist. The help you need might come from a friend or family member. Probably, it will come from all the above. In the end, our wounds need the touch and transformation of God.

But it's time to decide: Will you get the help you need because your kids and grandkids do not deserve the pain that you're asking them to bear?

It's time to make the call for help. Now. Will you?

You can do this,
Pastor Brian

> *Dear Jesus, I've tried to change this. I've tried to run away from this. And I've tried to numb this away. I guess I am having trouble admitting to myself, much less you, that I am causing pain just like I received pain. I ask that you give me the strength to face my pain and the pain I am passing on to those I love. You have my attention. Please use this moment to begin a transformation deep inside my soul. Fill me with forgiveness and grace. Give me the courage to make a phone call for help. In Jesus' name, Amen.*

24.

Acceptance

The days are long, but the years are short.
—A Parenting Proverb

To my friend whose teen is leaving for college,

I'm sitting here in my hotel room waiting to drop off my youngest daughter for college tomorrow. I'm reminded that we've gone through this before. Three years ago, when we dropped our oldest off and said our goodbyes, I wept uncontrollably. Seriously, it was incessant crying, and probably a bit embarrassing to my daughter. I think my youngest is wondering if I will do the same tomorrow. I'm sure I will.

You've shed these same tears. You know exactly what I am talking about.

My mind has been filled all day with images of her over the years. Big smiles. Deep laughs. Huge surprises. And lots of tears. It's been a great 18 years. And here we are. A carload full of necessities and a dad's heart full of memories. And this verse from my Bible:

> Start children off on the way they should go, and even when they are old they will not turn from it.
> —*Proverbs 22:6*

Here's the truth you and I need to remember: This is not the end. Sure, it's the end of an era. We're now empty nesters. I had no idea that it would be this hard. But it is not the end. In many ways, it is among many beginnings. First steps. First A's. First loves. And now, first time to live away from home. This is a moment where all my heart can see is what I am losing: her presence. She's thinking about everything she is gaining. New opportunities, new friends, and new ideas. This feeling is grief. Not that she died, but there is great loss.

All I know to say to you as parents, and for that matter, to my wife and me right now is: You will get through this. Your young adult will do great things. Life will be hard for her sometimes, and that's okay. That's how she will learn and grow. Jesus has her. Although it's hard to grasp sometimes, He loves your child more than you do. Your kids still love you, even if they feel awkward about showing it.

One more thing. It's OK that it hurts. I know it doesn't feel OK. But it's actually good. If sending your child away to college didn't hurt some, that would mean something wasn't right. As we've talked about, grief is a sign of the presence of love and, in some ways, a badge of honor.

The bottom line: Life is full of change whether you are ready for it or not. And this is the change you have raised them for. So, set them free. Cry your tears. Say your prayers. Release your fears. And trust them and Jesus. Mom and Dad, this is a good reminder to practice your faith.

This stage of parenting seems to most remind me of the stage where she took her first steps. It was so exciting, but it meant that so much more change was ahead. Steps mean walking and helping and serving.

It also reminds me of teaching her to ride her bike. The joy of watching and cheering as she peddled away. Of course, for her to pedal away, I had to let go. As much as I don't want to admit it to myself right now, it's what we raised her for. It's what we're supposed to do. Let them go.

Somewhere along the way, I forgot that I was supposed to be prepared to let go. Or maybe I didn't forget; I just didn't realize that letting go would be so hard on my heart. Or that it would come so quickly—as

Jordan Davis says in his song, "Next Thing You Know." Mom and Dad, you raised a good kid. It's OK that it's hard. Let go anyway. Stand back and cheer in amazement at what this human being you love so much can do!

This life change is largely about navigating two significant issues in your life—grief and identity.

It's grief. No other way to say it. Not in the sense of death but in the sense of change and loss. It's also gratitude and pride and hopes packed together with bags of college stuff waiting in some room in the house, along with pain and loss and just plain missing them. All the while thinking to yourself, I thought I had more time. Eighteen years in a blink. This went too fast.

You are great parents. That hasn't changed. But the kids are changing because they aren't kids anymore. And that's just plain hard.

It's even grief over losing your say. When my kids were little, I got used to having a say in what they did. By the time they were teenagers, I still lived in the illusion of control, thinking I had some say over their deepest thoughts when, in reality, they always were independent human beings with an independent will. Now, I am realizing that part of my grief orients around the season when I thought had more input over their decisions.

The most important step at this point in your journey is to grieve. Life is changing. Your kids are changing. You are changing. Change always comes with grief. Expect to feel sad some days. That's OK. Expect to look back with some regrets and some gratitude. Those are to be expected as well. But use this time to remember that as much as you love your kids, Jesus loves them, too. And the decisions they make from here are truly theirs to make.

It's no secret that we take pride in our kids. So much so that before we realize it, our identity is wrapped up in being so-and-so's mom or so-and-so's dad. This identity shift is very subtle and takes place while our kids are still little. When they go to school. When they enroll in dance, or baseball, or football. But by the time they reach their teen years and begin to pull away, we are so fully attached to this Mom or Dad identity that we don't want to let go of it, just like we struggle to let go of our kids. The reality is that you will always be a mom or a dad, but that role is not the essence of your identity.

This is a good moment to identify my illusions, "I'm a good dad because … or I'm a bad dad because …". It works both ways, by the way.

We beat ourselves up for the countless times we wish we had done things differently. If you really want to work through some pain in your life, think deeply about this particular regret: How often have you tried to push your kid to be who you wished you were growing up? And how often have you been really upset with your teenager because you saw something in them that you don't like about yourself, and you wanted to make them do it differently? In this sense, parenting can create a lot of illusions that trap our thinking.

It's not only grief you're struggling with as your children leave; you are likely struggling with your identity in Christ. Who has He made you to be as His child? Yes, you are a mom or a dad. That will never change. Your kids will always be welcome in your home. But you are so much more than a mom or a dad. You are a child of the King, who has been given incredible gifts to serve the King and this world. You are a masterpiece (Eph. 2:10). And, so are your kids. So, spend more of your energy trying to model Christ-rooted identity to them and entrust them to the One who loves them more than you do!

And while I'm at it, this particular life change is an opportunity to rediscover your spouse, your hobbies, your friendships, and a million other opportunities you set aside because it was important to prioritize your kids. It's good you did that. It's also good to rediscover who you are.

One more thing: This is a great opportunity to evaluate the opportunities in front of you to serve Jesus in the church and in your community. Your schedule has changed. What are your gifts, and how can you use them differently in this season to point people to hope?

Here's the bottom line: You love your kids, and although they're going to be a little weird about hugs and kisses when you move them into the dorm tomorrow, remember deeply that they still love you. Tonight, cry your eyes out. It's OK if it's a deep cry. Tomorrow, tell them you love them, and you are proud of them. Cry some more as you drive away. And trust them. You've started them in the way they should go. Let them go so they can find that way. They're excited for the future. You can be, too.

Grief feels impossible some days. Letting go is not necessarily the goal. Acceptance is. Letting go for today is cathartic for the soul.

You will get through this,
Pastor Brian

> *Dear Jesus, I know I'm not the only one going through this right now. I pray for my family and my friends who love our kids so much, yet we are experiencing intense emotion and grief as we let go. Comfort us. Somehow, this season was faster and shorter than we expected. Remind us that you love our kids, too. Remind us that you will be there with our kids and for our kids. Among the memories of great times and the guilt of feeling like we didn't do enough, help us to grieve this season, let go of our say, trust our kids, and continue to love them well. And as always, Jesus, help us to trust you with them. In Jesus' name, Amen.*

25.

Momentum and growth

Others, like seed sown on good soil, hear the word, accept it, and produce a crop—some thirty, some sixty, some a hundred times what was sown.
—Mark 4:20

To my friend who feels like a deer in the headlights,

You feel paralyzed by your pain. You can't decide what to do next because none of the options are the option you want—to get out of pain. You've mentioned that the longer you go, the more you struggle to hear God's voice. You're not sure that God is speaking, and if He is, you're not sure that your hearing is all that good. Not to mention, it really can be challenging to know what God wants you to do next. It's exhausting to feel stuck in your pain. I'm there with you much of the time.

Jesus told a parable that I think is particularly helpful to expose the spiritual reasons we feel like we can't move. It shows us the most important step we can take to get unstuck and create traction. It's found in Luke 8.

Jesus said that a farmer went to sow his seed, and some fell along the path, some fell on rocky ground, and some fell among the thorns while other seeds fell on good soil. The seed on good soil yielded a crop that was one hundred times more than was sown. The disciples didn't understand and asked for an explanation that Jesus made plainly clear.

> This is the meaning of the parable: The seed is the word of God. Those along the path are the ones who hear, and then the devil comes and takes away the word from their hearts, so that they may not believe and be saved. Those on the rocky ground are the ones who receive the word with joy when they hear it, but they have no root. They believe for a while, but in the time of testing they fall away. The seed that fell among thorns stands for those who hear, but as they go on their way they are choked by life's worries, riches and pleasures, and they do not mature. But the seed on good soil stands for those with a noble and good heart, who hear the word, retain it, and by persevering produce a crop.
> —*Luke 8:11-15*

The condition of the soil is reflective of the culture and condition of our hearts. When the condition of my heart is right, growth can happen, but when the culture of my heart is wrong, I block the work of God in my life.

How do I block the work of God in my life? Jesus reveals five conditions that block the work of the Gospel in our hearts:

- When I believe the lies of the enemy.
- When I harden my heart to what Jesus wants to do.
- When I keep my commitment shallow and am unwilling to endure the difficult parts of life and faith. This one is hard to hear.
- When I live distracted by the noise of busyness, worry, pleasure, etc.
- When I'm focused only on myself and unwilling to share the Gospel with others.

On the other hand, my growth accelerates as I long for the voice of Jesus to take root in my heart, and I obey. Be certain of this: *you are shaped by the voices you pay attention to and listen to most. Whether those voices are rooted in the media, in work, in friendships, or in our escapes, the voices I tune into most will shape not only my heart, but the next seasons of growth or decline.*

So, what helps the voice of Jesus take root? What kind of culture do I need in my heart for the voice of Jesus to take deep root in my life? This parable makes it clear.

I need urgency to hear from God. An urgency to listen to God's Word. This is how God speaks. God will never speak anything that contradicts His Word. An urgency to implement the Word once I have listened. I need to put hands, feet, and voice to the Word of God and work of God in my life. An urgency to persevere in faithfulness to the Word when life gets difficult. An urgency to share the Word and work of God with others around me.

Spiritually speaking, my greatest chance of growth and momentum happens when I am open, receptive, and working to obey God's Word. From that principle, I think it works the same way physically, emotionally, mentally, and relationally. A posture of openness, receptivity, and taking the right next step will only help the entirety of my life.

What does this say about the moments when I feel like I don't know what to do because I can't hear Jesus? Perhaps I am closed off, distracted, or pursuing other priorities. Or, when I'm tired and not sure how to find my next step? It might mean that I am not hungry to know and do the next right thing. Somehow, it's very easy when wrestling with pain to get so obsessed with what I want that I am not listening to anything else.

Growth happens when I long to know what God wants and persevere through difficulty to take steps of change for the better. When I have no energy left to take the next step, remember: *One percent beats zero percent. You can't change everything at once, but you can take one step forward. And then another. Traction happens when I long to hear the voice of Jesus and stack one right decision on top of another.*

You have the Voice of Jesus,
Pastor Brian

> *Jesus, I confess that I feel stuck spiritually, physically, emotionally. I'm so tired of treading water. And I need your voice to speak loudly in my life to show me where to go from here. Thank you that you came to us. Help me to embrace you, your Word, and your work with urgency. Give me strength, show me my next step, and give me the willpower and faith to take that step. And then another. And another. In Jesus' name, Amen.*

26.

Grace

A gentle answer turns away wrath, but a harsh word stirs up anger.
—Proverbs 15:1

The LORD detests the thoughts of the wicked, but gracious words are pure in his sight.
—Proverbs 15:26

Gracious words are a honeycomb, sweet to the soul and healing to the bones.
—Proverbs 16:24

To my friend who's living in "enemy mode," [53a]

You've lived in enemy mode so long you can't see it anymore. Many of us do. In America, we find our identity in our tribes, seek community only in our tribes, and feel better about ourselves when our tribe "wins."

Too often, this is our escape from pain. This tribalism creates an "us-vs-them" mentality that creates heroes and villains. Guess which category we identify with?

So, we think like this: Every person who votes differently than us is the enemy. Every Christian who interprets the Bible differently is the enemy. The people who don't look like us or think like us are the enemy. Family? Neighbors? Co-workers? If you don't like them, they are the enemy. It shows up in almost every aspect of American life: sports, politics, media, and work.

It's a curious thing about us Jesus followers: we're not really wild about Jesus' teaching about enemies:

> You have heard that it was said, 'Love your neighbor and hate your enemy.' But I tell you, love your enemies and pray for those who persecute you ...
> — *Matthew 5:43-44*

I understand how you might have gotten here. You've been hurt deeply by others, who, by the way, also live in enemy mode because they have treated you like the enemy. It's hard to know who started what—and where.

Relational scars are painful. We all have them. I know your scars run deep. As you've said, "What am I supposed to do about them?" Consider this: there are no relationships without scars.

Some wounds are so painful that they create trauma. Some of us are driven by them, can't trust others because of them, and struggle to move forward with them. We get stuck in our scars because of trauma and resentment. All of this reinforces enemy mode.

Some operate their life on the principle of payback. You hurt me. I will hurt you. If this is you, it's time to seek someone who will help you process this pain. Others seem to be able to show their scars to others, learn from them, and not be driven by them. They have released resentment and overcome hurt with good. They operate their life on the principle of grace.

We hear the word grace, and we immediately substitute it with the word forgiveness, but that's not quite right. Grace is much broader and bigger than forgiveness. Grace is Jesus giving me all of His blessings when I deserve none of them. Forgiveness is just one part of grace. If you think deeply about it, grace is what makes Christianity unique. God has given us everything good, including His Son, when I deserve nothing good.

There's no way forward in relationships without some scars. I heard a long time ago from Les and Leslie Parrot that conflict is the price we pay for a deeper level of intimacy.[54] Conflict is inevitable. Resentment doesn't have to be.

The reality is that I'm more like Jesus when I am less reactive and more gracious. I love this one from the Book of Romans.

> Do not be overcome by evil, but overcome evil with good
> —*Romans 12:21*

It's easy to look at our world and conclude that evil is not only present but often seems to triumph. It's disheartening at times. As silly as this sounds, when evil wins in our world, we long for heroes like those in the movies and cartoons to come and win the day. It would be great for "The Avengers" to hold evil at bay.

If the gang from "Star Wars" or even "Scooby Doo" could unmask evil and send it back where it came from, we would be more than thankful.

What if good triumphs over evil, not one cosmic battle at a time, and not one Avenger at a time, but one small daily choice for grace at a time by some everyday, ordinary person? The overwhelming good of collective grace would be amazing if only we practiced it.

Our problem is not that we don't like grace. We do. Especially when we're the ones receiving it. Our problem is that we do not practice grace enough ourselves.

Notice the word "practice." It must be repeated for us to begin to learn its rhythms. The practice of grace has a way of setting us free—eventually. But we must choose it and practice it in our hearts daily.

Christians, like many others, tend to practice payback and enemy mode as a way of life. Yes, we know it's not what our big Book says, but we're not very good at practicing the grace we claim to embrace. It's easy to return hurt for hurt, evil for evil. We see it play out around us every day.

In religious circles, when we are not practicing payback, we isolate ourselves in holy huddles, pretending that we are not like the world. We think we're better than those who practice evil for evil. We pretend that we are not capable of hurting one another, and when people in our huddle prove that they are quite capable, we kick them out. In the end, religiously speaking, we're left with a "circle of one" who thinks he is better than everyone else he's kicked out.

This is not the way.

Our problem is not that we don't find grace amazing. It's that we don't like to practice it when we're on the receiving end of the hurt and pain.

We've talked already about the adage "hurting people hurt people." It's human nature. It's also the result of sin and pride. You hurt me. I think I deserve to hurt you back.

What we may not realize, as people who follow Jesus, is that his grace is not meant to be theoretical. It's meant to be practiced. Not just by Jesus but by people who follow Him.

His grace is a new way of life. Yet, one of the last battlegrounds of maturity tends to be how I respond when I've been hurt. My relationships need the leaven of grace, especially my relationships with my enemies.

My internal autopilot is set on payback, but grace must change a lot in my soul to become my intentional response.

Romans 12:14-21 says grace looks like this: blessing, empathy, humility, forgiveness, and reactive kindness.

Above all, grace looks like Jesus. The verses say we should:

- **Bless those who persecute you; bless and do not curse.** Grace looks like blessing when what's natural is cursing. To curse is to wish evil on someone. To bless is to wish well for them. Blessing, especially when it isn't deserved and when, in fact, the exact opposite is deserved, is the very definition of grace.

- **Rejoice with those who rejoice; mourn with those who mourn.** Grace looks like empathy when what's natural is rejection. We must learn to enter into other people's worlds and other people's pain. Engage them in their real life. Rejoice with them when they do. Mourn with them when they do. It's impossible to do this if we abandon them, yell at them, and retaliate. We must meet them at the need of their heart! It's natural to rejoice when I rejoice. To escape when I need to mourn. To practice empathy with others, based on their needs, requires love that goes beyond myself. It points me right back to my need for Jesus, for my need for the love and grace of Jesus to be active in my heart.

- **Live in harmony with one another.** Do not be proud, but be willing to associate with people of low position. Do not be conceited.

Grace looks like humility when what's natural is pride.

"Live in harmony with" equals "be of the same mind toward." Thinking the same thing toward one another. It doesn't mean to think their thoughts. I am to be transformed by the renewing of my mind, thinking God's thoughts. I am not to think differently about one person than I do about another, based on race, gender, social class, place of birth—anything.

All the ways we categorize and stereotype, I am to acknowledge those and see them the way that Jesus does. This goes right to the core of our sinfulness. Conflict is almost always rooted in "I am better than you" and "you hurt me, so you deserve what I do to you."

Jesus says how you think of people and how you see people needs to change. How you treat people should not be defined by how they treat you. How you treat people should not be defined by where they were born. Jesus changes how I see people. He will not let me hate them. I bring pride. Jesus brings humility. It's natural for me to puff up and treat you based on what I think you deserve rather than how Jesus sees you. I must treat you as Jesus treats you, as a child created by God who is loved by God.

> Do not repay anyone evil for evil. Be careful to do what is right in the eyes of everyone. If it is possible, as far as it depends on you, live at peace with everyone.
> —*1 Peter 3:9*

Grace looks like making peace when what's natural is payback.

This is, quite literally, God making me like Jesus. God transforming me. These are next steps that must be intentionally embraced in the soul. Again, one of the last battlegrounds of maturity is how I respond when I have been hurt and attacked. Hurt for hurt is the normal human response. Instead of revenge, we must learn to respond to evil and hurt with good and grace.

In Romans 12, "be careful" equals "take thought beforehand." In other words, decide in advance to do what is right. I will do the right thing no matter what. It doesn't depend on whether they do the right thing. "In the eyes" means in the viewing or sight of everybody. I am releasing the hurt to the Lord, trusting that the Lord can bring justice as well as handle the consequences. I'm not just relying on myself to release the hurt. I am depending on the Lord himself.

> Do not take revenge, my dear friends, but leave room for God's wrath, for it is written: "It is mine to avenge; I will repay," says the Lord. On the contrary: "If your enemy is hungry, feed him; if he is thirsty, give him something to drink. In doing this, you will heap burning coals on his head."
> —*Romans 12:19*

Grace looks like reactive kindness when what's natural is retaliation.

This requires a lifetime of retraining your brain, heart, tongue, and soul. Retraining your reflexes to respond with kindness and goodness when you are treated with evil. Jesus taught us to turn the other cheek and go the extra mile. This is saying the same thing. This change forces me to depend upon my walk with Jesus. Overcoming evil with grace makes me like Jesus because it brings me to the end of me and points me to Jesus, asking Him to transform my heart.

When you've been wronged, you're going to feel the energy to do something. What you naturally feel the energy to do is retaliation. Take that energy back to your relationship with Jesus. Recognize that His good overcomes your evil. And practice overcoming evil with good toward others. When you cannot, and that will be often, return to your walk with Jesus and see in this moment, another chance to be shaped like Jesus.

My hurts and my pains are the exact laboratory Jesus uses to cause me to depend on Him, to learn his way of sacrifice, and to lay down my life for others. It's how I learn to be a living sacrifice (Romans 12:1-2). Grace overcomes. Grace wins. Grace breaks the cycle of hurt for hurt, evil for evil, the cycle of sin, pride and payback. Does this make sense?

Retaliation doesn't work, by the way. Retaliation guts my growth, and retaliation guts Jesus' credibility. Retaliation says, "I'm going to give you exactly what you deserve. Karma says, "You're going to get exactly what you deserve." Grace is entirely new and entirely different.

> Do not be overcome by evil, but overcome evil with good.
> —*Romans 12:21*

Grace is the story I need to repeat in my thoughts. I need to fully *experience* grace in order to fully *share* grace with others.

My dilemma is that I often go about trying to give away grace that I have not fully accepted or received myself. Sure, many Christians have accepted grace in *theory*, but don't embrace it in *practice*. I cannot give away what I am not currently experiencing. I can't give away what I do not have. I am a Christian saved by grace, but if the grace of Jesus is not alive in my heart, soul, and mind, it won't be what I share with others.

The bottom line: Grace looks like Jesus. Offering grace, especially when it isn't deserved, makes me more like Jesus when I choose it as my next step. And it wins others to Jesus because that's exactly how Jesus won me.

Your next steps need grace,
Pastor Brian

> *Dear Jesus, thank you for winning me with grace. For overcoming my evil with your good in my life. Take me out of "enemy mode." Make me more like you. A living sacrifice. Beyond forgiveness, help me to go on the offense and practice a lifestyle of blessing, empathy, humility, and kindness. Use the way we do this as Christians to overcome evil with good in our community and world. In Jesus' name, Amen.*

27.

Glory

When the perishable has been clothed with the imperishable, and the mortal with immortality, then the saying that is written will come true: "Death has been swallowed up in victory." "Where, O death, is your victory? Where, O death, is your sting?" The sting of death is sin, and the power of sin is the law. But thanks be to God! He gives us the victory through our Lord Jesus Christ.
—1 Corinthians 15:54-56

To my friend who is watching your wife wilt before your eyes,

You've told me many times that it's so hard to watch your spouse struggle with her disease. The disease is unfair, debilitating, and overwhelming. It's hard to watch the one you've loved for so long, who was so vibrant, become the one who needed your care. In many ways, it's impossible. Your wife was always the caregiver. Now, she is the one needing care. Long ago, you said to me, "Brian, it's like watching my favorite flower wilt right in front of me."

My heart breaks for you both. You two are dear to me. Family, really. I love you both, and I ache with you and for you. Truth is, I am already grieving as well.

We've talked about caregiving. It's hard to be a caregiver. I know you would trade places if you could. We've talked about grief. You're grieving before you lose her because, in some sense, you are losing her day by day. Caregiving is hard, and there's no doubt that your grief is real.

I want you to know some things beyond a shadow of doubt:

First, Jesus sees your servant heart. All the daily steps you take to serve. All the sacrifices you've made to care for her. He sees all of it. He knows your pain. After all, He loves her, too.

I wasn't there when you said your wedding vows, but I know I am watching a living example of "in sickness and in health as long as we both shall live." Thank you for modeling faithfulness to me. Your family is watching, too. Kids and grandkids, nieces and nephews are all watching and learning what it means to love your wife well and walk her home. Your church family is watching and learning as well.

Second, it's OK to ask for help—from family, friends, your church, and professionals. Many days, caregiving for the one you love can bring you to the end of you. It's one of life's ways of reminding us that we cannot do this on our own.

Third, life is short. Precious really. Nobody knows that better than you. There is a gift in knowing that time is short and that death is coming, but there are small things you can still enjoy together despite the hurting. Take deep breaths and enjoy the parts that are not hurting while you can. It's OK, even good, to do that.

And last, the disease has a way of planting painful memories that you would rather let go. Often, when your loved one is frazzled, or experiencing delusions, it's not her talking. It's the disease. It's OK to let go of those pain-filled memories. She is not defined by this disease, and your marriage is not defined by this season. She is a child of the King of Kings. You are a child of the King as well. He loves you both. Hold on to the memories that remind you of your loved one's identity, your identity, and your true relationship.

I know you've reached the place of peace where you are as ready as someone can be for Jesus to take her home. When the disease first began, you couldn't imagine life without her. But now that the disease is causing far more suffering, you don't want to see her continue to suffer. That journey of acceptance is a part of grief. And it's OK that you've resigned yourself to that reality. Such feelings aren't born of selfishness but of wanting what's best for her, even if it means a separation from you.

Since you both are grieving, I want to remind you of what lies ahead: Not just the grief aspects, but the heavenly ones. Heaven is, in some sense, a mystery, but in many senses, a reality that we can just begin to grasp. Some things we can know now. Some things we will know later.

Imagine her next steps. I want to give you a preview of what's to come for her after she breathes her last on earth. Imagine her first breath in Heaven.

One thing is very clear about heaven. Departing to heaven is better because heaven is to be with Christ. According to the Bible, heaven is better by far. That's somehow easier to grasp when seen against the backdrop of life when life is full of pain, tears, and suffering. Paul said:

> For to me, to live is Christ and to die is gain. If I am to go on living in the body, this will mean fruitful labor for me. Yet what shall I choose? I do not know! I am torn between the two: I desire to depart and be with Christ, which is better by far.
> —*Philippians 1:21-23*

I love the beautiful pictures of heaven and the new earth painted in the final two chapters of the Bible:

> Then I saw "a new heaven and a new earth," for the first heaven and the first earth had passed away, and there was no longer any sea. I saw the Holy City, the new Jerusalem, coming down out of heaven from God, prepared as a bride beautifully dressed for her husband. And I heard a loud voice from the throne saying, "Look! God's dwelling place is now among the people, and he will dwell with them. They will be his people, and God himself will be with them and be their God. 'He will wipe every tear from their eyes. There will be no more death or mourning or crying or pain, for the old order of things has passed away." He who was seated on the throne said, "I am making everything new!" Then he said, "Write this down, for these words are trustworthy and true." He said to me: "It is done. I am the Alpha and the Omega, the Beginning and the End. To the thirsty I will give water without cost from the spring of the water of life. Those who are victorious will inherit all this, and I will be their God and they will be my children.
> —*Revelation 21:1-7*

> Then the angel showed me the river of the water of life, as clear as crystal, flowing from the throne of God and of the Lamb down the middle of the great street of the city. On each side of the river stood the tree of life, bearing twelve crops of fruit, yielding its fruit every month. And the leaves of the tree are for the healing of the nations. No longer will there be any curse. The throne of God and of the Lamb will be in the city, and his servants will serve him.
> —*Revelation 22:1-3*

What are these beautiful pictures telling us? Simple, they are telling us that heaven is better by far. They tell us of everything that won't be in heaven.

- No more curse.
- No more threat to my life nor my relationships.
- No more death. No more cemeteries. No more funerals.
- No more mourning and grief.
- No more disease, sickness, nor suffering. No more Alzheimer's, dementia, Parkinson's. No more cancer.
- No more inpatient rehab facilities. No more hospice or hospitals.
- No more tears, crying, and wailing.
- No more sin or sinners.
- No more pain. Thank you, Jesus!

Heaven is, indeed, better. By far. Sometimes, people refer to the end of life as the end of the road. Short story. On the island of Kauai, Hawaii, the road that circles the island ends on two separate parts of the island. The main road goes most of the way around the island but, because of steep cliffs, cannot complete the circuit. On one side, the road ends at Polihale Beach. On the other end, the road ends at Ke'e Beach. Both are drop-dead beautiful, and in between is the otherworldly Napali Coast. Both lead to places that are more beautiful than I could imagine. At the end of the road at Ke'e Beach, there's a trail. The road may end, but the trail does not. Beyond the road, the hike on the Kalalau trail is one of the most beautiful hikes I've ever taken. Does the road end? Yes. Does the beauty end? Not at all. The end of the road is the beginning of some of the most beautiful places you can possibly imagine.

Christians often misunderstand heaven as clouds and harps and a never-ending worship service. That's not what the Bible says.

For many, death feels so final, so certain. For the believer, let's not forget that to die is gain. In heaven, God is at home. God's home is beyond description. Jesus invites us to His home. His place. His beauty. A place where everything that is wrong here is right there.

One day, He will literally bring that to a new earth. What lies ahead for her is the beginning of the trail. The beauty of heaven and the very presence of Jesus. For everything that isn't in heaven, the most important piece is who is there. Jesus himself. What lies ahead for her, because of her faith in Jesus, is more peaceful, more beautiful, and more magnificent than we can glimpse here on this side.

And then there's the transformation she will experience. Theologians call this final metamorphosis from death to resurrected bodies glorification. It's not that we receive glory, but that our transformed state finally represents the true glory of God. In this state, we are transformed to perfection and given resurrected bodies to reflect the glory of God forever.

The end of the road here is really the beginning of an infinite joy-filled forever that is better by far. Why? As I've mentioned, infinite reasons that are worth repeating: no more suffering, no more sickness, no more death, no more grief, and no more pain. *There is far more peace, far more beauty, far more love, far more servanthood, and there's a hand-scarred man who removes all our scars from this life. His scars remain, and we are made whole. Complete. Perfect. Glory.*

I'm praying for you. I love you. I am, and will be, here for you.

> You possess hope because Hope possesses her,
> Pastor Brian

> *Dear Jesus, I lift my suffering spouse to you, as you know their ups and downs in this world. I thank you for the gift they have been to me all these years, and the gift they have been to our family and friends. Most of all, I thank you that they know you, Jesus. And I thank you that one day, you will bring them home. Thank you immensely for the comfort and hope of heaven. Strengthen me, as I take their hand, and walk them home through what days they have left on this side. In Jesus' name, Amen.*

PART III

The Deep Dive

> If you're paralyzed in your pain, and you're not sure how to move forward from here, this last section of the book is for you. If you think, "Wow, I appreciate that you wrote letters to your friends, but I need you to write something to me."
>
> Realize this: The letters in the book aren't just random letters to my friends. *They are letters to you.* It is easier to recognize where someone else is stuck and what someone else needs to do than it is to look in the mirror and be honest with yourself about your own steps toward health. We're often too busy and too preoccupied with surviving our pain to focus on how to be stronger through it. The change you need to build perseverance rather than pity is embedded in the steps forward that are outlined in these letters. I want you to better understand the power that lies in these choices, and how these choices form a model we can use to be transformed from pity to perseverance.

28.

The Pity Vortex

As we've seen already, pain tempts me in a lot of ways that are awful for my soul. Pain tempts me to believe that my life isn't good enough or that my life is incomplete. That life is only about avoiding pain. That the only thing that defines my life is my pain. That I am nothing but my failures and my limitations. That my past defines my life. That my life cannot be changed. That God must not care because, if He did, I wouldn't be in pain. This is all a lie. Pain doesn't define my life.

Look back at that list. Pain promotes pity. Pain sucks me into what I call The Pity Vortex. You see lots of vortexes in nature. Hurricanes, tornadoes, whirlpools, black holes. A vortex creates a vacuum toward the center. Pain sucks literally, creating a suction of everything in my life toward pity.

After working with hundreds of people over the years, I've discovered that most of us fall into a repeated pattern of pain response. It's easy. In fact, it's natural to want to escape our pain. My observation after working with person after person is that when we experience the most excruciating parts of life, we want nothing but escape. But the choices we make and the attitudes we embrace while attempting to numb our pain create more pain in our lives and the lives of those around us. You've probably seen that in other people in the form of addiction. You may have observed it in your own life.

Here's the cycle I often see repeated in people who feel their life is doomed by pain. While these five choices are not purely linear, I observed this pattern more than not in people who embrace their identity as a victim of their pain. I call it The Pity Vortex.

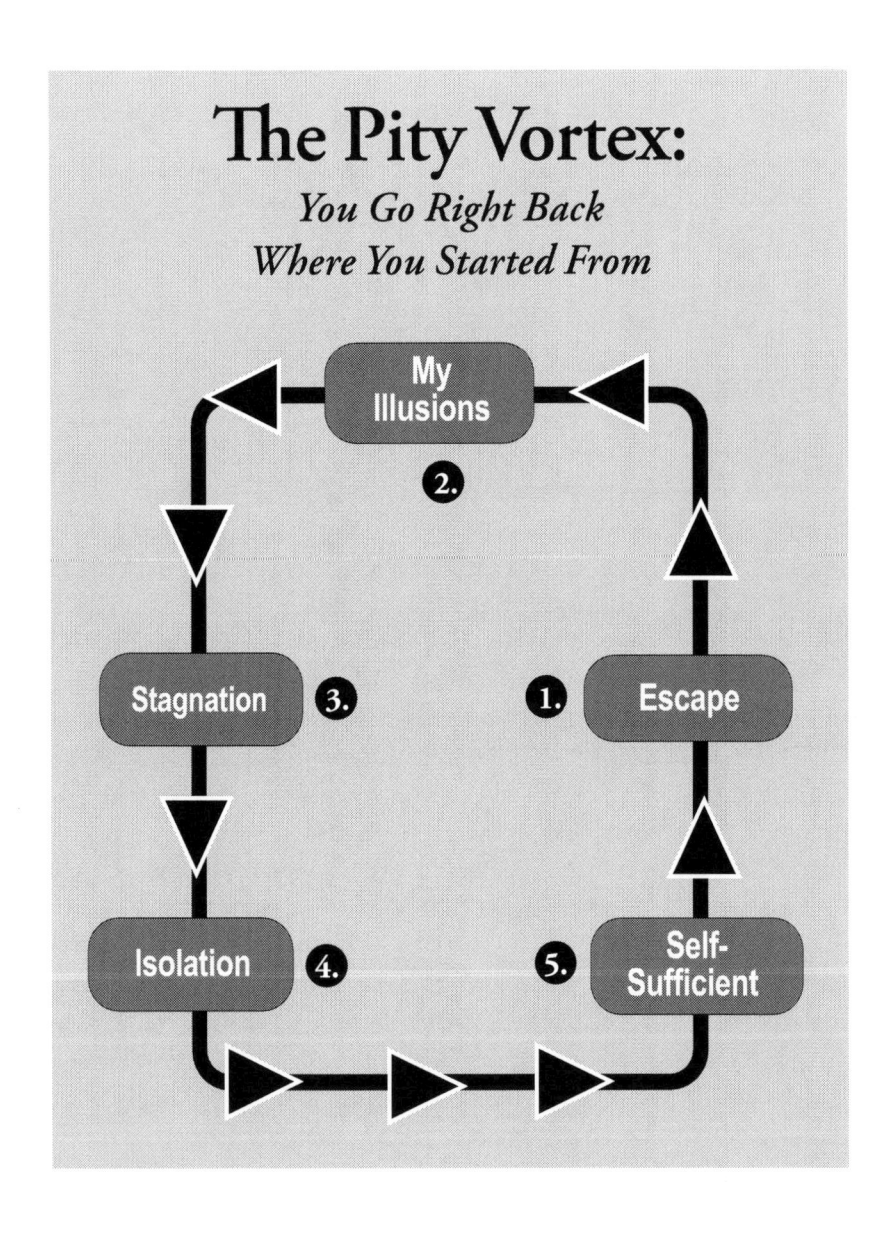

The Pity Vortex:
You Go Right Back Where You Started From

2. My Illusions
3. Stagnation
1. Escape
4. Isolation
5. Self-Sufficient

It's easy to get trapped in The Pity Vortex. In fact, it's not only common, it's natural. The pity cycle acts as a powerful vortex, a tornado swirl sucking us in and throwing us through the cycle. Add human nature and sin nature and you have a perfect formula for staying stuck in our pain. Also, Satan wants us to be stuck with a focus on ourselves because it takes our focus off Jesus.

Sometimes, we stay trapped in The Pity Vortex because the door is locked from the inside. Life often feels that way. Locked in from the inside with no access to the key. I'm not blaming you for your pain. But I am suggesting that many Christians allow themselves to be trapped by The Pity Vortex because of the choices they make.

When I'm trapped in The Pity Vortex, I'm convinced that I'm the victim and that there is nothing I can do about my pain. Nothing except to want out of it. And so, often, the most important thing in my life becomes escaping my pain.

I conclude that the Prime Directive is to escape my pain. And I seek to escape my pain through any means necessary. I run away from the source of the pain or ignore the source of the pain. I pretend it doesn't exist. I escape by numbing myself to pain in this world. Numbing usually involves overuse or abuse of something … prescription or illicit drugs, alcohol, pornography, the list goes on.

Let's drill down on the choices that relegate us to The Pity Vortex:

❶ I Decide that What's Most Important is To Escape My Pain

When life pushes us toward greater pain, we want nothing more than to push back. To escape that pain however we can. This becomes the most instinctual Prime Directive. Every child cries out, wanting Mom or Dad to make the pain go away. We're no different. Understandably, we seek healing. We go to doctors and therapists. However, when we can't make the pain go away, we begin to seek less healthy ways to numb it. Through drugs. Alcohol. Pleasure. Avoidance. Denial. Even through the creation of other kinds of pain to escape the pain we already feel; you can see that when a person inflicts emotional pain on others as an escape of their own. *But escaping and numbing never last.* Through it all, we not only stay trapped in our own pain, we create pain in those who care about us most. But we're not concerned about them because our personal Prime

Directive is to escape our own pain through any means necessary.

❷ I Decide to Find My Identity in My Illusions

Once we've decided that numbing the pain is our best way of escape, we must justify the unhealthy decisions we make. We conclude that we are defined by our pain, that our unique experience of pain and our desire to escape it justify our need to continue our quest to seek a pain-free life. So, we tell lies. Lies to our family. Lies to our friends. Lies to our boss and coworkers. Lies to God. And, perhaps most destructively, lies to ourselves. We begin to believe our illusions long before others do. Soon, our entire identity is found in the illusions that justify our need to numb our pain.

❸ I Decide, in Regard to Change, to Do Nothing

When our pain is still new, and we're still exploring healthy ways to end our pain, we find plenty of motivation to act. But the longer we fight the pain, the more our emotional and physical batteries get drained. Eventually, fatigue sets in. When it does, we might be inclined to see a doctor or counselor, but often, we do nothing, leaving us trapped in our fatigue and pain. As I am writing this, I'm wrestling with a headache. It's not a migraine today, but it's chronic. Today, I am pushing through, but my head is screaming "just stop and do nothing today." On any given day, that's OK. Sometimes, it's all you can do. But, eventually, doing anything requires more energy than you have to give.

❹ I Decide, in Regard to My Relationships, to choose Isolation

Trapped in our fatigue and pain, we find it difficult to reach out to the people we need for support. Sure, early on, there were plenty of people who said something like, "Call me if I can help." They meant it. We believed it back then. But we didn't think we needed them back then. Now, we're convinced they don't understand. Furthermore, we doubt they can really change anything for us. Instead of sharing our story so that we don't feel alone, instead of reaching out to a friend for a shoulder to cry on, instead of looking beyond ourselves and thinking about how our story can help someone else with their pain, we isolate ourselves from the world.

And we eliminate any accountability that might also come with the support and encouragement that person can give. In isolation, we often also find ourselves in depression.

5. I Decide to Find My Strength in Self-Sufficiency

Without the support and encouragement of friends, and without the help of any healthcare professionals, I find myself alone at the same time the pain is likely getting worse. I cling to my belief that I don't need God. I don't need grace. And I don't need other people. I'm just fine without them. Except I'm not. Notice the pride revealed in those statements. My reliance on me, and me alone, only increases the weight of the pain and intensity of the pain I feel. And if my primary pain to begin this whole thing was physical, it's not only physical pain anymore. Now, I feel the pain of rejection, the pain of failure, the pain of loneliness, and the pain of depression. Give it enough time, and I feel the pain of hopelessness. On the outside, I pretend to be fine—another illusion. On the inside, I'm dying.

1. I Decide, Again, that My Priority is to Escape My Pain Through Any Means Necessary

In all my pretending to be fine when I know I am not, I look for a way out. And I rinse and repeat the entire cycle. After a few trips around this vortex, the black hole of pity makes it easier and easier to justify the illusions, easier and easier to remove myself from those I need most, and easier and easier to numb the pain. This is precisely where addiction is born.

Escape. Illusion. Stagnation. Isolation. Self-reliance. Escape. The pull of The Pity Vortex often leaves us feeling trapped in a never-ending loop of desperation.

Pain often leaves us in a panic, tempting us to believe we are trapped with no hope of breaking free. One time, when my wife and I were on vacation, we stayed in a place that had a lock on the front door and a lock for the gate out front with a courtyard in between. When the time came to leave, the last thing on my mind was that gate. I was hyper-focused on making sure I didn't take the key to the house with me. You can see where this is going. We grabbed our bags, double-checked that we didn't forget anything, left the keys inside, and locked the front door. I forgot about the gate. Within seconds, we realized what we had done. We were trapped in the courtyard between the door, which was locked, and the gate, which was also locked. There was no way out without getting through that gate, and I just locked the keys out of reach. How we got out is a story for another time, but suffice it to say, we felt trapped. Pain and pity often leave us feeling trapped with no way out.

There must be a better way to live. A better way to approach pain. A better way to approach our response to pain and a better way to approach what's most important in life.

And I have great news for you: There is.

> *Jesus, please show me the way forward. This all makes sense. I can see this pattern of pity in my life. I know this is how I got into this mess. Please show me the way out. In Jesus' name, Amen.*

29.

The Perseverance Revolution

I cannot say to you, I know exactly what you are going through. But I can say I know the One who knows. And I have come to see that it's through the deepest suffering that God has taught me the deepest lessons. And if we trust Him for it, we can come through to the unshakeable assurance that He's in charge. He has a loving purpose. And He can transform something terrible into something wonderful. Suffering is never for nothing.[55]
—Elizabeth Elliot

There is a better way to suffer. To respond. To think. To live. As hard as it is to accept, pain is a part of life. "To suffer or not suffer" is not the question. Pity or perseverance is.

So, deep inside our souls, we must learn to live beyond a pain-free life. There's more to life than pleasure and pain. And there's more to life than running from one to the other. In fact, there are moments when the pain is truly helpful.

Think about it. How did you learn some of the greatest lessons of your life? Through pain or comfort? Pain can teach us empathy toward others, develop character and perseverance, and give us perspective toward what matters most. Next time you feel grief, think about how clarifying grief can be in life's most important relationships. Pain plays an important role in our lives. While that doesn't mean that we should all become masochists, it's a helpful reminder that my response to pain can make a galaxy of difference when I learn to change my mindset.

If you are alive, there is some pain in your life somewhere. If you are not currently in pain, count yourself thankful. But it won't last. The real question is not whether I will suffer or not suffer pain. *The real question is whether I will suffer alone or whether I will suffer with Jesus.*

If you've read all of this, and you don't believe in Jesus, I want to pause and say again that I am honored that you are considering my thoughts. Even more, I hope experiencing this book has given you pause and something serious to think about in your own life. In fact, I hope reading this book creates a sense of urgency because, often, we don't slow down long enough to think about life, death, suffering, and why we are all on this planet. If you feel an urgency now, lean in. Pay attention to what Jesus offers not just for your pain and suffering, but for your sins. Questions are good. I get it. Ask them. He has answers!

As difficult as it is to admit to myself, pain has a purpose. And my life is often stronger because of it. The pain of grief means the presence of love. The pain of heat on a hot pan prevents me from burning myself. Pain in my life creates compassion and empathy for others who experience a similar pain. The pain of hitting bottom creates motivation to seek help. When my muscles feel pain from my trip to the gym, or my hike along the beach, healing makes my muscles stronger. Muscles heal stronger when challenged and strained. Does it hurt? Yes. But when it heals, it heals stronger. The same is true for our hearts. The problem is that we often refuse to heal or refuse to let God heal the hurt inside of us. And so, we stay stuck in our pain. We short-circuit the healing process in the vortex of pity. Pain has a purpose. Healing the pain means healing the past—and our soul.

So, we need to pay attention to the tension. There are two paths to avoid: ignoring the pain and obsessing over the pain. Ignoring our pain is a competitive sport for some of us. Pain plays an important role in our lives but shouldn't play every role in our lives. It's also important to recognize that we sometimes focus too much on our pain, which can lead to staying stuck in it because we refuse to pay attention to anything else. Richard Ambron clarifies:

> Pain is the one sensation that is necessary for life because it alerts the brain that an injury has occurred, thereby eliciting a response to protect the wound from additional damage. It is also educational because it teaches us, usually at a young age, what to avoid. People born with defective systems for pain do not survive for long. While protective, pain can be onerous, and we live in an age where pain is viewed as an unwanted intrusion into our lives and is to be avoided. A high percentage of visits to a doctor are prompted by pain, and many hospitals now have entire clinics devoted to pain management. Fortunately, the pain from minor cuts, burns, or abrasions typically diminishes within a day and can be alleviated by over-the-counter medications. Pain becomes a problem when it is prolonged. [56]

When life is overwhelming, we're fragile. Grow a little stronger, and we're delicate. Harden a bit by experience, and we're survivors. But shouldn't we be more than survivors? When we learn to rely on God and the work that Jesus does in our lives, we become resilient, even anti-fragile. We don't just survive; we thrive. We overcome by living the abundant lives we're called to.

> For our light and momentary troubles are achieving for us an eternal glory that far outweighs them all.
> —*2 Corinthians 4:17*

So, where do we find hope? In our relationship with Jesus. How does that help? I call it The Perseverance Revolution.

Everybody must decide what to do with their pain. Remember: Pain turned inward is depression. Pain turned outward is anger. But pain turned upward toward God is hope. Might there be anger? Yes. Might there be doubt? Yes. But neither can dilute the hope rooted in Him—and hope never disappoints.

> Not only so, but we also glory in our sufferings, because we know that suffering produces perseverance; perseverance, character; and character, hope.
> —*Romans 5:3-4*

Thinking back through The Pity Vortex, I'm going to encourage you to reverse your thinking, reverse your decisions, and reverse the cycle. This revolution strengthens us from the inside out. Like The Pity Vortex, the Perseverance Revolution is a cycle, but it moves in a clockwise, not counterclockwise, direction. I want to begin in a more foundational place: your identity.

These five choices are not "Five Easy Steps to a Pain-Free Life." And I recognize that it's not always as clearcut and sequential as this makes it look. But I do see this pattern repeated among those who grow stronger in the face of suffering.

New Way:
The Perseverance Revolution

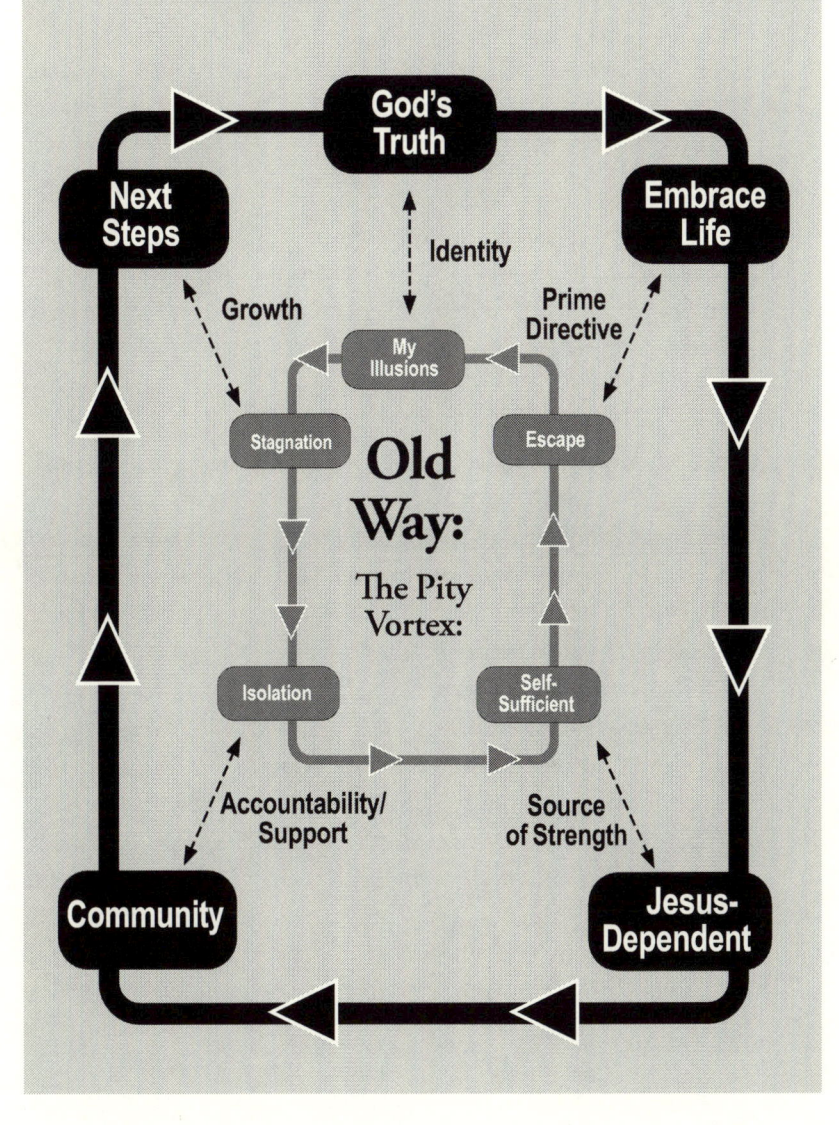

God's Truth — Identity

Next Steps — Growth

Embrace Life — Prime Directive

My Illusions

Stagnation

Escape

Old Way:
The Pity Vortex:

Isolation

Self-Sufficient

Community — Accountability/Support

Jesus-Dependent — Source of Strength

The Choice
to Find My Identity in God's Truth

When pain screams that God has abandoned me and God doesn't care about my pain, the Bible reminds me that I am a son or daughter of God. Perhaps more than any other, Henri Nouwen reminds us that we will spend our entire lives working to embrace this truth: I am the beloved of God.

> Every time you feel hurt, offended or rejected, you have to dare to say to yourself: "These feelings, strong as they may be, are not telling me the truth about myself. The truth, even though I cannot feel it right now, is that I am the chosen child of God, precious in God's eyes, called the Beloved from all eternity and held safe in an everlasting embrace."[57]

Understanding who I am and, more specifically, who I am in Christ will fight against all the lies and illusions I attempt to sell myself and others to justify my need to numb my pain. *I build my life on the best foundation when I lean into my identity as God's loved child.*

The Choice
to Embrace My Broken and Beautiful Life Even When Life is Brutal

As mentioned, it's normal to seek healing in the face of pain. I encourage that. I pray healing for myself and for you. I believe, as we will see, that one day, all pain will be healed. But while we wait in this world with pains that often linger, it matters that I embrace my life.

If you think about it, when we're living in chronic pain, we're grieving the life we used to live without pain.

With that in mind, let's take into consideratiopn the well-known five stages of grief: Denial, anger, bargaining, depression, and acceptance.

I don't believe that those five common experiences happen in exactly that sequence. But I do find in my own life that as I wrestle through them all, I'm moving in a healthier direction as I learn to accept my new reality. Life might be full of pain, even chronic pain, but that doesn't mean that I can't find gratitude, joy, contentment, or even grace in this beautiful mess we call life.

My perspective about life is healthier when I lean into the goodness God provides while I'm in pain.

The Choice
to Live Jesus-Dependent for Moment by moment Strength

If I'm going to live abundantly despite my pain, I need to find a source of strength that is stronger than I am. Earlier, I wrote about how easily we can see ourselves as having superpowers. This pride keeps me from admitting a more fundamental reality: I am not God. And I need Him.

As hard as it is to admit, Jesus does not exist simply to relieve my pain. To be clear, I need Jesus to forgive my sins, not just heal my pain. Theologically speaking, our pains are at least loosely connected to our sins. Not necessarily a one-to-one correlation, but certainly, a correlation between the pain of humanity and the sinfulness of humanity.

The bottom line is I need a strength that is out of this world. And I have a Savior who is. *I'm stronger when leaning on Jesus rather than leaning on myself.*

The Choice
to Lean into Support and Accountability with God's People

I can't embrace my beautiful mess alone. I need Jesus. And while Jesus is all I need for salvation, I need the support of other people so that I can move forward with life despite my pain. Jesus began with a circle of twelve. I need a circle of people as well. I need people who believe my pain is real. I need people who love me for the flawed, broken child of God I am. I need people to encourage and support me when I simply want to give up. I need people to lean in and check on me when I am tempted to lean out and isolate myself. I need people. Period.

Jesus set up just this kind of community when He launched the Church. I know—churches often don't live up to this kind of loving, supportive community. If that is your church experience, I grieve with you. But I know in the depth of my soul that it is possible to find a supportive, loving, truth-telling community that will embrace you for who you are while also challenging you to become who God made you to be. I pastor one that does that for me and others on an ongoing basis. *I'm more resilient in the connectedness of community.*

The Choice to Change by Taking My Next Step Forward

Implementation always beats stagnation. There is a way forward, but I must embrace the next step in front of me. You and I must keep moving. A little progress is better than no progress. Have you ever been around a stagnant body of water when it's hot? It attracts bugs, and more than not, it stinks. And then dries up. We're not that different. When the heat is turned up, we dry up. No matter what your next step toward health is, it's crucial to take the next right step. Life will sometimes scream at you, "Just stay in bed. Forget the world. Don't make any attempts to change." Stagnation breeds indecision. And indecision breeds anxiety. And anxiety breeds inaction. In that moment, I don't have to have everything figured out. I don't have to know the entire plan. But I do need to learn a habit that will help me forever. The habit is to learn to take that first baby step, and when I can, just like a child learning to walk, take another one. *I'm mentally tougher when I'm moving forward.*

Rest and Repeat

When I boldly step out in faith to trust that Jesus will be there to help me embrace the life He has planned, I find a graceful, merciful Savior who is more than willing to help me become more like Him.

I believe one of the best examples of all of this is found in 2 Corinthians 12. Paul, who was the cause of much suffering among some (he had a past) and who experienced a lot of suffering both physically and mentally, explains how he desperately asked God to remove a thorn in his flesh.

Sounds painful. Scholars debate whether this was physical pain, stomach sickness, eye problems, or perhaps some internal anguish.

Wrote Paul:

> Even if I should choose to boast, I would not be a fool, because I would be speaking the truth. But I refrain, so no one will think more of me than is warranted by what I do or say, or because of these surpassingly great

revelations. Therefore, in order to keep me from becoming conceited, I was given a thorn in my flesh, a messenger of Satan, to torment me. Three times I pleaded with the Lord to take it away from me. But he said to me, "My grace is sufficient for you, for my power is made perfect in weakness." Therefore I will boast all the more gladly about my weaknesses, so that Christ's power may rest on me. That is why, for Christ's sake, I delight in weaknesses, in insults, in hardships, in persecutions, in difficulties. For when I am weak, then I am strong.
—*2 Corinthians 12:6-10*

Notice that, like you and me, Paul pleaded with the Lord to take it away. It's natural to want our pain gone. Yesterday. But notice also that Paul accepted everything the Lord said. And embraced his life. In this one passage, we see Paul live out The Perseverance Revolution.

First, he refused to fake something. He refused to pretend he was strong so that others would think more of him than he deserved. His identity was secure in Christ. He didn't need to pretend.

Second, after asking God to remove the thorn in his flesh and accepting the answer that Jesus gave, Paul embraced his life in weakness. In fact, he leaned into his weaknesses and difficulties because they provide the backdrop against which Jesus will shine brightly to the world around him.

Third, Paul found strength in the grace of Christ which is sufficient for him. Paul was not sufficient in himself. He was not enough. The grace of Jesus was enough.

Fourth, he shared his story with the Corinthians, both receiving support and giving them encouragement through their troubles. By the way, we're still receiving strength from Christ today because Paul shared his story. If you think about it, this is quite revolutionary.

Fifth, as we read later in 2 Corinthians 12, Paul is making plans to visit the church in Corinth and continue to take action that will strengthen this unhealthy church. Paul refuses to be a victim and continues to take action to live out God's purpose for his life.

Finally, and crucially, Paul was honest with God and himself. Specifically, Paul was willing to admit that he is fragile. *It turns out the only way to an anti-fragile life is to admit my weakness and learn to depend on the only anti-fragile life there is—Jesus.*

If you wish one of my letters was written to you, remember, as I said, *these are for you, not just to some "inner Jesus circle."* Each letter addresses the way forward, the way to get unstuck and move toward healthy choices. Toward truth over illusion, toward embracing life rather than escaping pain, toward Jesus-dependence rather than self-sufficiency, toward community rather than isolation, and toward next-steps rather than stagnation.

Embedded in these letters is a sequence of steps that, when prayed through and followed, will strengthen you, provide perspective, and create perseverance in your life. On the next page is a summary of the primary point of each letter. Consider for a moment how powerful the growth and momentum in your life would be if you dedicated a day a month to each of these practices. In fact, I want to challenge you to take a 30-Day Perseverance Challenge by focusing on one of these ideas a day for the next 30 days. Meditate, pray about, and let it soak into your soul.

> *Dear Jesus, I confess that more than not, my pride makes me want to appear strong, so that others will think more of me. Please change my focus away from others to you. And help me to fall on your grace, lean on your power, rest in your presence, rely upon your Word, and trust in what you allow in my life. In Jesus' name, Amen.*

The 30-Day Perseverance Challenge

Identity

Truth Rather than Illusion
p. 40

My thinking about life and pain will change when I refocus my thoughts not just on who I am, but who I am in Christ.

Loved
p. 49

I'm often content to be anonymous, to be a nobody. Jesus is not. I am often content with my illusions. Jesus knows that I and everyone I know need to know that I am loved as His child.

Joy
p. 55

What happens to me is external. What happens in me is internal. What Jesus has done for me is eternal. Choose joy.

Humility
p. 61

Pride and insecurity open the door for everything wrong in my life. Humility opens the door for more of Jesus in my life.

Breathe
p. 67

I am not sufficient to heal myself. I need to slow down and focus on the deeper parts of my life below the surface.

Redemption
p. 73

God uses us to minister to others because of our brokenness, not just in spite of our brokenness. My life is a showcase of His grace, love, and relentless pursuit of me, even when I am at my worst.

What's Most Important

Embracing My Life Rather than Escaping My Pain
p. 78

Living well means embracing my broken, but beautiful life with Jesus, especially when life is brutal. I don't obsess with my pain but immerse myself into the love and hope of Jesus.

Peace
p. 89

Jesus offers me His peace because He offers Himself. For all the trouble that life brings my way, troubled times may have to be endured, but they don't have to be feared.

Hope
p. 97

Jesus' grief was not shallow because His love was not shallow. Like Jesus, I grieve because I love. No love. No grief. Jesus grieved with hope, and so can I.

Providence
p. 105

God did not abandon me. Jesus suffers with me. In fact, Jesus suffers for me. Jesus is not immune to our suffering because He plunged headfirst into it.

Lament
p. 113

I need to learn to feel my emotions, not suppress them. Sit with them, not run from them. Legitimize them, not minimize them. Process them, not ignore them. And understand them and learn from them, not pretend they do not exist. Suppression creates a place that enslaves my soul.

Gratitude
p. 123

My life will be filled with grumbling or gratitude. Pain makes it easy to choose grumbling. Jesus provides perspective. I need to choose gratitude.

Source of Strength

Jesus-Dependence Rather than Self-Sufficiency
p.128

Every single day is an invitation from Jesus to live like my entire life depends on my connection to Him because it does.

Weakness
p. 137

I have to hit the bottom of my own strength to admit that I need His.

Self-Honesty
p. 145

Elijah had an emotionally honest conversation with God. This is the part I usually skip. I don't want to give God honest answers because that would mean admitting the truth not only to God but to myself.

Resurrection
p. 153

God rarely gives me answers. He gives me something far better—Himself. Jesus gives me Himself in my pain and grief. He can because He is the resurrection and the life.

Waiting
p. 161

When I give up too early based on incomplete information about what Jesus is going to do in the days ahead, I short-circuit the healing process and the strengthening process. When I wait on Jesus to work with great expectation, do you know what that is called? Hope.

Confidence
p. 169

Rebuild my life by rebuilding my confidence on God's unhindered ability to work through my chaos. On Jesus' unhindered ability to finish what He started. On His Spirit's unhindered ability to work through doctor appointments and physical therapy and one step forward and two steps back.

Relationships

Community Rather than Isolation
p. 176

If I am going to get through what I am going through, I cannot do it without the encouragement, support, and accountability of community. Specifically, the community of faith.

Vulnerability
p. 183

We need each other. Need others to see the real us. Need to drop the pretending and let them see our fears, anxieties, and worries. When we are real, others around us have permission to be real as well. Together, we find collateral hope.

Reaching Out for Help
p. 189

It's healthy to be honest enough with myself to admit that I need to reach for help.

Forgiveness
p. 197

Forgiveness doesn't ignore the real hurt, pain, and trauma. It acknowledges that those pains are very real, and that's just the reason Jesus came and died. There's real and present danger in my tendency to want to receive forgiveness but not give forgiveness. I need to name what I don't want to forgive.

Community
p. 205

Sometimes, we need others to help carry burdens that would crush us if carried alone. Other times, we need the accountability of being reminded to carry our own responsibilities. Community offers both.

Love
p. 211

The church has the answer in the love and grace of Jesus if we will only live it.

Change

Next Steps Rather than Stagnation
p. 218

Taking pivotal steps works like compound interest working in my favor. Ignoring those steps and living stagnant works like compound interest as well, leaving a mountain of debt I owe myself.

Transformation
p. 225

Change only happens when I take first steps and next steps. Staying the same might be normal, but it isn't helpful. Pity pulls me toward stagnation. Jesus propels me toward transformation when I do not resist Him.

Acceptance
p. 231

Grief feels impossible some days. Letting go is not necessarily the goal. Acceptance is. Letting go for today is cathartic for the soul.

Momentum and Growth
p. 237

Traction happens when I long to hear the voice of Jesus and stack one right decision on top of another.

Grace
p. 241

Jesus' grace is my new way of life. Yet, one of the last battlegrounds of maturity tends to be how I respond when I've been hurt. My relationships need the leaven of grace, especially my relationships with my enemies.

Glory
p. 249

Heaven is far more peace, far more beauty, far more love, far more servanthood, and a hand-scarred man who removes all our scars from this life. Jesus' scars remain, and we are made whole.

The Perseverance Revolution:
Every single day is a choice between Pity and Perseverance.

30.

Addiction and the Perseverance Revolution

Step 1. *We admitted we were powerless over alcohol—that our lives had become unmanageable.*
Step 2. *Came to believe that a Power greater than ourselves could restore us to sanity.*
Step 3. *Made a decision to turn our will and our lives over to the care of God as we understood Him.*
Step 4. *Made a searching and fearless moral inventory of ourselves.*
Step 5. *Admitted to God, to ourselves, and to another human being the exact nature of our wrongs.*
Step 6. *Were entirely ready to have God remove all these defects of character.*
Step 7. *Humbly asked Him to remove our shortcomings.*
Step 8. *Made a list of all persons we had harmed, and became willing to make amends to them all.*
Step 9. *Made direct amends to such people wherever possible, except when to do so would injure them or others.*
Step 10. *Continued to take personal inventory and when we were wrong promptly admitted it.*
Step 11. *Sought through prayer and meditation to improve our conscious contact with God as we understood Him, praying only for knowledge of His will for us and the power to carry that out.*
Step 12. *Having had a spiritual awakening as the result of these Steps, we tried to carry this message to alcoholics, and to practice these principles in all our affairs.*[58]

—The 12 Steps of Alcoholics Anonymous

Addiction sucks. You might not believe that, but if you are an addict, the people around you do because they see, better than we see, what the addiction has made of us. And it ain't pretty. We're often the last to know that we are an addict. We become polished at deceiving ourselves so we can hang onto that one thing we think numbs our pain away. It might be alcohol or prescription drugs. It might be spending money we don't have on something we don't need, or it might be pornography. Sometimes, it's too much of a good thing, like food or drink or travel, that becomes toxic for our lives. And sometimes, we open the door and invite things we know are toxic to come right in.

You tend to recognize toxic behavior when you see it in other people. It has a smell to it. It's much easier to observe in other people than in ourselves. More than not, toxic behavior is self-centered and self-seeking. Destructive and harmful. Controlling and manipulative. Why am I talking about toxic behavior? Because addictive behavior, often rooted in pain, is toxic.

What's more, addiction creates more pain, and multiplies pain. There's no avoiding it. Some of us know we are addicts and know this to be true. Some of us refuse to admit we are addicts, but we know that the pain is real. Others of us joke about being addicted to coffee, soda, or desserts. At some level, we are all addicted to something: selfishness, sin, pride, etc.

There are two clear indicators of addiction in your life:

First, when you can't not do something, it manages you more than you manage it. Occasional indulgence is not an addiction. But when you can't say no to something, often with increasing frequency, you are an addict. It may be behaviors you've thought of as addiction for a long time: gambling, food, alcohol, illicit drugs, medication, pornography, spending. Also, it might be something that's relatively new to humanity—screen time, social media, gaming.

Second, when whatever you cannot say no to is hurting your life, and often the lives of those around you.

What should you do if you believe you have an addiction? Find a recovery group. It might be an Alcoholics Anonymous group, a Narcotics Anonymous group, a Celebrate Recovery group. No matter what, please find help. This book is not meant to replace your recovery group, but it can supplement your recovery journey because it is built on the same principles and same foundation in the Bible.

You will not be able to find recovery and healing alone. You might notice that there is significant overlap between the twelve steps of AA, the eight principles of Celebrate Recovery, and this book. That's because they are all rooted in the same source: the Bible. Seriously, study the development of AA and you'll find roots in various places in the Bible. The Bible changes lives because Jesus changes lives.

Proverbs 6 says there are six things that the Lord hates, seven that are detestable to Him.

> There are six things the LORD hates, seven that are detestable to him: haughty eyes, a lying tongue, hands that shed innocent blood, a heart that devises wicked schemes, feet that are quick to rush into evil, a false witness who pours out lies and a person who stirs up conflict in the community.
> —*Proverbs 6:16-19*

I think you'll find that most of these, if not all these, are descriptive of toxic, addictive behavior.

- Prideful eyes that look down on ourselves and others.
- A willingness to lie to avoid accountability.
- Behavior that is destructive, harmful, poisonous, even murderous.
- A spirit that devises a plot to manipulate and control.
- A bent or an autopilot driven by what is harmful, hurtful, and evil.
- Lies that cover up lies.
- Behavior that passes on the pain and conflict to others.

When you read the book of Proverbs, you can plainly see that some people are righteous. Some people are wicked. Some people are foolish. And some people are wise. Addictive and toxic behaviors are often foolish and/or wicked.

Furthermore, the book of Proverbs outlines for us a variety of foolish behaviors. I act like a fool when I (said in my best "I pity the fool" Mr. T voice):

- Live like there's no God or live like I am God. (Proverbs 14:1)
- Say everything that pops into my head. (Proverbs 10:8)
- Refuse advice and correction. (Proverbs 12:15)

- Think I am right all the time. (Proverbs 26:12)
- Refuse to change. (Proverbs 13:20)
- Live in love with my own opinions. (Proverbs 18:2)
- Live on the constant edge of defensiveness and conflict (Proverbs 20:3)
- Trust only in myself. (Proverbs 28:26)
- Give full vent to my anger. (Proverbs 29:11)

Do you recognize any of these in yourself? Why do I offer this list of foolish behaviors? Because 99 out of 100 times, we must hit bottom and experience the utter foolishness, pain, and consequence of our behaviors to come to the starting point of recovery: *I have a problem, and I cannot fix it.*

So, where do you begin? Where do I begin?
I love the story of Jesus and the disabled man found in John 5.

> Sometime later, Jesus went up to Jerusalem for one of the Jewish festivals. Now there is in Jerusalem near the Sheep Gate a pool, which in Aramaic is called Bethesda and which is surrounded by five covered colonnades. Here a great number of disabled people used to lie—the blind, the lame, the paralyzed. One who was there had been an invalid for thirty-eight years. When Jesus saw him lying there and learned that he had been in this condition for a long time, he asked him, "Do you want to get well?"
> —*John 5:1-6*

Jesus asked the man, "Do you want to get well?" What kind of question is that? Of course, he wants to get well. He's been unwell for 38 years. It seems like a dumb question until we learn "the rest of the story." After being healed, this man returned to the same place and went right back to his old life. Jesus knew the human tendency to say we want to be well, but not want to change. Change is hard work. It's easier to stay the same than it is to do the hard work of healing. Furthermore, this man's entire life and earnings had been defined by his condition. Jesus' question is legitimate. Many of us struggle with the mental paralysis this man struggled through. We must be ready to answer Jesus. Do you want to get well? Do you want abundant life?

It's natural to want to escape pain. But it's not healthy to let the desire to escape take over our lives. Sometimes, I'm just like this paralytic. It's my move, but I can't move. Sometimes I am paralyzed because I don't know what to do. Because of mental paralysis. Or because of emotional paralysis. Others might be stymied by religious or spiritual paralysis.

Healing and recovery all begin with an admission: I have a problem. I need to admit to myself with absolute clarity that I have a problem, and I cannot fix this. I need to be totally and brutally honest with myself. I need extreme clarity regarding my life. I must want to be well and acknowledge that I am not.

Usually, everybody around me knows I am not well before I do. The reason we say that an addict needs to hit bottom is that we are so good at deceiving ourselves into the belief that we are OK when we aren't. We tell ourselves that it's not that big of a deal when it is. This is the illusion—that I am not really hurting anyone when the truth is, I am hurting myself and others. I need to stop lying to myself and others. Stop justifying my behavior. Stop playing the victim. Stop blaming everyone but myself. I have a problem, and I cannot fix it on my own. I am powerless.

Part of this self-honesty needs to include a willingness to look at the problems and the pain behind the problems. I might not be able to say no to something that is hurting my life and the people in my life. Much of the time, the driving force behind my addiction is not alcohol or pornography or social media that I can't resist. There are deeper issues, deeper problems, and deeper pains, and when I admit to myself and others that I have a problem, I also need a willingness to peel back the layers of my problem and pain, piece by piece. Underneath my addiction is often something I'm trying to escape. We abuse alcohol or drugs to avoid some other pain. We numb ourselves so that we don't have to face the pain of the deeper issue. We use the addiction to cope with our bigger pain, not realizing that we are simply transferring the pain, often from ourselves to others.

What is the source of my pain that I want to escape? Go deeper. Why do I feel the way I do? What am I really trying to escape? Why does this bother me so much? What is the core hurt I am feeling that I do not want to feel?

Acknowledging that I am powerless to heal myself brings me to this honest admission: I need a real power source to find the strength to fuel this self-honesty. I need a power greater than myself to help me begin to say no to the wrong things and yes to the right things. The 12 Steps point us to a "Power greater than ourselves" and the need to make "a decision to turn our will and our lives over to the care of God as we understood Him." Let me be clear: If the God you turn to is not real or does not have real power, none of this will work. I need to ask Jesus for the grace to make me whole. I am not just a product of what happens to me in this world, nor am I simply a product of what happens in me. I can be the result of the healing work of the creator of the universe.

Grace is what Jesus offers. It's everything good that Jesus offers, all bundled into one word. It's His forgiveness and His mercy wrapped together with a relationship with Him, plus His power, His blessings, His work in my life, and so much more. I don't deserve it. But He doesn't operate on the basis of what we deserve. He operates on unconditional love.

From here, all of my next steps spring from looking to Jesus for the strength and power He offers that I do not have on my own. Life is a journey of taking the next right step. There are many to work through.

When I say healing, we often picture the final result. We believe we are healed when we no longer wrestle with addiction. While I have heard rare stories of instantaneous change where a person never struggles with alcohol again, I believe these instances to be few and far between.

The reality of healing and recovery for most of us is a lifelong process. Theologically speaking, we need the beginning of justification, the Spirit's work of sanctification, and the final healing of glorification to be set free for eternity from our addiction. *That's a long way of saying that I need the work of Jesus in my life for the rest of my life. Healing and recovery are a process.*

Many of the next steps I take will force me to look deeper to explain the hurts, pains, and problems behind my addiction. If you need biblical justification for these steps, start with the book of James, then read the Sermon on the Mount in Matthew 5-7. Furthermore, the 12 Steps point me to the power of community.

The path out of toxic, addictive behavior begins with knowing that—sit down, please—*I am nothing but foolish.* I do not have the wisdom of God, and I need the wisdom of God. It may sound contradictory, but admitting your weaknesses is an asset, not a liability. Wisdom is found in learning from the ultimate source of wisdom, the Bible. Wisdom is found in the heart of God. And wisdom is found in learning from the experience of those wiser than me who follow Him.

Wisdom has a name: Jesus.

> Surely I am only a brute, not a man; I do not have human understanding. I have not learned wisdom, nor have I attained to the knowledge of the Holy One. Who has gone up to heaven and come down? Whose hands have gathered up the wind? Who has wrapped up the waters in a cloak? Who has established all the ends of the earth? What is his name, and what is the name of his son? Surely you know!
> —*Proverbs 30:2-4*

Life is healthier with Jesus, less toxic, less addictive. That said, you must be "all in" with Him. A little dabbling with Jesus isn't going to work. Life is better when I move into the house of wisdom, not just stop by for a sip now and then.

Addiction is a relationship. And a lifestyle. It's just a relationship with the wrong things. Addiction is laying down my life for something that isn't God but that I am making into my god. Following Jesus is also a relationship. Following Jesus is also a lifestyle. And He is God. So, He can truly help.

Hitting bottom brings clarity to my inability to do anything. Faith brings clarity to Jesus' ability to make me new again. Jesus brings clarity and strength for my next steps.

Dear Jesus, I confess that I am hopelessly lost on my own. That I have no power to overcome not only my addiction, but my deeper sins, pains, traumas, and hurts. Forgive me for denying my foolish, sinful behavior. I admit that without you, I am the problem. Please be the wisdom of God in me. May your Spirit breathe wisdom into every aspect of my life. Make me healthy, not harmful. Make me tough, but not toxic. Help me to think as you think, Jesus. I confess that I need you to be the source and strength of not only my salvation, but my entire life change. I turn my life, my will, and my choices over to you. In Jesus' name, Amen.

31.

Where to Begin If You Don't Know Where to Start

If you don't know where to start with God, I want to tell you a story, but not before first posing a question. Where do you start with Jesus when you don't know anything about where to start? The answer lies in a few words: Admission, repentance, faith, and commitment. We'll get to that.

What's the worst thing you can lose? What gives you the most panic when it's lost? Thirty years ago, I would have said my wallet. Twenty years ago, I would have said my credit card. Today, many would probably say their phones. I would say my wife and kids.

When you lose something, you find out how far you are willing to go to find what needs to be found. When my youngest daughter was in middle school, she lost her phone. (And, yes, I do have permission to tell this story). For days, then months, we searched for this phone. She'd say, "I don't know. I can't find it." And being the great dad that I am, I blamed her for not being responsible. We had long talks about being responsible for your things. We searched and searched—and never found the phone. Tore her room apart. Looked all over the house. Nope. Anguish. Frustration. Lament.

Months later, I was standing in our living room, and it hit me like a ton of bricks. I walked into the garage, reached up on a high shelf out of sight, and pulled down the phone. I walked back in with the phone that she "lost." She didn't lose her phone. I did. One day, we were going somewhere as a family, and she gave me some attitude, and I disciplined her. I took away her phone. We left in a hurry, and I left the phone somewhere she couldn't get to it. Up high. Out of reach. In the garage.

I'm the one who needed the speech about being responsible for your things. I'm the one who lost what needed to be found. She felt joy. Me? Not so much. Why am I telling us all of this?

When we lose something, our response indicates how important and valuable that lost thing is to us. Agree? We all know the panic of losing our phone, wallet, keys, credit card, or passport. And we all know the joy of finding what was lost.

Jesus told a similar story. There were many tax collectors, who were considered traitors, and sinners who were all gathering around to hear Jesus. And the ultra-religious types began to mutter under their voices that Jesus welcomed sinners and eats with them. How dare he?

Then Jesus told them this parable.

> Suppose one of you has a hundred sheep and loses one of them. Doesn't he leave the ninety-nine in the open country and go after the lost sheep until he finds it? And when he finds it, he joyfully puts it on his shoulders and goes home. Then he calls his friends and neighbors together and says, 'Rejoice with me; I have found my lost sheep.' I tell you that in the same way there will be more rejoicing in heaven over one sinner who repents than over ninety-nine righteous persons who do not need to repent. "Or suppose a woman has ten silver coins and loses one. Doesn't she light a lamp, sweep the house and search carefully until she finds it? And when she finds it, she calls her friends and neighbors together and says, 'Rejoice with me; I have found my lost coin.' In the same way, I tell you, there is rejoicing in the presence of the angels of God over one sinner who repents."

—Luke 15:4-7

Jesus continued: "There was a man who had two sons . . . ."

You probably know the next story about the man who had two sons. One son said, "Dad, you're as good as dead to me. Give me my share of the inheritance." He left, went away to a far-off land, and squandered that inheritance. He was gone for what seemed like forever. But Dad never stopped watching the horizon for his lost son to come home. One day, the son changed his mind, and came home to become a servant in his dad's household. Dad, seeing his son far off, welcomed him home, threw a joy-filled party to celebrate, killed the fattened calf, and prepared to celebrate. Dad was always looking for his son to come home. We talk a lot about the dad. Lately, I'm wondering about the Mom.

The point: When you come to Jesus, to God in the flesh, the way that Dad feels is exactly how God feels about you. Take note that all three of these parables in Luke 15 are largely about the joy in heaven and the joy of God that breaks out when the lost are found! That's how God, Jesus, and heaven feel about you!! God's love isn't earned. It's received. You are loved and valued by Jesus, by God, before you ever took your first breath, and before you ever committed your first sin, and before you ever came to the realization that you are utterly broken. Before you ever thought, "I am hopeless," you were loved. And you are loved.

When I find something that's been lost for a long time, it seems like a miracle. Indeed, when Jesus finds me, it is.
Jesus plunged from heaven to earth to bring heaven to earth on a search and rescue mission that brings incredible joy to heaven. And the lost get found. The miracle of all miracles is that Jesus came seeking what was lost—you and me.

This doesn't have to read like a fairytale. It's real. All of it.

I don't want to make any assumptions about you. You may believe this. And you're thinking, "Right on." You may not believe this. You might even think I'm crazy. Or maybe right now, for the first time ever, you see God in a different light, and you're open to what Jesus wants to do in your life.

How does this work? How do the lost get found? How can you and I be found by Jesus? You need to know that Jesus did more than enter our painful world as a good teacher.

1. Admission—Admit you are lost and in need of finding.

It's what the tax collectors and sinners were doing. It's the opposite of what the religious types were doing. They didn't need to be found by God. In the minds of the ultra-religious, they were never lost. Sinners, on the other hand, know they are lost, know they are sinners, and know they need rescue. You and I need to admit to ourselves and to God that religion isn't the answer. Jesus is. This is not about being good enough for God. It's about admitting that I know I will never be good enough, and Jesus came searching for me anyway.

The Prodigal Son had something that we often do not: a sense of urgency that motivated him to turn back to his father. If you are feeling that urgency right now, I'd urge you to turn to Jesus today. Admit that you are a sinner in need of forgiveness. That you fall short of what God intended and that you will never be able to be what God intended on your own. Your life, like mine, is full of selfishness and pride. I'll never be able to change that about myself. I need Jesus to change what I cannot change, and I need to turn to Him.

2. Repentance—Turn away from your sins to Jesus who died for you.

The biblical word here is repentance, which means to turn around or change my mind and direction. The Gospel says that you are God's priority. How far is God willing to go to recover what was lost? Jesus was willing to go from heaven to earth so that heaven could rejoice. But He went further than that. Jesus was willing to go to death, to the cross, so that heaven could find you and me. Remember, I couldn't earn this if I tried.

This is not empty talk. There's deep meaning behind these words because they are backed up not just by talk but by sacrifice. Jesus died for you. It's personal.

3. Faith—Put your faith (your trust) in Jesus.

Believe that not only are you hopelessly lost without God, but that you are completely loved and treasured by God. The shepherd treasured the lost sheep. The woman treasured her lost coin. The father treasured his lost son. That's why they all went searching. God expresses joy over my salvation. The angels of God rejoice when I put my trust in Jesus and his sacrifice. This is the Bible's way of saying that God expresses joy at your salvation. Faith is about more than salvation, and it isn't just a "get out of hell" card. Faith is a day-to-day trust in a living Jesus who gives what I need to be treasured every day.

4. Commitment—Surrender your life to Him.

Commit your life to Him by believing that Jesus rose from the dead, is alive today, and is coming to live inside of you.

Jesus doesn't just change your eternal destination. He comes to bring heaven to your life now. He comes to live in you, comfort you, empower you, and walk with you every single day. You and I get to walk in the love of Jesus every single day. We have the Bible to help us understand what Jesus is like and how to live out this life of grace. It's important that we live every day with urgency about the love of Jesus for other outcasts just like you and me.

Losing something clarifies and magnifies its worth, value, and priority in my life. If you are filled with any sense of guilt or shame that screams into your soul that God couldn't possibly love and treasure you, read again any of the Gospel stories in the Bible. They are found in Matthew, Mark, Luke, and John.

If you and I are willing to move heaven and earth to find a lost phone, what do you think it means that Jesus would leave heaven, be born to a virgin, live a perfect life, bring hope and healing to sinners, die for our sins on the cross, and rise again to life on the third day?

It means that you are loved, treasured, and wanted by Jesus.

If you've prayed today to put your faith in Jesus, would you let me know at brian@myfriendsinpain.com.

> *Dear Jesus, thank you that the lost still get found, and that you still offer grace to outcasts like me. I admit that I am a sinner, and I turn from my sins to you. I believe you died for my sins on the cross, even though I do not deserve it. I believe you rose again and are alive today. Please love me, take over my life, change me, and make my heart like yours. In Jesus' name, Amen.*

32.

Overcoming

To My Friend Who Still Has Pain,

We've come a long way together. If this book has been helpful to you, would you please consider reviewing it online, sharing it on social media, or giving it to a friend who needs its message as much as you? Maybe your church would like to start a small group using this book as curriculum.

I promised in the beginning that I was not selling snake oil and that I would not be able to eliminate your pain. If I could, I wouldn't be human. Jesus was both divine and human. And He did something much bigger than snap his fingers to eliminate our pain.

I'm hopeful that by now, you've found some new perspectives, some changes to make in your thinking, some stories of inspiration, and some ideas for next steps. Likewise, I'm hopeful that, by now, you understand the value of making healthy choices that lead to perseverance rather than pity.

More than anything, I hope you've found hope in Jesus, who guarantees a day when there will be no more death, mourning, crying, or pain. Lean into Him. Stay focused on your dependence on Jesus. Abandon your illusions. Lay out your feelings in brutal honesty as though Jesus is present and listening—because He is. Instead of looking for the easy off-ramps for pain, seek a day by day dependence on Jesus for strength you do not have.

When He provides relief, be grateful. And when He does not, be grateful for the chance to live another day. But never lose sight of this—there are people who need you and the story of how you learned to listen to Jesus, live in His truth, and practice his way of grace. His grace truly is sufficient for you. Grace is enough. Jesus is enough when I am not enough.

Life is not fair. We all know that. Life is not only "not fair," but life for many people is just plain brutal. Consider those who lived a hundred or more years before our era. People died. Young and old. Pandemics aren't a new thing. The bubonic plague. World War II. The Holocaust. For most of history, life for humans has been agonizing. It's enough to make a pessimist, an agnostic, an absurdest out of all of us. But it doesn't have to. Just because life is not fair does not mean that God is not fair.

When you read the Bible from cover to cover, you see a few things very clearly. Humans are inhumane toward each other. We're all broken and marred by sin. God repeatedly intervenes to bring hope to the hopeless. Humans rebel against God with regularity.

Jesus plunged headfirst into our sin-filled and pain-filled world to rescue us from the effects of our sin and change our world with grace, love, hope, and peace. His death paid the price for our sins, and His resurrection empowers the change we need. Jesus left the Church (you and I) here on earth to bring heaven to earth. One day, this world as we know it will end. But His hope, grace, love, and peace will last forever. If this world is all there is, I'd be a pessimist or a nihilist or an absurdest, too. But this world is not all there is. For that matter, we're not all there is.

> Some time ago, I got to know to a guy who has lived through tremendous pain and hardship, yet he found God to be better than fair.
> *Jesus was faithful.*

When he was a baby, a doctor got him hooked on a highly addictive drug. He almost didn't survive it.
God saw him through it.

In his childhood, he almost died from a traumatic brain injury.
He grew up and finished school.

In late childhood, he suffered numerous breathing problems that landed him in the hospital.
He is still breathing today.

In his teenage years, he felt abandoned and considered suicide.
Jesus was there with him.

In his twenties, he lost several friends because of both healthy and poor decisions.
He has many friends today.

Throughout his twenties and thirties, he lost several family members and experienced deep grief.
He found great comfort, even hope, in his grief.

In his thirties, some thought he failed in his line of work.
He is not a failure.

He was laid off from his next job due to a recession.
God provided.

He moved his family halfway across the country, where they didn't know anyone, to begin a new job.
Jesus was on the move.

Throughout his career in leadership, he's made several difficult decisions that helped some, but caused others to reject him.
He is still loved.

In multiple seasons, he suffered depression.
He still has hope.

Throughout his life, he felt many regrets.
He works to choose joy and gratitude.

In his forties, his body started to fall apart.
He is still serving others today.

Jesus was faithful and will continue to be faithful.
I know because I am that guy.

There will always be moments where the pain hurts more than anyone but God understands. Maybe that's just the point. There is someone who understands. His name is Jesus. Every single day is a choice between pity and perseverance.

It's your choice.

Pain sucks, but life doesn't have to.
Pastor Brian

Endnotes

[1] Ambron, Richard. The Brain and Pain. Columbia University Press, 2022. p. 14.

[2] Nouwen, Henri J. The Return of the Prodigal Son: A Story of Homecoming. Convergent Books, 1992. p. 99.

[3] Macknik, Stephen L., et al. Sleights of Mind. Henry Holt and Co., 2010. pp. 8-9.

[4] Macknik, Stephen L., et al. Sleights of Mind. Henry Holt and Co., 2010. pp. 12-13.

[5] Macknik, Stephen L., et al. Sleights of Mind. Henry Holt and Co., 2010. p. 10.

[6] Comer, John M. The Ruthless Elimination of Hurry: Emotionally Healthy and Spiritually Alive in the Chaos of the Modern World. Waterbrook, 2019. p. 56.

[7] Nouwen, Henri J. Life of the Beloved: Spiritual Living in a Secular World. Crossroad Pub Co., 1992. pp. 44-54.

[8] Keller, Timothy. The Reason for God: Belief in an Age of Skepticism. Penguin Group, 2008. p. 181.

[9] "Dear Sigmund." M.A.S.H., created by Larry Gelbart, Richard Hooker, Season 5, Episode 7, 20th Television, 1976.

[10] Berg, MS, Sara. "Pandemic Pushes U.S. Doctor Burnout to All-time High of 63%." American Medical Association, 15 Sept. 2022, https://rb.gy/utjw72.

[11] Baldisseri, Marie R. "Impaired Healthcare Professional." National Library of Medicine, 1 Feb. 2007, pubmed.ncbi.nlm.nih.gov/17242598/. Kaliszewski, Michael PhD. "Substance Abuse in Doctors According to Physician Specialty." American Addiction Centers, 14 Sept. 2022, americanaddictioncenters.org/healthcare-professionals/substance-abuse-in-doctors-according-to-physician-specialty.

[12] "Ten Facts About Physician Suicide and Mental Health." American Foundation for Suicide Prevention, americanaddictioncenters.org/healthcare-professionals/substance-abuse-in-doctors-according-to-physician-specialty.

[13] Gaultiere, Bill. "The Wounded Healer As a Spiritual Guide (Henri Nouwen)." Soul Shepherding, www.soulshepherding.org/wounded-healer-spiritual-guide-henri-nouwen/. "Usually people who appreciate the wounded healer symbol associate it with Henri Nouwen. But the idea is not original to him. He got it from the famous psychiatrist Carl Jung's application of an ancient Greek Myth about Chiron (Ky-ren), a Centaur (with the upper body of a human and lower body of a horse). Most Centaurs were savage, but Chiron was knowledgable about medicine, wise, and nurturing and became famous for his healing powers. Paradoxically, Chiron suffered from a wound that never healed. Surprisingly, his wound gave him great knowledge, compassion, and power to heal. Many people came to him at his home at the foot of Mt. Pelion to learn from him and be healed of ailments. Chiron was a wounded healer."

[14] "Churchill's Phony "Success" Quotes." Richard M Langworth: Senior Fellow, Hillsdale College Churchill Project, Writer and Historian, 26 Mar. 2011, richardlangworth.com/phoney-success.

[15] Macknik, Stephen L., et al. Sleights of Mind. Henry Holt and Co., 2010. p. 6.

[16] "Johannes Kepler." New World Encyclopedia. www.newworldencyclopedia.org/entry/Johannes_Kepler.

[17] Farivar, Cyrus. "Why Star Trek's Prime Directive Could Never Be Enforced." Ars Technica, 6 Sept. 2016, arstechnica.com/tech-policy/2016/09/why-star-treks-prime-directive-could-never-be-enforced/.

[18] Ambron, Richard. The Brain and Pain. Columbia University Press., 2022. pp. 195-196. "There is ample anecdotal evidence that this happens. For example, postsurgical patients exhibited significantly reduced pain when paying attention to music. Thus, the awareness of the music effectively distracted them from the pain. Moreover, the greater the relevance of the distraction, the greater the reduction in painfulness. Attending to an image of a beautiful sunset, or to a religious icon of particular relevance, is a powerful distractor. We know from our own experiences that under certain circumstances we can become oblivious to all sensations, as exemplified by the absent-minded professor who is so focused on an idea that he or she is not aware of what is happening around them."

[19] "Beauty in Broken Things: A Guide to Kintsugi." Konmari, 1 Jan. 2023, konmari.com/beauty-in-broken-things/.

[20] Thiele, F. In L. Coenen, E. Beyreuther, & H. Bietenhard (Eds.), New international dictionary of New Testament theology. Zondervan Publishing House., 1986. Vol. 3, p. 1152.

[21] Keller, Timothy. The Reason for God: Belief in an Age of Skepticism. Penguin Group, 2008. p. 234.

[22] Van der Kolk, Bessel. The Body Keeps the Score. Penguin Publishing Group., 2014. pp. 67-68.

[23] Ambron, Richard. The Brain and Pain. Columbia University Press, 2022. pp. 194-195.

[24] Ambron, Richard. The Brain and Pain. Columbia University Press, 2022. p. 14.

[25] Anderson, Jamie. "Blog." All My Loose Ends, 1 Mar. 2014, allmylooseends.com/2014/03/lights-wink/.

[26] Keller, Timothy. The Reason for God: Belief in an Age of Skepticism. Penguin Group, 2008. pp. 30-31.

[27] Wardle, Terry. "CNLP 309: Terry Wardle on Why So Many Leaders Cave Under the Pressures of Leadership, Why Leaders Implode Morally, and How to Grieve Your Leadership Losses." Carey Nieuwhof Leadership Podcast, careynieuwhof.com/episode309/.

[28] Sean Nemecek, " A High Risk Profession: Pastors and PTSD." https://pastorsoul.com/2019/06/26/a-high-risk-profession-pastors-and-ptsd/

[29] Sullivan, Marissa P. "Mark Dance Equips Pastors to Finish Well in New Book, 'Start to Finish'." Lifeway Newsroom, 16 May 2023, news.lifeway.com/2023/05/16/mark-dance-equips-pastors-to-finish-well-in-new-book-start-to-finish/.

[30] Van der Kolk, Bessel. The Body Keeps the Score. Penguin Publishing Group, 2014. p. 54.

[31] Van der Kolk, Bessel. The Body Keeps the Score. Penguin Publishing Group, 2014. pp. 82-83.

[32] Van der Kolk, Bessel. The Body Keeps the Score. Penguin Publishing Group, 2014. pp. 89-90.

[33] Ambron, Richard. The Brain and Pain. Columbia University Press, 2022. pp. 192-193.

[34] Ambron, Richard. The Brain and Pain. Columbia University Press, 2022. pp. 197-198.

[35] Scazzero, Peter. Emotionally Healthy Discipleship. Zondervan, 2021. p. 192.

[36] Ambron, Richard. The Brain and Pain. Columbia University Press, 2022. pp. 190-191.

[37] Ambron, Richard. The Brain and Pain. Columbia University Press, 2022. p. 15.

[38] Ambron, Richard. The Brain and Pain. Columbia University Press, 2022. pp. 221-222.

[39] "An Origin Story." Fringe, created by J.J. Abrams, Alex Kurtzman, Roberto Orci, Season 5, Episode 5, Bad Robot, 2012.

[40] Beuchner, Frederick. "Quotes › Authors › F › Frederick Buechner." AZ Quotes, www.azquotes.com/quote/859029.

[41] Stanley, Charles. "Quotes › Authors › C › Charles Stanley." AZ Quotes, www.azquotes.com/quote/281083.

[42] Ambron, Richard. The Brain and Pain. Columbia University Press., 2022. pp. 175-176.

[43] "Some 38th Parallels." M.A.S.H., created by Larry Gelbart, Richard Hooker, Season 4, Episode 20, 20th Television, 1976.

[44] William O'Flaherty. "2020 Confirming C.S. Lewis Quotes - Episode 5." Essential C.S. Lewis, 15 Aug. 2020, https://essentialcslewis.com/2020/08/15/wccslq-5-weekly-confirming-c-s-lewis-quotes-episode-5/

[45] Peck, M. Scott. The Different Drum. Simon & Schuster, 1988.

[46] "Community Building Stages." Chattanooga Endeavors, 1 Jan. 2023, chattanoogaendeavors.org/service/community-building/stages/.

[47] Smedes, Lewis B. "Lewis B. Smedes Quotes." BrainyQuote, 1 Jan. 2023, www.brainyquote.com/quotes/lewis_b_smedes_135524.

[48] This quote is also sometimes attributed to Nelson Mandela. It is a helpful quote no matter the source.

[49] Van der Kolk, Bessel. The Body Keeps the Score. Penguin Publishing Group, 2014. pp. 70-71. "The brain-disease model overlooks four fundamental truths: (1) our capacity to destroy one another is matched by our capacity to heal one another. Restoring relationships and community is central to restoring well-being; (2) language gives us the power to change ourselves and others by communicating our experiences, helping us to define what we know, and finding a common sense of meaning; (3) we have the ability to regulate our own physiology, including some of the so-called involuntary functions of the body and brain, through such basic activities as breathing, moving, and touching; and (4) we can change social conditions to create environments in which children and adults can feel safe and where they can thrive. When we ignore these quintessential dimensions of humanity, we deprive people of ways to heal from trauma and restore their autonomy."

[50] Van der Kolk, Bessel. The Body Keeps the Score. Penguin Publishing Group, 2014. pp. 97-98.

[51] Hughes, Langston. Good Morning, Revolution: Uncollected Social Protest Writings. Citadel Press, 1992.

[52] Van der Kolk, Bessel. The Body Keeps the Score. Penguin Publishing Group, 2014. p. 58.

[53] Rohr, Richard. "Transforming Pain." Center for Action and Contemplation, 17 Oct. 2018, cac.org/daily-meditations/transforming-pain-2018-10-17/.

[53a] Wilder, Jim, and Ray Woolridge. Escaping Enemy Mode: How Our Brains Unite or Divide Us. Northfield Publishing, 2022. pp. 20-23. Thank you, Jim and Ray, for this concept.

[54] Parrott, Les, and Leslie Parrott. "5 Tips for Fighting Well with Your Spouse." Symbis Assessment, 5 Jul. 2015, www.symbis.com/blog/5-tips-for-fighting-well-with-your-spouse/.

[55] Elliot, Elizabeth. Suffering Is Never for Nothing. B&H Publishing Group, 2019. pp. 1-2.

[56] Ambron, Richard. The Brain and Pain. Columbia University Press, 2022. pp. 11-12.

[57] Nouwen, Henri J. Life of the Beloved: Spiritual Living in a Secular World. Crossroad Pub Co., 1992. pp. 44-54.

[58] "The Twelve Steps." Alcoholics Anonymous, 1 Jan. 2023, www.aa.org/the-twelve-steps.

Acknowledgments

One of them, when he saw he was healed, came back, praising God in a loud voice.
—Luke 17:15

No one overcomes the traumas of life alone, much less is able to write about the experience. I am deeply thankful and greatly indebted to:

My family. You've stood beside me, nursed me back to health, and joined in on my crazy ideas, including this book. I still remember the first time we talked about me writing a book over a decade ago. You've read, edited, encouraged, and improved everything here. My life is rich because I have you.

Joe, Cam, Keith, Benton, Ron, Jeff, and Charles. "No man is a failure who has friends." You don't all know each other, but you all know me. Aren't you lucky? Your encouragement, support, and accountability shore up my soul when I'm running on empty. You inspire me to follow Jesus more profoundly and listen to others more compassionately. I can only hope to help others the way you have helped me.

My editorial team, led by Bob Welch. This book would not exist without your deliberate advice, careful reading, and supportive accountability. At every point you made a recommendation, my thoughts became more concise and helpful. Thanks for believing in me, moving this forward, and bringing this project to reality.

My pastor friends too numerous to count. Most of us pastor normal-sized churches without fame or fortune. Don't mistake that for insignificance, as you create environments that help people love and be loved by Jesus by name. You're more "local corner" and "mom and pop" than Walmart or Amazon. Many of you live across parts of the world where Jesus is misunderstood at best, if known at all. The kingdom wouldn't be all it is without you. Nearly every letter in the New Testament ends with a list of names, many of whom are unsung heroes who made an extraordinary difference by faithfully loving others where God placed them. Just like that, you inspire me.

My health care team. Your patients come and go. Few return to say thanks. Count me among those thankful that you have compassionately attempted to help, even if we haven't yet achieved the results we want.

All the people at SoulCare Press. You care for the people who take care of other people. May your tribe increase.

My readers. No book of this nature would be complete without people who risk reading, wondering, and believing. Thank you for taking a leap of faith with me.

Harvest Community Church in Eugene, Oregon. You have been my friends through more ups and downs than we can count. I hope our journey together inspires you to more love and grace, because that's precisely what you've done for me.

To contact the author:

brian@myfriendsinpain.com

Made in the USA
Middletown, DE
16 February 2025